S0-AOQ-597

M. Gervautz
A. Hildebrand
D. Schmalstieg (eds.)

Virtual Environments '99

Proceedings of the Eurographics Workshop
in Vienna, Austria,
May 31–June 1, 1999

Eurographics

SpringerWienNewYork

Univ.-Prof. Dr. Michael Gervautz
Dr. Dieter Schmalstieg
Institute of Computer Graphics,
Technical University, Vienna, Austria

Dr. Ing. Axel Hildebrand
ZGDV Computer Graphics Center,
Darmstadt, Germany

© 1999 Springer-Verlag/Wien
Printed in Austria

Typesetting: Camera-ready by authors
Printing: Novographic, A-1238 Wien
Binding: Papyrus, A-1100 Wien

Printed on acid-free and chlorine-free bleached paper

SPIN: 10728684

With 78 Figures

ISSN 0946-2767
ISBN 3-211-83347-1 Springer-Verlag Wien New York

Preface

This book contains the scientific papers presented at the 5th EUROGRAPHICS Workshop on Virtual Environments '99, which was held in Vienna May 31st and June 1st. It was organized by the Institute of Computer Graphics of the Vienna University of Technology together with the Austrian Academy of Sciences and EUROGRAPHICS. The workshop brought together scientists from all over the world to present and discuss the latest scientific advances in the field of Virtual Environments.

31 papers where submitted for reviewing and 18 where selected to be presented at the workshop. Most of the top research institutions working in the area submitted papers and presented their latest results. These presentations were complemented by invited lectures from Stephen Feiner and Ron Azuma, two key researchers in the area of Augmented Reality. The book gives a good overview of the state of the art in Augmented Reality and Virtual Environment research.

The special focus of the Workshop was Augmented Reality, reflecting a noticeable strong trend in the field of Virtual Environments. Augmented Reality tries to enrich real environments with virtual objects rather than replacing the real world with a virtual world. The main challenges include real time rendering, tracking, registration and occlusion of real and virtual objects, shading and lighting interaction, and interaction techniques in augmented environments. These problems are addressed by new research results documented in this book. Besides Augmented Reality, the papers collected here also address levels of detail, distributed environments, systems and applications, and interaction techniques.

We believe that this selection of outstanding research results yields a book that is valuable not only for scientists, but also for engineers and developers working on applications of Virtual Environments.

Michael Gervautz, Axel Hildebrand and Dieter Schmalstieg

International Program Committee

Peter Astheimer (Germany), Ron Azuma (US), Jean-Francis Balaguer(CH), Massimo Bergamasco (Italy), Mark Bilinghurst (US), David Boyd (UK), David Breen (US), Sabine Coquillart (France), Carolina Cruz-Neira (US), Leonid Dimitrov (Austria), Steve Feiner (US), Bernd Froehlich (Germany), Martin Goebel (Germany), Michitaka Hirose (Japan), Hans Jense (Netherlands), Gudrun Klinker (Germany), He-Dong Ko (Korea), Robert van Liere (Netherlands), Bowen Loftin (US), David Mizell (US), Heinrich Mueller (Germany), Junji Nomura (Japan), Axel Pinz (Austria), Larry Rosenblum (US), Bill Sherman (US), Jaoying Shi (China), Gernot Schaufler (US), Dieter Schmalstieg (Austria), Jose Teixeira (Portugal), Daniel Thalmann (CH), Rolf Ziegler (Germany)

Additional Referees

Gerhard Eckel, Christian Faisstnauer, Francois Faure, Andrew Forsberg, Anton Fuhrmann, Gernot Göbbels, Luis Gonvalves, Dieter Koller, Stephan Mantler, Ivan Poupyrev, Greg Welch, Michael Wimmer

Contents

Systems and Applications

Interaction

Validity-Preserving Simplification of Very Complex Polyhedral Solids

Carlos Andújar, Dolors Ayala, and Pere Brunet

Universitat Politècnica de Catalunya, Dept. LSI, Diagonal 647
E-08028 Barcelona, Spain
{andujar, dolorsa, pere}@lsi.upc.es

Abstract. In this paper we introduce the Discretized Polyhedra Simplification (DPS), a framework for polyhedra simplification using space decomposition models. The DPS is based on a new error measurement and provides a sound scheme for error-bounded, geometry and topology simplification while preserving the validity of the model. A method following this framework, Direct DPS, is presented and discussed. Direct DPS uses an octree for topology simplification and error control, and generates valid solid representations. Our method is also able to generate approximations which do not interpenetrate the original model, either being completely contained in the input solid or bounding it. Unlike most of the current methods, restricted to triangle meshes, our algorithm can deal and also produces faces with arbitrary complexity.

1 Introduction

Geometry simplification deals with generation of 3D models that resemble the input model but involve less faces and vertices. A concept closely related is the approximation error —a quantification of the difference between the original model and the simplification. *Level of Detail* is concerned to the possibility of using different representations of a geometric object having different levels of accuracy and complexity. Multi-resolution models provide several level-of-detail representations of a geometric model and have become a powerful tool in many computer graphics applications, including CAD, Virtual Reality and Scientific Visualization, as they can accelerate the handling of complex models by omitting unessential computation and reducing storage space in visualization [12], [6], transmission over networks [7], query acceleration, collision detection, visibility analysis and acoustic modeling. Simplification is also used for reducing the verbosity of 3D models, adjusting the accuracy to the application's requirements and multi-resolution interactive modeling.

1.1 Solid Simplification vs. Surface Simplification

Most of the simplification methods published so far are concerned with a subproblem of geometry simplification which will be called *surface simplification.* In surface simplification the approximation error is measured by some distance defined on the points *on the surface*, regardless of the enclosed volume, if any. We introduce a new approach for the geometry simplification problem, the *solid simplification* (Table 1). Solid simplification measures the error using the points *inside the solid*, and hence it has more freedom for modifying the geometry and the topology (genus and shells).

1.2 Previous Work on Surface Simplification

Most of the current simplification methods are devoted to triangle meshes. An approach is *incremental* if simplification proceeds through a sequence of local boundary updates which reduce the face count. Different local operators have been proposed, such as vertex removal [13], edge collapse [7] and face removal. Current methods are not suitable for the simplification of solids because they produce invalid solids, they are unable to simplify topology, or the error is not bounded.

A simplification method for the special case of orthogonal polyhedra is presented in [4] and extended for general polyhedra in [1]. Unfortunately, both methods usually increase the number of components of the solid. Another approach based on sampling and low-pass filtering is presented in [3], but it does not provide a suitable bound for the error.

1.3 Contribution

In this work we introduce the *Discretized Polyhedra Simplification*, a framework for polyhedra simplification (Section 2) and a new algorithm, Direct DPS (Section 3), that generates error-bounded solid approximations, and is capable of reducing the topology of the input solid. The results and conclusions are shown in Section 4.

Table 1. Surface simplification vs. Solid Simplification

	Surface Simplification	Solid Simplification
Underlying entity	surface (2D)	point-set model (3D)
Basis for error control	points on the surface	points inside the volume
Topology simplification	very limited	high degree of freedom
Previous work	intense research	papers are still rare
Applications	visualization-oriented	more general

2 Discretized Polyhedra Simplification

The DPS framework models a family of simplification methods which have in common the use of an intermediate space decomposition scheme to generate a multi-resolution family of solid representations. The DPS framework involves five components: a decomposition scheme, an error metric, and discretization, reconstruction and face reduction processes. The DPS pattern (Figures 1 and 3) shows the integration of these components.

Decomposition Scheme A space decomposition scheme allows sound topology simplification. Only regular decompositions, such as voxelizations and maximal division classical octrees (MDCO) [5] are of interest for uniform error control.

Error Metric Almost all the simplification methods use a metric based on the points of the surface; such a metric is called *on-metric*. On-metrics are not appropriate for solid simplification since they limit the topology reduction. The DPS framework is based on a new approach for error measurement, the *in-metrics*, i.e., based on the points *inside* the solid. Symmetrically, *out-metrics* are based on the points *outside* the solid. The following distances represent these three approaches: *In-Hausdorff* distance is the symmetric Hausdorff distance defined over the points *inside* the volume enclosed by the solids. A solid P' is said to approximate P within a bound ε iff

$$\forall p \in P \; \exists p' \in P' \mid dist(p, p') < \varepsilon \text{ and } \forall p' \in P' \; \exists p \in P \mid dist(p, p') < \varepsilon . \quad (1)$$

The *On-Hausdorff* (resp. *Out-Hausdorff*) is the symmetric Hausdorff distance defined over the points *on the boundary* (resp. *outside* the solid). The In-Hausdorff is a good quantification of the difference between two solids and allows topology simplification (especially shell reduction).

Discretization The discretization process consists on the conversion of the input solid P into a multi-resolution family of decomposition representations. The discretization proceeds through a space subdivision producing the more accurate model followed by iterative grouping of adjacent cells creating coarser representations. Grouping in octrees is achieved by pruning the deepest level.

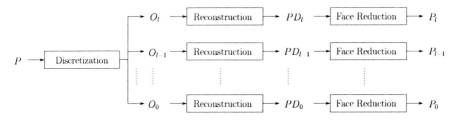

Fig. 1. The DPS framework. O_k stands for a $2^k \text{x} 2^k \text{x} 2^k$ division of the space

Reconstruction The reconstruction process consists on the generation of a polyhedral representation PD_k for each member O_k of the multi-resolution family of decomposition models. Since classic decomposition schemes are approximate representations of polyhedral solids, there exist many ways to interpret the underlying object, e.g. Marching Cubes [8]. The reconstruction must guarantee that the distance between PD_k and P is bounded. This can be accomplished by using an octree as the decomposition model and confining the boundary of PD_k to particular cells of the octree.

Face Reduction The face reduction is the incremental simplification of each intermediate polyhedron PD_k by topology-preserving transformations. Avoiding application of topology reduction operators over the B-Rep is the key for producing manifold boundaries.

3 The Direct Method

Direct DPS (Figure 3) is a solid simplification method following the DPS pattern (Figure 1). A maximal division classical octree (Section 3.1) is used as the decomposition scheme; the approximation error is measured using the In-Hausdorff distance (the extension to support the Out-Hausdorff distance is straightforward); the direct reconstruction is a region-based combination of an orthogonal reconstruction (Section 3.4) and an extended DMC (Section 3.5), and the face reduction is based on merging of adjacent faces (Section 3.7). In each iteration the octree is pruned removing the last level (Figure 3).

3.1 Maximal Division Classical Octree

The Maximal Division Classical Octree [5], denoted as $MDCO(P, l)$, is an octree representation of P, containing White (W), Black (B), Grey (G) and terminal grey (TG) nodes with all TG nodes belonging to the last level l. The boundary of P is completely contained in the set of TG nodes. For now on we will refer to sets of nodes using calygraphic letters, i.e. $\mathcal{B}$ is the set of B nodes, and so on. MDCO cells are defined by three closed intervals yielding to a quasi-disjoint decomposition. A TG node is a *border node* BTG^W, if at least one of its 26-neighbor nodes is W. Otherwise it is an *interior node*, ITG^W. The symmetric definitions for BTG^B and ITG^B, which are useful for the Out-Hausdorff distance extension, are obtained exchanging the role of B and W nodes. Surface inside interior nodes do not need to be reconstructed:

Property 1. Each maximally 26-connected subset of the set $\mathcal{B} \cup \mathcal{ITG}^W$ is enclosed inside a 6-connected subset of $\mathcal{BTG}^W$ nodes.

3.2 Error Control

A polyhedron P' is said to be *In-feasible* (resp. *Out-feasible*) with respect to a MDCO iff W nodes are outside P', B and ITG^W nodes are inside P', and the boundary of P' intersects all BTG^W nodes.

It is straightforward to proof [2] that if P' is In-feasible (resp. Out-feasible) with respect to $MDCO(P, l)$ then the In-Hausdorff (resp. Out-Hausdorff) distance between P and P' is bounded by $\varepsilon = \sqrt{3}/2^l$, i.e. the length of the diagonal of terminal nodes.

3.3 Parameterization of Orthogonal Reconstructions

The *White Surface* $WS(O)$ is the cuberille surface that separates W nodes from the rest of nodes. Symmetrically, the *black surface* $BS(O)$ separates B nodes from the rest. Note that $WS(O) = BS(\overline{O})$.

Definition 1 (δ_i-**offset of WS**). *Let δ be a fraction of the unit. δ_0-offset(WS) is defined as WS; for $i \geq 1$ δ_i-offset(WS) is the result of covering δ_{i-1}-offset(WS) with sub-nodes of size δL that lie inside a TG node and are 26-adjacent to δ_{i-1}-offset(WS).*

Symmetrically, we can define the δ-offsets of BS. The δ parameter represents the thickness of the offset relative to the length L of TG nodes. Discrete offsets can be described using the Minkowski addition operator: the volume enclosed by δ_i-offset(WS) is $\mathcal{B} \cup (\mathcal{TG} - (\mathcal{W} \oplus \mathcal{O}_{\delta i}))$ and the volume enclosed by δ_i-offset(BS) is $\mathcal{B} \cup (\mathcal{TG} \cap (\mathcal{B} \oplus \mathcal{O}_{\delta i}))$, where '$\oplus$' is the Minkowski addition operator and $\mathcal{O}_n$ is a cube of length $2Ln$ centered at the origin, L being the length of TG nodes.

3.4 The Orthogonal Reconstruction

The *Orthogonal Overflow Solid*, OOS, is the volume enclosed by 0.25^1-offset(WS). Symmetrically, the *Orthogonal Underflow Solid*, OUS, is enclosed by the 0.25^1-offset(BS). The difference between these orthogonal solids are given by $Nodes(Surf(OOS(O) \; xor \; OUS(O))) = \mathcal{ITG}^W \cup \mathcal{ITG}^B \subset \mathcal{TG}$.

Property 2. [2] The OOS boundary is two-manifold.

Property 3. [2] $OOS(O)$ is In-feasible with respect to O.

Property 4. [2] BTG nodes are stabbed by a single component of the OOS surface and each octant of a BTG node contains at most one vertex of the OOS.

Property 5. [2] All OOS vertices have degree three or six. $V3$ vertices (Figure 2) can be splited into two vertices $V2$ and a $\overline{V2}$, resulting a minimum degree solid, i.e. all its vertices have degree three.

An orthogonal reconstruction can be generated by calculating the set of BTG nodes. A complete B-Rep can be obtained from this set computing first the vertices using a look-up table as in [4] but indexed by local 26-neighborhood and the faces using a domino-matching algorithm. This reconstruction process improves [4] because it does not separate connected regions.

Before the OOS construction, if TG are converted to B and W nodes 26-adjacent to new B are converted to TG, then OOS is a bounding volume of the input solid. Symmetrically, if TG become W and 26-adjacent B become TG, then OOS will be completely contained in the input solid.

3.5 Discretized Unambiguous Marching Cubes

Some simplification methods based on MC [8] use vertex colors to extract a polyhedral surface from a 3D grid. Our approach uses the 26-neighborhood of TG nodes instead of vertex colors. Meanwhile, vertex color information can be derived from the MDCO such that the reconstruction of the resulting 3D digital picture is topologically equivalent to an OOS:

Theorem 1. *Given a MDCO O, there exists a 3D digital picture $\mathcal{P}$ such that the extraction of an isosurface from $\mathcal{P}$ is non-ambiguous and generates a surface S topologically equivalent to OOS(O) enclosing an In-feasible volume, provided that the extraction guarantees that all stabbed edges, and only them, are intersected by S.*

Proof. The proof is based on a constructive method to obtain the 3D digital picture $\mathcal{P}$ from the MDCO O, called *induced grid*. The grid points of $\mathcal{P}$ are defined as the corners of the octants resulting by subdiving once the terminal nodes of O. A grid point v of $\mathcal{P}$ is white if v has contact with a W node of O; otherwise it is black. If neighbor grid points of $\mathcal{P}$ are arranged into voxels, as usual in isosurface extraction, the only possible configurations are the planar, non-ambiguous classes [2], so extraction methods such as MC generate a closed surface. It is straightforward to see that this surface S is topologically equivalent to $OOS(O)$, and that limits an In-feasible solid.

The DMC [10] is an extension of MC based on a discretization of the planes in 13 different orientations, so coplanar triangles can be merged forming large faces. Given a MDCO O, the Unambiguous Discretized Marching Cubes solid, UDMC, is defined as the polyhedron generated by the DMC algorithm from the grid induced by O. The UDMC only uses the non-ambiguous, planar classes of DMC and creates In-feasible, valid solids.

3.6 Direct Solid

Direct DPS uses a mixed reconstruction combining the OOS and the UDMC in a region-basis producing the *Direct Solid*. In order to guarantee the surface continuity, the regions are selected so that the boundary nodes of these regions does not include incompatible nodes. The Direct Solid keeps the main properties of OOS and UDMC: it is two-manifold and In-feasible. Regions coming from the OOS have the minimum degree property.

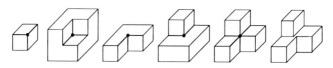

Fig. 2. OOS vertices. *From left to right:* $V1$, $\overline{V1}$, $V2$, $\overline{V2}$, $V3$ and split of $V3$

3.7 Face reduction based on face-merge

The interest for a three-degree solid arises from the fact that the dual graph of a minimum degree solid is a triangulation. In triangle meshes there are no coplanar restrictions on the vertices, so they can be moved without producing non-planar faces. The dual equivalent of vertex displacements is the modification of support planes. Since all the OOS vertices have degree three, the vertices of the adjusted faces can be recalculated by intersecting their three incident faces.

Our face reduction process preserves validity and feasibility using a face-merge operator, which is the dual of the edge-collapse. The face-merge has several interesting properties: it preserves topology and it preserves the degree of the vertices. The face-merge takes as input the two adjacent faces f_1, f_2 to be merged. Both faces are replaced by a single face f, losing the shared edge e and the shared vertices v_1 and v_2. The third face incident in v_1 (v_2) is f_3 (f_4). The only computed value is the plane for the new face, which determines the position of the new face's vertices V by intersecting the incident faces.

Our face-reduction differs from a classic surface simplification in many ways. The face reduction starts from a two-manifold solid whose geometry and topology has been reduced during discretization and reconstruction; the input surface inside a MDCO node is quite simple; the face reduction takes profit of local properties of the Direct Solid such as minimum degree and finally MDCO nodes provide the error control for the In-Hausdorff distance.

Selection of Faces Faces f_1, f_2 must fulfill the following constraints in order to preserve topology: f_1 and f_2 must share exactly one edge; $nvert(f_1) + nvert(f_2) \geq 7$; $nvert(f_3) \geq 4$ and $nvert(f_4) \geq 4$.

New Plane Computation The plane of f fixes the third degree of freedom of vertices in V. The separation of positive and negative points (end points of node edges that must be stabbed by the new plane) is a linear separability problem. Two sets of points are linearly separable iff their convex hulls do not intersect. The new plane computation is a linear programming problem involving three unknowns [2] (recall that a flat in $I\!R^d$ has d degrees of freedom). This plane can be computed in optimum O(n) time using the method proposed in [9]. Unfortunately, the number of constraints n depends on the number of nodes intersected by f_1 and f_2. The number of constraints can be reduced by storage and incremental update of upper and lower convex hulls. The alternative fast heuristic we implemented proceeds computing the normal of the non-planar polygon defined by V and computing the distance to the origin by one-variable linear-programming.

Preserving Validity In order to guarantee that the new solid is In-feasible, the face merge must fulfill these two conditions: the new face is contained and intersects exactly the same set of nodes than the merged faces and the resulting boundary is non-self-intersecting. Self-intersection test is computationally cheap because each BTG octant is used exclusively by a single sheet.

8

4 Results and Discussion

We tested Direct DPS on a solid model with 1,366 faces (Figure 3) and compared the results with a free implementation of mesh decimation (Table 2). To draw the comparison we had to triangulate the test object (2,728 triangles) and the faces returned by Direct DPS. Taking the number of triangles as the basis for the comparison, Direct DPS produced less triangles than mesh decimation in accurate approximations but more triangles in coarse ones. Regarding the number of faces, Direct DPS always produced less faces than mesh decimation. Mesh decimation produced self-intersections specially in coarse levels, while Direct DPS preserved validity. Mesh decimation did not simplify topology while Direct DPS reduced the genus. Since Direct DPS faces were triangulated after simplification, resulting triangles had better aspect ratio.

Table 2. Number of faces returned by Direct DPS (*second column*) and mesh decimation (*third column*) on the test object of Figure 3

depth	#f Direct	#t decim.	max. error	time (MIPS R4600)
8	122 (248 t)	294	0.6%	114 s
7	86 (176 t)	217	1.2%	26 s
6	64 (132 t)	161	2.1%	8 s
5	56 (116 t)	80	4.5%	4 s
4	34 (68 t)	59	6.1%	2 s

Since the original polyhedron is not used beyond discretization, running times of reconstruction and face reduction do not depend on the complexity of the original polyhedron, so cheap simplifications are cheap to compute (e.g. 3D thumbnail generation); Direct DPS is not affected by degeneracies of the input surface, and produces two-manifold solids even with non-manifold inputs so Direct DPS can be viewed as a lossy conversion from non-manifolds to manifolds.

Compared to mesh simplification, Direct DPS minimizes the number of planes by using arbitrary faces, so it is especially suitable for BSP-based applications. In occlusion analysis, Direct DPS provides a fast and sound way of computing big occluders from a complex scene, specially in reverberation path calculation, used in acoustic modeling, where significant high tolerances can be used. Due to its ability to produce bounding or bounded approximations, it is also suitable for collision detection.

5 Concluding Remarks and Future Work

The contributions of this paper are: a) the identification of the solid simplification problem, which addresses two limitations of current simplification methods, topology reduction and validity preservation; b) a characterization of the error

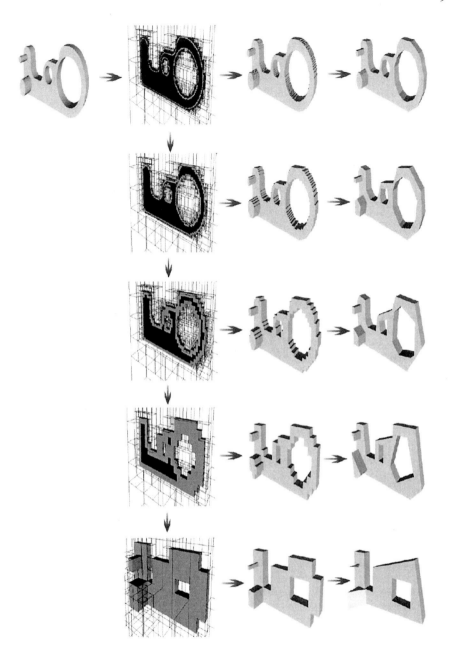

Fig. 3. *From left to right:* input polyhedron, multi-resolution of octrees (front grey nodes have been culled to keep black nodes visible), reconstructed solids and final multi-resolution

metrics and a new distance suitable for topology simplification; c) a framework for polyhedra simplification supporting the In-Hausdorff distance in a simple and robust way; d) a concrete solid simplification method, Direct DPS, which produces concise, error-bounded representations of valid, two-manifold objects, with faces of arbitrary complexity.

Future work includes the improvement of the face reduction to minimize the effect of local minima, such as adjusting more than one face at a time or using deformable models. A reconstruction still based on the MDCO but directed by the input polyhedron is being studied.

Acknowedgements The authors would like to thank Jarek Rossignac, Greg Turk and Renato Pajarola for their helpful comments.

References

1. C. Andújar, D. Ayala, P. Brunet, R. Joan, and J. Solé. Automatic generation of multiresolution boundary representations. *Computer Graphics Forum*, 1996.
2. Carlos Andújar. The discretized polyhedra simplification: A framework for polyhedra simplification based on decomposition schemes. Technical report, Universitat Politecnica de Catalunya, LSI-98-XR, 1998.
3. Taosong He at al. Controlled topology simplification. *IEEE Transactions on Visualization and Computer Graphics*, 2(2):171–184, 1996.
4. D. Ayala, C. Andújar, and P. Brunet. Automatic simplification of orthogonal polyhedra. In D.W. Fellner, editor, *Modelling Virtual Worlds Distribuited Graphics*, pages 137–147. Internationallen Workshop MVD'95, Infix, 1995.
5. P. Brunet, R. Juan, Isabel Navazo, J. Sole, and D. Tost. *Scientific Visualization. Advances and challenges*. Academic Press, 1988.
6. T.A. Funkhouser and C.H. Sequin. Adaptive display algorithm for interactive frame rates during visualization of complex virtual environments. In *Proc. SIGGRAPH*, pages 247–254, 1993. Computer Graphics Proceedings, Annual Conference Series.
7. H. Hoppe. Progressive meshes. *Computer Graphics*, 30(Annual Conference Series):99–108, 1996.
8. William Lorensen and Harvey Cline. Marching cubes: A high resolution 3d surface construction algorithm. In *Proc. SIGGRAPH*, pages 44–50, 1987. Computer Graphics vol. 21 no. 4.
9. N. Megiddo. Linear-time algorithms for linear programming in 3d and related problems. *Siam J. Computer*, 12(4):759–776, 1983.
10. C. Montani, R. Scateni, and R. Scopigno. Discretized marching cubes. In *Visualization'94*, pages 281–287. IEEE Computer Society Press, 1994.
11. Isabel Navazo. *Contribucio a les tecniques de modelat geometric d'objectes polimerics usant la codificacio amb arbres octals (written in Catalan)*. PhD thesis, Universitat Politecnica de Catalunya, 1986.
12. J. Rossignac and P. Borrel. Multiresolution 3D aproximations for rendering complex scenes. In *Modeling in Computer Graphics*. Springer-Verlag, 1993.
13. W. J. Schroeder, J. A. Zarge, and W. E. Lorensen. Decimation of triangle meshes. In *Proc. SIGGRAPH*, pages 65–70, 1992. Computer Graphics vol. 26 no. 2.

View-Dependent Topology Simplification

Jihad El-Sana and Amitabh Varshney

Department of Computer Science, State University of New York at Stony Brook,
Stony Brook, NY 11794-4400
{jihad,varshney}@cs.sunysb.edu

Abstract. We propose a technique for performing view-dependent simplifications for level-of-detail-based renderings of complex models. Our method is based on exploiting frame-to-frame coherence and is tolerant of various commonly found degeneracies in real-life polygonal models. The algorithm proceeds by preprocessing the input dataset into a binary tree of vertex collapses. This tree is used at run time to generate the triangles for display. Dependencies to avoid mesh foldovers in manifold regions of the input object are stored in the tree in an implicit fashion. This obviates the need for any extra storage for dependency pointers and suggests a potential for application to external memory prefetching algorithms. We also propose a distance metric that can be used to unify the geometry and genus simplifications with the view-dependent parameters such as viewpoint, view-frustum, and local illumination.

1 Introduction

Interactive visualization of large geometric datasets in computer graphics is a challenging task due to several reasons. One of the main reasons is that the sizes of several present geometric datasets are one or more orders of magnitude larger than what the current graphics hardware can display at interactive rates. Further, the rate of growth in the complexity of such geometric datasets has outpaced the advances in the graphics hardware rendering capabilities. As a result, several algorithmic solutions have been proposed to bridge this gap between the actual and desired rendering performances on such large datasets. These include visibility-based culling, geometric multiresolution hierarchies, levels of detail in illumination and shading, texture mapping, and image-based rendering. The focus of this paper is on defining geometric multiresolution hierarchies to enable a view-dependent simplification of the geometry as well as topology of the model for interactive walkthroughs of high complexity polygonal datasets.

For some graphics systems such as those used in mechanical tolerancing and medical volume visualization preservation of the topology of the input dataset is an important criterion. However, for a wide variety of real-time graphics applications where interactivity is essential, preservation of the topology of the input polygonal dataset is often not a requirement. For such applications geometry simplification has been shown to yield significantly lower complexity approximations if performed with genus simplification than without. In this paper we demon-

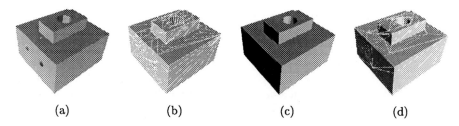

(a)   (b)   (c)   (d)

Fig. 1. Genus-simplification based on light direction

strate a technique for performing topology simplifications in a view-dependent manner. In our approach a hierarchy of vertex-pair collapses is identified to form a *view dependence tree*. Appropriate levels of detail are selected from this tree at runtime to generate view-dependent simplifications. We also propose a distance metric that uses the coordinates and the normals of vertices, to define view- and light-dependent topology and geometry simplifications for polygonal environments in a unified manner.

2 Related Work

Related work on geometry simplification has been well surveyed in several recent papers [2, 3, 6, 9, 12]. In this paper we shall overview the related work in genus simplifications and view-dependent simplifications. These two categories have almost no overlap with the notable exception of [13].

2.1 Genus Simplifications

Rossignac and Borrel's algorithm [16] uses a global grid to subdivide a model. Then the vertices of one cell are collapsed to a single vertex and the polygonal mesh is appropriately updated. This approach can simplify the topology if the desired simplification regions fall within a grid cell. He *et al* [8] have used an low-pass filter to perform a controlled simplification of the genus of a volumetric objects. However, polygonal objects need to be voxelized. El-Sana and Varshney [5] perform genus simplification by extending the concept of α-hulls from points and spheres to triangles. Their approach is based on convolving individual triangles with a L_∞ cube of side α and then computing their union. The convolution operation effectively eliminates all holes that are less than size α.

Several algorithms for topology simplification are based on vertex-pair collapse method, though not in the context of view-dependent renderings. Schroeder [18] has introduced vertex-split and vertex-merge operations on polygonal meshes for modifying the topology of polygonal models. The simplification is based on the Euclidean distance and the vertex splits are performed along feature lines and at corners. Garland and Heckbert [6] present a quadric error metric that can be used to perform genus as well as geometric simplifications. The error at a vertex v is stored in the form a 4×4 symmetric matrix. The algorithm proceeds by performing vertex-pair collapses and the error is accumulated from one vertex to the other by summing these matrices. Popović and Hoppe [15] introduce the operator of a generalized vertex split to represent progressive changes to the geometry as well as topology for triangulated geometric models. Progressive use of this operator results in representation of a geometric model as a *progressive simplicial complex*.

2.2 View-Dependent Simplifications

Most of the previous work on generating multiresolution hierarchies for LOD-based rendering has concentrated on computing a fixed set of view-independent levels of detail. At runtime an appropriate level of detail is selected based on viewing parameters and displayed. Such methods are overly restrictive and do not take into account finer image-space feedback such as light position, visual acuity, silhouettes, and view direction. Recent advances to address some of these issues in a view-dependent manner take advantage of the temporal coherence to adaptively refine or simplify the polygonal environment from one frame to the next. Since most of the work in view-dependent simplifications is closely related to the concept of progressive meshes we briefly overview them next.

Progressive meshes have been introduced by Hoppe [9] as an elegant solution for a continuous resolution representation of polygonal meshes. Progressive meshes are based upon two fundamental operators – edge collapse and its dual, the vertex split, as shown in Figure 2. In this example the vertices $n_0 \ldots n_6$ comprise the *neighborhood* of the edge pc. A polygonal mesh $\hat{M} = M^k$ is simplified

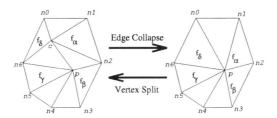

Fig. 2. Edge collapse and vertex split

into successively coarser meshes:$M^k \overset{ecol_{k-1}}{\to} M^{k-1} \overset{ecol_{k-2}}{\to} \ldots M^1 \overset{ecol_0}{\to} M^0$ by applying a sequence of edge collapses. One can retrieve the successively higher detail meshes from the simplest mesh M^0 by using a sequence of the dual transformation, vertex-split: $M^0 \overset{vsplit_0}{\to} M^1 \overset{vsplit_1}{\to} \ldots M^{k-1} \overset{vsplit_{k-1}}{\to} (\hat{M} = M^k)$

Merge trees have been introduced by Xia *et al* [19] as a data-structure built upon progressive meshes to enable real-time view-dependent rendering of an object. Let the vertex p in Figure 2 be considered the parent of the vertex c (as c is created from p through a vertex split). The merge tree is constructed in a bottom-up fashion from the high-detail mesh $\hat{M}$ to a low-detail mesh M^0 by storing these parent-child relationships in a hierarchical manner over the surface of an object.

View-dependent simplification is achieved by performing edge-collapses and vertex-splits on the triangulation used for display depending upon view-dependent parameters such as lighting (detail is directly proportional to intensity gradient), polygon orientation, (high detail for silhouettes and low detail for backfacing regions) and screen-space projection. Since there is a high temporal coherence the selected levels in the merge tree change only gradually from frame to frame. Unconstrained edge-collapses and vertex-splits during runtime can be shown to result in mesh foldovers resulting in visual artifacts such as shading discontinuities. To avoid these artifacts Xia et al propose the concept of dependencies or constraints that necessitate the presence of the entire neighborhood of an edge before it is collapsed (or its parent vertex is split). Thus, for the example shown in Figure 2, the neighborhood of edge pc should consist exactly of vertices $n_0 \ldots n_6$ for c to collapse to p. Similarly, for the vertex p to split to c, the vertices adjacent to p should be exactly the set $n_0 \ldots n_6$.

View-Dependent Progressive Meshes Hoppe [10] has independently developed an algorithm that is similar to Xia et al [19]. Whereas Xia et al use the Euclidean distance metric and collapse the shortest edge first to construct the merge tree, Hoppe proceeds in a top-down fashion by minimizing an energy function first defined in [9]. Hoppe uses screen-space projection and orientation of the polygons to guide the run-time view-dependent simplification. Like the approach of Xia et al, this approach also requires constraints to prevent mesh foldovers. However, unlike [19], Hoppe [10] empirically observes that for some distance metrics (such as the energy minimization function described there), the vertex-split/edge-collapse constraints limited to only the four faces f_α, f_β, f_γ, and f_δ as shown in Figure 2 are adequate. However, this in general is not a sufficient requirement for other distance metrics, such as the shortest-edge-first, for which the entire neighborhood has to be stored as a constraint for vertex-split/edge-collapse. In Section 4.2 we propose to define these constraints in an implicit manner thereby obviating the need to store them explicitly.

Guéziec et al [7] have developed a surface partition algorithm for a progressive encoding scheme for surfaces in the form of a directed acyclic graph (DAG). The DAG represents the partial ordering of the edge collapses with path compression. De Floriani et al [4] have introduced the multi-triangulation(MT). The change of level of detail in MT is achieved through a set of local operators that affect fragments of the mesh. The dependencies between the fragments of the mesh are used to construct a DAG of these fragments. This DAG is used at run time to guide the change of the resolution of each fragment.

Schilling and Klein [17] have introduced a refinement algorithm that is texture dependent. They measure the texture distortion in the simplified mesh by mapping the triangulation into the texture space and then measuring the error at vertices and edge intersections. In the vertex hierarchy they store the sequence of the simplification operations and the texture distortion with each operation. Klein *et al* [11] have developed an illumination-dependent refinement algorithm for multiresolution meshes. The algorithm stores maximum deviation from Phong interpolated normals and introduces correspondence between the normals during the simplification algorithm. In order to avoid aliasing artifacts they recompute the normals at the vertices. In the vertex hierarchy they store the geometric error and maximum normal deviation at each triangle.

2.3 View-Dependent Topology Simplifications

Luebke and Erikson [13] use a scheme based on defining a *tight octree* over the vertices of the given model to generate hierarchical view-dependent simplifications. In a tight octree, each node of the octree is tightened to the smallest axis-aligned bounding cube that encloses the relevant vertices before subdividing further. If the screen-space projection of a given cell of an octree is too small, all the vertices in that cell are collapsed to one vertex. Adaptive refinement is performed analogously. Marshall *et al* [14] have developed a view-dependent topology simplification algorithm based on a clustering approach and simplification metric. The simplification metric minimizes changes to the final image rather than changes to the input model.

3 Overview

We present a technique for performing geometry and genus simplifications in a view-dependent manner. We first construct a hierarchy of vertex-pair collapses to construct a *view dependence* tree. We would like to note here that the view dependence tree differs from trees constructed in the previous literature [10, 19] in that it allows genus simplifications and it does not store any explicit constraints. Details of how we construct the view dependence tree are given in Section 4. In general for n vertices $O(n^2)$ vertex pairs are candidates for collapse. In our current implementation we only consider $O(n \log n)$ candidate vertex pairs by constructing an octree and considering only the nearest neighbors across adjacent cells as candidates.

We have tried several distance metrics and have found that the combination of the vertex coordinates with the normals yields the most acceptable results. We discuss this multi-attribute metric further in Section 5. Almost all view-dependent simplification criteria make use of vertex normals. We discuss how tests for backfacing regions, view-frustum, foveation, and local illumination can be performed in a natural fashion by using our distance function. Our algorithm that makes use of these criteria results in a visually better view-dependent simplification of a scene, than purely Euclidean-distance metrics. We discuss these criteria further in Section 5.

4 View Dependence Tree Construction

A view dependence tree is a generalization of the merge tree introduced by Xia *et al* in two important ways. First, a view dependence tree is capable of performing genus-reducing simplifications whereas a merge tree can only perform genus-preserving geometric simplifications. Second, a view dependence tree does not store any explicit constraints. Instead implicit constraints are used to ensure runtime consistency in the generated triangulations. We next describe these two important differences.

4.1 Simplifying Genus

An edge collapse combines two vertices that are connected by an edge. A vertex-pair collapse is a generalization of an edge collapse that combines any two vertices. For a dataset with n vertices, $O(n^2)$ vertex pairs are possible. An algorithm that selects from amongst these in a sorted order would take time $O(n^2 \log n)$ – too slow for most practical applications.

To generate the candidate vertex pairs more rapidly we construct an octree over the vertices of the object. For each cell C_i of the octree we include the closest pair of vertices $(\mathbf{P_1}, \mathbf{P_2})$ such that $\mathbf{P_1}$ lies in C_i, and $\mathbf{P_2}$ lies in C_j, where C_i and C_j share a common subdividing plane Π_{ij}. This results in $O(n \log n)$ candidate vertex pairs. We have found that this method works better than selecting vertex pairs based on Delaunay tetrahedralizations or grid-based methods.

Once the vertex pairs have been selected, these together with all the edges of the model are considered for possible collapses to build the view dependence tree in the shortest-edge-first order. The distance metric that we have used to compute the shortest edge is given by Equation 1 in Section 5. The resulting view dependence tree is constructed much along the lines of a merge tree, except for handling of constraints that is discussed next.

4.2 Implicit Constraints

In construction of a view dependence tree we keep track of the identification numbers of the vertices. If the model has n vertices at the highest level of detail they are assigned vertex-ids $0, 1, \ldots, n-1$. Every time a vertex pair is collapsed to generate a new vertex, the id of the new vertex is assigned to be one more than the greatest vertex-id thus far. This process is continued till the entire view dependence tree has been built. The order of the selection of vertex pairs to collapse is made on the basis of the following criteria:

1. *Shortest Distance First:* We store all candidate vertex pairs in a priority heap and select the vertex pair that has the shortest distance based on some distance metric. For our current implementation we use a multi-attribute distance metric defined by Equation 1.
2. *Avoid Mesh Foldover:* If the vertex pair collapse occurs along an edge (i.e. is non-genus-reducing), and performing this collapse does not result in the normals of any of the final triangles from being "flipped" with respect to the pre-collapse triangles then we flag this collapse as valid, otherwise we go back and test criteria (1) above with the next shortest edge.

For certain applications in which long and thin sliver triangles are not desirable an additional test can be added to the above list that will flag a vertex pair collapse as invalid if it results in creation of sliver triangles. All of the above tests are done during the preprocessing stage; they are too costly to be performed at runtime to determine view-dependent triangulations. The outcomes of these tests are represented in the sequence in which the vertices are collapsed during the preprocessing and are reflected in the vertex ids.

4.3 Runtime Traversal

The list of vertices that are used for display at any frame i is defined as the set of *active vertices* for that frame. Active vertices for display in frame $i + 1$ are determined by collapsing or splitting from amongst the active vertices for frame i based on the view-dependent criteria. The list of triangles that are displayed in frame i comprise the set of *active triangles* for that frame. The determination of active triangles for frame $i + 1$ proceeds in an interleaved fashion with the determination of active vertices for frame $i + 1$ from frame i. Every time a display vertex of frame i collapses or splits in frame $i + 1$ we simply delete and add appropriate triangles to the list of active triangles. For frame 0 we initialize the lists of active vertices and active triangles to be the entire set of vertices and triangles, respectively, in the model.

Before a vertex is split or collapsed at runtime we make a few simple checks based on vertex ids to ensure the consistency of the generated triangulations and avoid mesh foldovers. These can be simply stated as:

- *Vertex Split:* A vertex p can be safely split at runtime if its vertex-id is greater than the vertex-ids of all its neighbors.
- *Vertex Pair Collapse:* A vertex pair (p, c) can be collapsed if the vertex-id of the resulting vertex is less than the vertex-ids of the parents of the union of the neighbors of vertices p and c.

The two above checks can be efficiently implemented by storing two values with every active vertex – (a) the maximum vertex-id of all its neighbors and (b) the minimum vertex-id of the parents of all its neighbors. During each frame each active vertex is visited once to evaluate its potential to split or collapse. If an active vertex passes the view-dependent tests outlined in Section 5 these two values stored locally at the vertex can be used to determine whether it will be safe to split/collapse. These values are updated only when an active vertex or one of its neighbors actually splits or collapses.

5 Unifying Geometry and Topology

One of the important issues in combining genus simplification with geometry simplification is quantifying and prioritizing the changes in the genus of an object relative to changes in its geometry. Consider for example the object shown in Figure 3(a). Using simple Euclidean-distance-based metrics we find that the distance between A and B is larger than that between B and C. The decision to collapse vertices B and C will be topology-modifying whereas the collapse of A and B will be a geometry simplification.

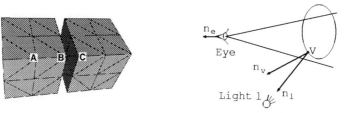

(a) Geometry and topology simplification (b) View-dependent simplifciaction

Fig. 3. View-dependent topology simplifications

Currently there are two techniques for deciding which collapse to perform first: (a) *Geometry First:* Perform as many genus-preserving geometry simplifications as possible. When it is no longer possible to perform any geometry simplifications any further for a given error bound, perform genus-reducing simplification. This is the approach taken in [18, 5]; (b) *Equal Preference:* Treat genus-preserving and genus-reducing simplifications on an equal basis and make decisions based only by the spatial distance in R^3. This is the approach taken in [6, 13].

We would like to be able to prioritize genus-preserving and genus-reducing simplifications between the two above extremes. We observe that genus-reducing simplifications are almost always characterized by a large difference in the normals of the surfaces that are merged. This suggests the use of the following distance function between two points $\mathbf{P_0} = (\mathbf{v_0}, \mathbf{n_0})$ and $\mathbf{P_1} = (\mathbf{v_1}, \mathbf{n_1})$:

$$dist(\mathbf{P_0}, \mathbf{P_1}) = \frac{\|\mathbf{v_0} - \mathbf{v_1}\|_2}{(1 + \mathbf{n_0}.\mathbf{n_1}) + \epsilon} \qquad (1)$$

where $\mathbf{v_i} = (x_i, y_i, z_i)$ and $\mathbf{n_i} = (n_{i_x}, n_{i_y}, n_{i_z})$ denote the position and normal respectively of point $\mathbf{P_i}$ and ϵ is a user-specified preference factor that prioritizes the genus-preserving and genus-reducing simplifications. As an example, when $\epsilon = 0.1$, genus-preserving geometry simplifications (that involve collapsing two similarly oriented vertices) would be preferred over distances 21 times greater than genus-reducing simplification (that involve collapsing two oppositely oriented vertices).

As shown in Figure 3(b) most of the view-dependent simplifications can be cast in terms of computing the distance between two points with coordinate positions and normals. Let us assume that the eye is located at position $\mathbf{e}$ and has associated with it a vector $\mathbf{n_e}$ that is the oppositely oriented with respect to the look-at vector.

- *Triangle Position and Orientation:* This involves computing the distance between $(\mathbf{v}, \mathbf{n_v})$ and $(\mathbf{e}, \mathbf{n_e})$. If the triangle is backfacing, this will yield a large value assisting in backface simplification. If the triangle is near the center of the screen and facing the viewer, Equation 1 yields a small value of the distance assisting in implementing foveation, i.e. high detail in the direction the eye is looking at. Foveation can be used to mimic the high visual acuity at the center of the human retina [1].

– *Lighting-based Adaptive Simplification:* If the triangle under consideration is front facing we use the minimum of the distance between $(\mathbf{v}, \mathbf{n_v})$ and $(\mathbf{l}, \mathbf{n_l})$ and the distance between $(\mathbf{v}, \mathbf{n_v})$ and $(\mathbf{e}, \mathbf{n_e})$ to compute the requisite level of detail for illumination.

6   Results and Discussion

We have implemented our approach on a SGI Onyx2 with Infinite Reality graphics and tested it on several models. The times for preprocessing appear in Table 1. We would like to point out that our code has not yet been particularly optimized. The results of our approach for the above models appear in the Figures 1– 6.

Dataset	Vertices	Triangles	Preprocessing Time	
			View-Dependent Tree	Octree
Bunny	35947	69451	10.3 s	1.4 s
Pipes	107754	206352	58.1 s	87.5 s
AMR	173042	339444	1 m 55 s	5 m 10 s
Torp	464720	736516	12 m 46 s	19 m 12 s

Table 1. Preprocessing times for various models

Figure 1 shows the results of lighting-dependent genus simplification. Figure 4 shows the results of view-frustum-guided simplifications. The yellow rectangle in the center of each image shows the outline of the screen-space projection of the view frustum. As can be seen the detail outside the view frustum has been considerably simplified in Figure 4(b). Figure 5 shows the original and two progressively lower levels of detail of the Auxilliary Machine Room dataset from a notional submarine dataset. We would like to point out that on an average traversal of the view dependence tree takes up only 8 – 10% of the time to draw each frame; rest of the time is being taken up in drawing the triangles that have been determined. Figure 6 shows view-dependent simplifications for a procedurally generated model of pipes. Most of the simplification in this case is because of genus-reducing simplifications. This might be an appropriate place to compare our work with that of Luebke and Erikson's [13] as two instances of view-dependent topology simplification work. In Luebke and Erikson's [13] approach fine control over the simplification of the topology is not easy to achieve. For example, a hole that exists on the border of three or more cells may become larger as result of the collapse of the vertices of the adjacent cells. Since our primitive operation of a vertex-pair collapse is simpler than that of collapsing

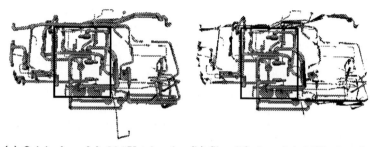

(a) Original model: 86.5K triangles (b) Simplified model: 21K triangles

Fig. 4. View-frustum-guided genus simplification

all vertices in an octree cell, we believe that our method will be able to provide a finer level of control for more realistic rendering. However, identification of candidate vertex pairs takes more time than simply constructing an octree over input vertices.

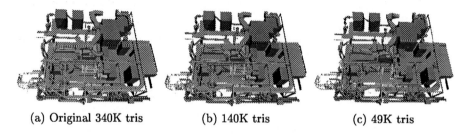

(a) Original 340K tris   (b) 140K tris   (c) 49K tris

Fig. 5. Three LODs from the view dependence tree for Auxilliary Machine Room

We have observed several advantages in making the split and collapse constraints implicit and storing the values to be checked locally:

1. *Local Accesses:* Explicit constraints the way they are stored in previous work [10, 19] result in several non-local accesses resulting in unnecessary paging for large datasets or on computers with less memory. Implicit constraints overcome these drawbacks and suggest possibilities for developing external memory algorithms for view-dependent visualization of datasets that do not even fit into the main memory of the visualization workstation.
2. *Change-Sensitive Processing:* Explicit constraints need to visit every neighbor of an active vertex to determine whether or not it can split/collapse. This might result in visiting of a node several times, once from each of its neighbors, often unnecessarily. With implicit constraints, the way we have defined them, the algorithm needs to visit a node of the view dependence tree only when its associated active vertex actually splits or collapses. Thus the processing time is now proportional to the actual number of changes as opposed to potential changes.

3. *Memory Savings:* Implicit constraints require only two integers to be stored per node of the view dependence tree as opposed to a pointer to every vertex in the neighborhood. This results in a modest savings of about 30% in the storing of the tree.

7 Conclusions and Future Work

We have presented the concept of view-dependence trees to perform genus-reducing simplifications for large polygonal datasets. These trees are more compact, faster to navigate, and easier to build than prior work. Further, we have also introduced a distance metric that can be used for prioritizing genus-reducing simplifications with respect to geometry-reducing simplifications in a view-dependent manner. This metric is particularly useful in that it is able to unify the distance function being used in genus-preserving versus genus-reducing simplifications with the other criteria in defining view-dependent simplifications.

We see scope for future work in designing external memory algorithms for visualization of datasets whose sizes exceed that of the main memory, by taking advantage of the localized and compact structure of view dependence trees. Also, there is scope for better defining the normal and coordinate values of a new vertex as a result of vertex pair collapse by using methods similar to those of Garland and Heckbert [6]; we currently use the average normal and average coordinate values of the two vertices.

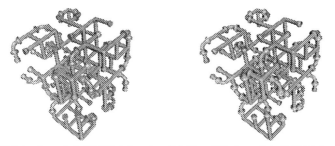

(a) Original model: 25.7K triangles (b) Simplified model: 7.2K triangles

Fig. 6. View-dependent simplification of the procedural pipe model

Acknowledgements

This work has been supported in part by the NSF grants: CCR-9502239, DMI-9800690, ACR-9812572 and a DURIP instrumentation award N00014970362. Jihad El-Sana has been supported in part by the Fulbright/Arab-Israeli Scholarship and the Catacosinos Fellowship for Excellence in Computer Science. The figures 1, 4, and 5 show mechanical parts from the dataset of a notional submarine provided to us by the Electric Boat Division of General Dynamics.

References

1. E.-C. Chang and C. Yap. A wavelet approach to foveating images. In *Proceedings of the 13th International Annual Symposium on Computational Geometry (SCG-97)*, pages 397–399, New York, June4–6 1997. ACM Press.
2. P. Cignoni, C. Montani, and R. Scopigno. A comparison of mesh simplification algorithms. *Computers & Graphics*, 22(1):37–54, February 1998. ISSN 0097-8493.
3. J. Cohen, A. Varshney, D. Manocha, G. Turk, H. Weber, P. Agarwal, F. P. Brooks, Jr., and W. V. Wright. Simplification envelopes. In *Proceedings of SIGGRAPH '96*, pages 119 – 128. ACM SIGGRAPH, ACM Press, 1996.
4. L. De Floriani, P. Magillo, and E. Puppo. Efficient implementation of multi-triangulation. In *Proceedings Visualization '98*, pages 43–50, 1998.
5. J. El-Sana and A. Varshney. Topology simplification for polygonal virtual environments. *IEEE Transactions on Visualization and Computer Graphics*, 4, No. 2:133–144, 1998.
6. M. Garland and P. Heckbert. Surface simplification using quadric error metrics. In *Proceedings of SIGGRAPH '97 (Los Angeles, CA)*, pages 209 – 216. ACM SIG-GRAPH, ACM Press, August 1997.
7. A. Gueziec, F. Lazarus, G. Taubin, and W. Horn. Surface partitions for progressive transmission and display, and dynamic simplification of polygonal surfaces. In *Proceedings VRML 98, Monterey, California, February 16–19*, pages 25–32, 1998.
8. T. He, L. Hong, A. Varshney, and S. Wang. Controlled topology simplification. *IEEE Transactions on Visualization and Computer Graphics*, 2(2):171–184, 1996.
9. H. Hoppe. Progressive meshes. In *Proceedings of SIGGRAPH '96 (New Orleans, LA, August 4–9, 1996)*, pages 99 – 108. ACM SIGGRAPH, ACM Press, 1996.
10. H. Hoppe. View-dependent refinement of progressive meshes. In *Proceedings of SIGGRAPH '97*, pages 189 – 197. ACM SIGGRAPH, ACM Press, 1997.
11. R. Klein, A. Schilling, and W. Straßer. Illumination dependent refinement of multiresolution meshes. In *Computer Graphics International*, June 1998.
12. P. Lindstrom and G. Turk. Fast and memory efficient polygonal simplification. In *Proceedings Visualization '98*, pages 279–286, 1998.
13. D. Luebke and C. Erikson. View-dependent simplification of arbitrary polygonal environments. In *Proceedings of SIGGRAPH '97 (Los Angeles, CA)*, pages 198 – 208. ACM SIGGRAPH, ACM Press, August 1997.
14. D. Marshall, A. Campbell, and D. Fussell. Model simplification using directional clustering. In *Visual Proceedings*, page 174. ACM/SIGGRAPH Press, 1997.
15. J. Popović and H. Hoppe. Progressive simplicial complexes. In *Proceedings of SIGGRAPH '97*, pages 217 – 224. ACM SIGGRAPH, ACM Press, August 1997.
16. J. Rossignac and P. Borrel. Multi-resolution 3D approximations for rendering. In *Modeling in Computer Graphics*, pages 455–465. Springer-Verlag, June–July 1993.
17. A. Schilling and R. Klein. Texture-dependent refinement for multiresolution models. In *Computer Graphics International*, June 1998.
18. W. Schroeder. A topology modifying progressive decimation algorithm. In *IEEE Visualization '97 Proceedings*, pages 205 – 212. ACM/SIGGRAPH Press, 1997.
19. J. Xia, J. El-Sana, and A. Varshney. Adaptive real-time level-of-detail-based rendering for polygonal models. *IEEE Transactions on Visualization and Computer Graphics*, pages 171 – 183, June 1997.

Adaptive tessellation of connected primitives for interactive walkthroughs in complex industrial virtual environments

M. Krus[†‡], P. Bourdot[†], A. Osorio[†], F. Guisnel[‡] and G. Thibault[‡]

[†] LIMSI/CNRS, UPR 3251   [‡] EDF/DER, IMA/TIEM/CAO
BP 133   1, av du Gle de Gaulle
F-91403 Orsay Cedex   F-92141 Clamart Cedex

Email : Mike.Krus@edfgdf.fr, pb@limsi.fr, osorio@limsi.fr,
Francoise.Guisnel@edfgdf.fr, Guillaume.Thibault@der.edfgdf.fr

Abstract. Geometrical primitives used in virtual environments are converted to an important amount triangles at rendering time. The meshes of the resulting simplifications usually introduce discontinuities between neighboring object. We extend a simple adaptive tessellation method which adapts the amount of triangles to the viewing conditions with connection information to ensure that the meshes of connected primitives remain continuous. An ergonomical study has validated this approach for applications using virtual environments.

Keywords: adaptive tessellation, virtual environments, user evaluation.

1 Introduction

The scenes used for virtual simulators of complex and hostile industrial environments contain a large number of technical networks (piping, cable trays, ventilation) which are usually modeled by combinations of simple primitives such as cylinders, tori and cones. These primitives are converted to triangles at rendering time, leading to a huge triangle count. In order to maintain a sufficient frame rate, the amount of resulting triangles must be reduced.

Many methods have been proposed to simplify meshes and build several levels of details which can be used at different distances from the observer. These algorithms often remain unsatisfactory because they increase the size of the database. In addition, they do not respect the topology of the objects and the relationship between neighboring objects. Thus, discontinuities appear in rendering for objects which were initially connected.

We have chosen a method of real time adaptive tessellation of the primitives based on the distance from the viewpoint. In order to prevent the creation of visual artifacts and ensure a "continuity" in the mesh, we describe the relations between primitives by the graph of their connections. By evaluating the density of points required at each connection, it is possible to manage the fitting between the tessellations of the connected primitives, producing a mesh which contains the lowest number of triangles acceptable for a given viewpoint.

The following section presents the context of this research. Section 3 presents our adaptive tessellation algorithm. Finally, sect. 4 presents the results of an ergonomical study conducted to evaluate the quality of the tessellation and give a sample of the measured performance gains.

2 Background

2.1 Industrial Context

Industrial installations such as power plants contain many technical networks such as piping for fluids, cable layouts and ventilation. They are usually modeled for CAD or VR applications using simple primitives such as cylinders, tori, boxes or pyramids, which are converted to triangles at rendering time. This produces an enormous amount of triangles which needs to be reduced to achieve an interactive frame rate for VR applications. The traditional approach was introduced in 1976 by Clarck who suggested the use of *levels of detail* [1]. Several versions of the same object are produced with decreasing number of triangles (see fig. 1 with 1906 and 368 triangles). While reducing the number of faces, LOD algorithms introduce a number of problems (see sect.2.2). Our approach is to use specific characteristics of these primitives to render them adaptively based on the current viewpoint.

Fig. 1. Two versions of the same object

The major applications for this technology are training simulations [2], project review during the design phase, interactive walkthroughs for intranet based mission preparation or for the general public in visiting centers.

2.2 Related work

Levels of details. Simplification of arbitrary meshes is usually achieved by polygonal simplification (see [6] for an overview). Some type of heuristic is used to identify features of the geometry which should be preserved or removed. For example, polygons in planar area are merged into bigger ones. The tolerance on the deviation from the plane can be relaxed to decrease the number of resulting polygons. These heuristics are needed because topological information concerning the object is usually not available.

When using simple primitives such the ones we are concerned with, we could use an off-line tessellation algorithm which would produce several meshes for each primitive at different levels of details. However, this, as well as polygonal simplification methods, has several drawbacks:

– Since every primitive has several different representations, the size of database increases significantly. For scenes which initially contain an important number of primitives this can be a considerable handicap.

- It is not easy to know how many simplifications should be built and at what distance they should be used. It is a matter of finding a balance between the required quality of rendering and the size of the database. However, that knowledge is very application specific.
- Furthermore, a popping effect is usually noticeable when two representations of an object are swapped because the differences between them can be quite significant.
- Since topological information is not available, there is no way for the simplification algorithms to know that, for example, a given set of polygons form a cylinder. They are thus usually incapable of producing simplification which preserve that topological constraint.
- Different objects which are connected, i.e. topologically share some of their vertices and edges, often appear disconnected when simplified, leading to discontinuities and cracks in the mesh (see fig. 2(a)), particularly visible on low end image generators which do not support antialiasing. This happens because the primitives are simplified independently of each other and that the knowledge of their connection is not used by (or not available for) the simplification algorithms. Some algorithms resolve this problem by leaving border vertices unchanged. However, in the case of simple primitives such as cylinders, no simplification could then be performed since all vertices are on a border.

(a) Non connected primitives   (b) Connected primitives

Fig. 2. Mesh discontinuities for adjacent primitives

Adaptive meshes. Some algorithms are capable of producing *geomorphs* which contain an entire range of simplifications [3, 4]. From the simplest form of a mesh, any level of detail can be obtained by selectively adding a number of triangles based on information compiled during the simplification process. This greatly reduces the popping effect since the difference between two successive meshes can be as small as one triangle. [5] extends this method so that parts of the object facing towards the observer will contain more triangles than other parts. These methods are well suited for complex meshes like terrains; however they introduce a significant overhead for simple primitives such as those we are interested in. Additionally, the connections between objects remain ignored.

Performer's *Active Surface Definition* (ASD, see [9]) enables several pre-computed levels of details to be combined in a single structure. At rendering time, based on distance, a mesh is constructed by interpolating between two of the simplifications, producing a morphing effect. Using the ASD, the amount of detail is not uniform over the entire mesh. This method is well suited for terrain models which span a large part of the scene so that some parts are close and others are far from the observer. However, extra care needs to be taken for parts of different objects which are connected usually by insuring that the connection points are not simplified.

It is not clear whether the use of such techniques, given their complexity, would yield a significant increase in the rendering performance of simple primitives. A way of applying these algorithms would be to merge the triangles of the primitives of a given pipe branch and build geomorphs or ASD structures from that. However, animation or manipulation within the simulator of individual primitives would then be impossible. Furthermore, using on single large object would reduce the efficiency of view frustum and occlusion culling (in our framework, as described below, only visible primitives are considered for adaptive tessellation).

Scene based simplification. Luebke and Erickson propose a way of adaptively simplifying entire scenes formed of simple triangles ("polygon soup") [7]. The scene is partitioned using a hierarchical structure. A single vertex is chosen for all vertices in a given node of the hierarchy. At rendering time, traversing of each branch of the hierarchy is halted when the screen size of the current node becomes inferior to a given area. Thus parts of the structure which are further away and which project to smaller areas on the screen are traversed less deeply and the corresponding geometry is simplified.

This method achieves adaptive tessellation of any collection of triangles. However it does not respect the topology of the objects. Furthermore, the hierarchical structure which is used to partition the scene needs to be updated whenever an object moves which makes it impractical for applications requiring animations.

3 Adaptive tessellation

Since traditional LOD algorithms perform poorly on the type of scenes we are concerned with, we decided to use adaptive tessellation of the primitive and enhance it by introducing connection information to produce continuous meshes (fig. 2(b)).

One additional constraint was that our design needed to be integrated in a modern library designed to build virtual environments which are based on a scene graph in which basic primitives (defined in their own coordinate system) are composed by translation and rotation in a hierarchical way. This is convenient because it often corresponds to hierarchical compositions of objects in the application domain (like the various part of an engine). Additionally, simple animations can be performed by changing the transformation, without needing to modify each vertex of all object individually.

3.1 Basic geometric primitives

The main type of primitives we manage adaptively in our system are those with a circular section such as a cylinder, a torus or a cone. The number of triangles needed to approximate the curvature of the objects can be very important. Adaptive tessellation is used to select a number of points on the section of those primitives.

Connected primitives have two connections which are used to build the list of vertices, normals and texture coordinates for the primitive. If two primitives of the same type are placed in the scene in such a way that they share an extremity (the end points and the radius coincide) then a shared connection is constructed. Tessellation is evaluated at each connection and a mesh is constructed between two connections to represent a given primitive. In effect, constructing a mesh of several connected primitives can be viewed as a non uniform extrusion along a path linking the different connections, with constraints being propagated from one to the other (see sect. 3.2).

In order to determine if two primitives are connected, the ending points of each primitive need to be compared. If the primitives are expressed in different coordinate systems, the points need to be converted into a common systems. This increases the number of computations and introduces errors. In order to combine efficient connection detection with traditional primitives, we have introduced a double representation:

- *Connectable Primitives* which are defined in the current coordinate system. For example, a cylinder would be defined by the two end points and the radius. Connections between these primitives are managed by the *connection controller*.
- *Instance Primitives* which do not contain any geometry and are used in the scene graph. They each create a connectable primitive which is registered with the connection controller. When the graph is traversed, the transformations are applied to the primitives which update the parameters of the associated connectable primitive.

The torus is tessellated adaptively both on the section and on the number of segments used to rotate from one extremity to the other by a given angle around the axis of the torus (see the wheel of the tap in fig. 1). In our implementation, each step in the rotation is represented by an implicit connection to which other primitives cannot connect. This way, we have a uniform way of building vertices, normals and texture coordinates for all the primitives. The number of these implicit connections depends on the angle covered by the torus.

3.2 Building a mesh

In our current implementation, the connectable primitives are either cylinders, cones or tori. Each circular connection is defined by a radius, a center and a normal. For cylinders and cones, the normal is the axis of the primitive. For tori, it is the tangent of the arc defined by the major radius. A connection is either *bound* if it connects two different primitives, or *free* if it only belongs to one primitive (as is the case for the first or the last one in a list of connected primitives). The basic steps in the algorithm for constructing a mesh are:

- construct points, normals and texture coordinates;
  update these if one of the parameter of the primitive changes.
- for each frame and each primitive:
  - select a number of points for each connection.
  - build a mesh.

Constructing vertices. Points for each connection are constructed by using the simple parametric equation of the circle in the XY plane. The points are then translated to the origin of the connection and rotated so that the Z axis of the circle lies along the direction of the normal for the connection. However, special care needs to be taken to make sure that points of the two connections of the same primitive are aligned with each other. Otherwise some primitives would appear twisted.

This is done by defining an *up vector* in the direction where the first point of the circle will be. It is either the X axis or the Z axis depending on whether the normal of the connection lies along the Z axis or not. Given a list of connected primitives as explained in sect. 3.3, an up vector is chosen for first free connection. That up vector is then propagated from one connection to the other depending on the type of the primitive:

- if the primitive is a cylinder or a cone, the up vector is simply copied from the first connection to the second. Changing the up vector between two extremities of a cylinder or a cone would introduce a twisting effect which would be noticeable.
- if the primitive is a torus, the up vector is rotated around the axis of the torus by the same angle as the torus. This is done in steps for each of the implicit connections. Thus, the rotation of the up vector is made smoothly over all the connections as shown in fig. 3.

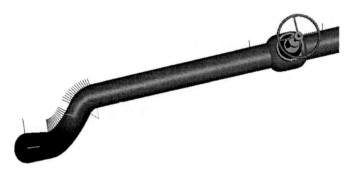

Fig. 3. Propagating the *up vector*

Selecting vertices. The adaptive tessellation algorithm selects a number of points from those stored in the connection. The selection criteria should ideally be based on the screen size: the smaller the primitives are, the lesser will the curvature be noticeable and fewer triangles will be needed to represent them. However screen size can be expensive to compute. In the case of the primitives we are using, two factors are considered to select an appropriate tessellation at each connection:

- *the distance:* more details are required for closer objects. For each object, the ergonomical study (see sect. 4) has enabled us to define a range of distances between which tessellation should vary linearly from the highest to the lowest possible value. Distance is measured at the center of each connection. This means that connected primitives can have a different number of vertices at each connection and that the resulting mesh would not be uniform.
- *the radius of the primitives:* the smaller the radius, the fewer vertices are used. This factor is in fact used to modify the value of the distance range discussed above. If a cylinder of one meter diameter reaches it's lower tessellation level at a distance of one hundred meters, then a cylinder of fifty centimeters diameter will reach it at only fifty meters.

We do not use the length of the cylinder as a factor for computing tessellation because the primary feature which makes a cylinder identifiable as one is the curvature which is controlled by the radius. Length has very little impact on the perception of the curvature.

Initially we tried selecting vertices continuously, adding points one by one as the primitive moves closer to the observer. However this produces a rotation effect since points are packed gradually closer to each other and additional points are added to close the circle. We have thus chosen to constrain the number of vertices so that it remains a multiple of three. This maintains three "stable" directions as the tessellation evolves suppressing the rotation effect.

Building triangles. Given a number of points for each connection, a triangle strip is build connecting the vertices. If the number of vertices is not the same for both connections, the strip will contain degenerate triangles (reduce to a segment). While this is generally not desirable, it has no effect on the rendering (since points and normals coincide) and enables to retain the use of strips which are quicker to render.

3.3 Managing connections

As explained in sect. 3.2, constraints need to be propagated from one connection to the other so that points remain aligned. For animation purposes or because of user interactions within the simulator, the position and orientation of a primitive might change. Each time this happens, the connection information needs to be updated. This is done in three steps:

1. The validity of all existing connections is checked. The non-valid connections are deleted and replaced by free connections for the each disconnected primitive.
2. Primitives with free connections are compared to each other to determine if new connections are established. If no connection can be found, the free primitives are placed in a temporary list.
3. Finally, constraints are propagated from one primitive to the other starting with those in the list constructed in the previous step. Given a primitive of that list, an up vector is chosen for its free connection and is recursively propagated from connection to connection (until a free connection is reached) using the method described in sect. 3.2.

This ensures that constraints can be propagated without having to explicitly build lists of primitives: the connections are used to get the chaining information.

4 Evaluation and Performance

Experiments. The aim of these experiments was to evaluate the loss of information when simplifying virtual 3D objects. Reddy showed that the caracteristics of the human visual system can be used to control the simplification objects [8]. We extend these results by showing that simplifications can be used at levels which are perceivable because cognitive processes facilitate the recognition of objects. We tested the perceptual behavior of various types of users to determine the effect of field knowledge: workers from the piping and plumbing service of the CNPE (Energy Production Unit) of Tricastin; computer scientists and engineers, expert in VR applications; people non experts in either production installations or VR applications. The experiments were designed and conducted by A. Drouin, S. Tonnoir and M.-A. Amorim, of EDF.

Fig. 4. Four taps for the experimentation

- Different versions of standard taps were displayed with various levels of tessellation and view angles (see fig. 4. The subjects were ask to adjust the distance of the objects to the distance they thought was most appropriate. We could thus reconstruct the curve of perception levels for 3D objects based on the distance from the observer.
- The same objects were presented close up at various angles and the tessellation was gradually decreased until the user pressed a key to indicate that he had sensed a change in the representation of the object. This enabled us to optimize the maximum number of triangles needed when the objects are presented close up.
- Having tested the perception of the tessellation, we still needed to test if participants were capable of identifying randomly presented taps based on the mental representation they had acquired. A close up view of a highly detailed version of each of the objects was displayed side by side by a random view of any object at any tessellation level, any orientation, and any distance. The user was asked to decide whether both displayed objects were identical.

Fig. 5. Comparing real and virtual scenes

- The last experiment was intended to study the behavior of participants when they are required to process a complex environment of geometric and architectural configurations. We wanted to find out if an excessive degradation would impact on the efficiency of the simple viewpoint finding task. A picture of the real scene was displayed above a 3D model of the scene in which the user was ask to navigate until he would find the point of view corresponding to where the picture had been taken from (see fig.5). The subjects were divided in four groups. Adaptive tessellation was activated for the first group but the three others where shown three different fixed levels of tessellation.

Results. The first three experiments proved that the appropriate tessellation for the circular section of the primitives should range from 6 vertices to 18. The minimum tessellation for a cylinder of one meter diameter should be reached at 30 meters.

The last experiment showed that adaptive tessellation improved the performance of subjects within the environment. High levels of fixed tessellation lower the frame rate and hinder the navigation. The lowest level of tessellation distorted the objects too much and made identification more difficult. The frame rate and triangle count for the adaptively tessellated environment were comparable to those obtained for a fixed tessellation of 12 vertices. However, triangles were better distributed since closer objects had more details than further ones. This lead to fewer identification errors and to a better recognition of objects in the environment.

Results also showed that dynamic visual perception is influenced by the operative knowledge as well as by the task that is assigned to the subject. The perception and recognition strategy of industry workers was influenced by their prior knowledge of the types of objects and installations used in the experimentation. It usually help them recognize simplified objects by accepting greater degradations and filtering out some parts of the object which were not important for the recognition (as the supporting pipes). However, it also sometimes lead them to consider only foreground objects and ignore pertinent information in the background, which introduced a few more errors in the navigation.

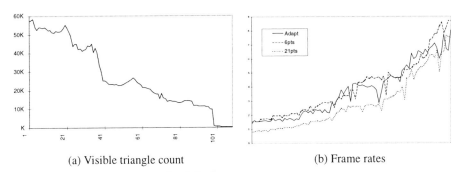

(a) Visible triangle count   (b) Frame rates

Fig. 6. Performance measures

4.1 Performance

We have implemented this algorithm using the OpenGL Optimizer library. It is coupled to a view frustum and an occlusion culling algorithm so that only visible primitives are evaluated for adaptive tessellation. The performance measures where made on an environment representing a forty meters long corridor with one side covered with various pipes (see fig.5). It contains about 2300 primitives leading to maximum of 50K triangles. The observer simply walked down that corridor while the frame rate and the number of displayed triangles were measured.

As shown in fig. 6(a), the number of triangles rises slowly as the users moves closer the objects and drops sharply when close objects move out of the view frustum. Figure 6(b) shows the frame rate for adaptive tessellation, and constant tessellation levels such that each cylinder is represented by six and twenty one vertices (which are the minimum and maximum values determined by the ergonomical study). The frame rate increases gradually as fewer objects are visible. The figure shows adaptive tessellation performs always better than constant high levels of tessellation which are required to maintain object comprehension.

5 Conclusion

In order to reduce the amount of triangles used to represent simple primitives, we have presented an extension of a tessellation algorithm which already which adapts the number of triangles to the observation distance. In this context, we showed that it is useful to manage connection information so that the meshes of adjacent primitives remains continuous. Using the connections, the alignment constraints can be propagated from one primitive to the next. The connections are updated each time an object moves within the scene.

An ergomical study was conducted to determine the appropriate levels of tessellation for a given distance. It has also shown that adaptive tessellation improves the performance of the user within the virtual environment by raising the frame rate while preserving the appearance of visible objects.

We plan to extend our design by including other factors to modulate the tessellation such as the incidence of the viewing direction, the speed of the object with respect to the observer or the peripheral location. Additionnaly, we intend to evaluate the inclusion of other types of primitives within our framework.

References

1. J. H. Clark. Hierarchical geometric models for visible surface algorithms. *Communications of the ACM*, 19:547–554, 1976.
2. A. Drouin, A. Schmid and G. Thibault. Training of Nuclear Workers using Virtual Environments. *IAEA Specialist's Meeting on Maintenance Training Centers for Nuclear Power Plants*, Charlotte, NC, October 1998.
3. M. Eck, T. DeRose, T. Duchamp, H. Hoppe, M. Lounsbery, and W. Stuetzle. Multiresolution Analysis of Arbitrary Meshes. In *SIGGRAPH '95*, August 1995.
4. H. Hoppe. Progressive meshes. In *SIGGRAPH'96*, 1996.
5. H. Hoppe. View-dependent refinement of progressive meshes. In *SIGGRAPH'97*, 1997.
6. M. Krus, P. Bourdot, F. Guisnel, and G. Thibault. Levels of detail and polygonal simplification. *ACM's Crossroads*, 3.4, 1997.
7. D. Luebke and C. Erikson. View-dependent simplification of arbitrary polygonal environments. In *SIGGRAPH'97*, 1997.
8. M. Reddy. Perceptually Modulated Level of Detail for Virtual Environments. PhD thesis, University of Edinburgh, 1997.
9. Silicon Graphics, Inc. *IRIS Performer Programmer's Guide*, 1998.

An Optical Tracking System for VR/AR-Applications

Klaus Dorfmüller

ZGDV Computer Graphics Center, Visual Computing Department,
Rundeturmstr.6, D-64283 Darmstadt, Germany
EMail: Klaus.Dorfmueller@zgdv.de
WWW: http://www.zgdv.de/www/zgdv-vc/

Abstract. In this paper, an optical tracking system is introduced for the use within Virtual and Augmented Reality applications. The system uses retroreflective markers which are attached to a special designed interaction device. The construction of the device allows us to gather six degrees of freedom. In order to achieve high tracking precision we introduce a calibration algorithm which results in sub-pixel accuracy and is therefore well applicable within Augmented Reality scenarios. Further the algorithm for calculating the pose of a rigid body is described. Finally, the optical tracking system is evaluated in regard to its accuracy.

1 Introduction

Realtime interaction within Virtual Environments in Virtual Reality (VR) and Augmented Reality (AR) applications is one of the essential objectives, which should be provided in a proper manner. Especially the way of interacting with virtual objects should be implemented in an intuitive way. Furthermore the interaction should not tether the user, and it should be robust and precise. Common VR-systems use the wide-spread magnetic trackers, which suffer from electrical interference caused by included magnetic currents and eddy patterns initiated by metallic objects and external sources of radiation such as computer monitors or projectors. In addition, magnetic systems limit the range of user interaction.

Since Augmented Reality applications often make use of video cameras, realtime optical tracking became an important issue within this area. Since optical tracking has been a research topic within Computer Vision applications for quite some time, many methods have been proposed for camera calibration, image segmentation, feature tracking, structure estimation, motion prediction and motion smoothing. Although this gives a rather comprehensive basis the practical drawbacks and limitations of using these methods together with real-time VR and AR applications are still unknown. Indeed, one can find commercial optical tracking systems like Biovision^{TM}, Biomechanics^{TM} and Adaptive Optics Associates^{TM}, but since they are related to different subjects, the setup is not suitable to Augmented Reality. As an example often large and heavy cameras are applied, which cannot be mounted on the user's head. Furthermore, the systems usually do not allow to make any kind of application specific extensions. As a result it is impossible to perform a calibration on the fly. These systems are mostly restricted to special applications like natural movements for character animation. Besides these technical drawbacks commercial optical systems usually are very expensive.

Due to the limitations of magnetic trackers, an optical tracking system was developed, which overcomes many of the drawbacks of conventional tracking systems. We mainly apply this tracking system in combination with a projection table. Hereby we want to provide an intuitive, non obtrusive human computer interface for an intuitive interaction with virtual environments (cf. 1(a)). Since we are able to achieve sub-pixel accuracy by tracking six degrees of freedom, the system seems to be well applicable within AR applications as well. We especially consider the calibration method which could be extended to a dynamic estimation of th external and internal camera parameters as very beneficial in AR. Thus, as a practical matter, the system will allow to change the focal length of the cameras, which makes Augmented Reality applications more flexible. A possible scenario for using the described optical tracking system within interactive augmented reality applications is shown in Fig. 1(b). Two video cameras

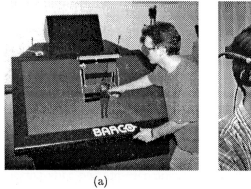 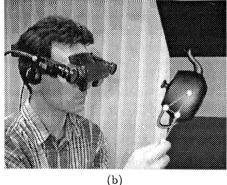

(a)   (b)

Fig. 1. Optical tracking applications

for an accurate position determination are mounted on the user's head and are fitted with infrared filters. The system is able to track retroreflective landmarks, to determine the absolute orientation, and an interaction device simultaneously.

2   Related Work

Since on the one hand there is a strong demand in new ways of man- machine interaction, and on the other hand current standard computer technology enables to perform various real-time image processing applications, many research groups are developing methods for optical head tracking [12, 3], hand tracking [6, 10, 11] or even full body tracking [17]. The captured signals are sometimes further processed in order to perform gesture recognition [6, 17]. Some Augmented Reality [7] make use of adapted algorithm coming from robotic applications, where the position an orientation of moving cameras is calculated relative to well known edges or marker positions (see [18]). They use one or more CCD cameras mounted on the user's head and determine the head's position and orientation relative to predefined patterns. Predefined patterns are necessary to simplify and accelerate the segmentation process.

Koller *et al.* [7] use one PAL CCD camera. Based on an initial calibration method in order to estimate the camera's position, they are able to apply collision detection methods if the user is interacting with virtual objects. Their calibration includes the estimation of internal camera parameters like the focal length. The usage of full PAL images creates interlace effects which require special segmentation algorithms, especially when the camera or the object moves. In addition, the position estimation cannot be performed very precise, because of the time difference between acquiring both half images. In order to predict the position of artifical landmarks, which are usually attached at the walls and to yield 3-d camera position and orientation, they apply an Extended Kalman Filter.

Another optical tracking system was introduced by Madritsch and Gervautz [9]. Their hardware system consists of two Silicon Graphics Indy Workstations with CCD cameras and infrared LEDs. Due to their unsynchronized cameras, the 3-d position determination is not very precise while the beacon is moving. They apply a standard calibration, which was presented for exampe by Tsai [15], with radial lens distortion parameters. This technique is a time-consuming process that usually requires special equipment[1] and a great deal of care.

Affine object representations are used for example by Kutulakos, Vallino and Seibert [8, 13]. They avoid an Object-to-World and a World-to-Camera transformation. Hence, they are able to renounce a camera calibration, but they lose information which results in restricted interaction possibilities.

DeMenthon and Davis [4] have introduced a small iterative algorithm which determines the object pose. Within their method, they do not require an initial pose estimate and they prevent a calculation of an inverse matrix. As the input, their algorithm detects the image points which belong to the 3-d object.

State *et al.* [14] show a hybrid tracking approach. They combine vision-based trackers with magnetic trackers in order to get the robustness of magnetic and the accuracy of optical systems. The synchronization of both tracking systems is not an easy task, in fact it is almost impossible, but it is needed for a precise 3-d position calculation. In addition, their tracking system works in a restricted area due to necessary cables.

---

[1] In order to use Tsai's calibration technique at the projection table, it is necessary to have a large pattern. Furthermore, it is very cumbersome to execute a coplanar movement of a calibration pattern.

In this paper, an optical tracking system is described, which uses retroreflective markers with infrared light in order to achieve a fast segmentation process. The system uses two video cameras, because of the advantages which are well known from 3-d Computer Vision [16], which imply a high precision in regard to position estimation.

A calibration algorithm is described in Sect. 2, which is able to determine intrinsic and extrinsic camera parameters during the tracking of a rigid body in real-time. Section 3.2 shows how to estimate the object pose from given 3-d position values. These 3-d input values are not necessarily part of the rigid body. The algorithm determines automatically the 3-d point belonging to the rigid body within the 3-d point cloud.

3   The Optical Tracking System

As the system is used in combination with the projection table under reduced lighting conditions, an infrared light source is mounted on each camera. Choosing retroreflective balls as tracking markers came out to be a good approach for a precise center of gravity determination. Furthermore, an accurate position calculation is necessary while the user moves the balls. Specifically, if the user rotates the input device, the determination of the rotational parameters needs a high precision marker position detection. Therefore, the system is equipped with progressive scan cameras, which are externally synchronized. Both cameras are pointed towards the center of the projection plane and are placed one meter to the left and to the right of the table in regard to the corners of the projection table. After proceeding the camera calibration, which is described in the next section, the centre of gravity of all markers is calculated. The marker matching between left and right image centers is solved with the epipolar constraint which makes use of the fundamental matrix determined from the calibration algorithm. For more details see [5, 18]. The result are 3-d positions given in the projection plane coordinate system, which is right handed and the centre is lying in the middle of the plane, the x axis belonging to the width and z coming out of the plane. Afterwards, the object pose of the interaction device shown in Fig. 1(b) can be determined. The position and rotation values are transmitted over network to the rendering system.

3.1   System Calibration

The calibration step is very easy to perform because the system uses an adaptive calibration method[2], which was first developed by Azarbayejani and Pentland [1, 2]. Thus, our system can adaptively calibrate a stereo rig by tracking a single moving point acquired from each of two cameras. As a result, the calibration data may be entered by just waving a flashlight around (see left and right camera

---

[2] Adaptive means, that camera parameters are altered to get better estimated values. The process requires no knowledge on the user's side.

Fig. 2. The system calibration

measurements given in Fig. 2). The result is a calibrated camera system where 3-d points are given in the coordinate system of the right camera. A detailed description of this technique is given in [5]. The principle of the calibration technique, which increases pixel accuracy, is shown in Fig. 3. First, a measured

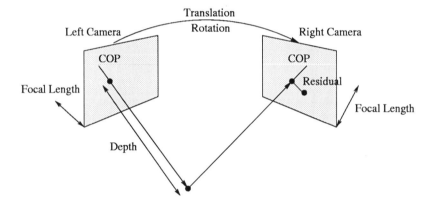

Fig. 3. The calibration principle

point in the left camera's image plane is re-projected onto a 3-d position in the left camera coordinate system with the knowledge of a pre-estimated depth, focal length and centre-of-projection (COP). Second, the resulting 3-d point is transformed to the coordinate system of the right camera. Third, the 3-d point is projected onto the right camera image plane using the pre-estimated focal length. Comparing this result with the measured image point of the right camera enhances the pixel accuracy. This works by modeling the camera transformation values, both focal length parameters and the depth value of the measurement, in a state vector of an Iterated Extended Kalman Filter (IEKF). After a pre-estimation is done, the filter iteratively alters the state in order to reduce the residual vector until a variance threshold is achieved.

38

3.2 Object Pose Estimation

In order to calculate the rotation of an object, at least three points are needed. Since they have to be identified unambiguously, the interaction device uses three sphere markers to form an unique rigid body. Fig. 4 shows the marker locations at P_a, P_b and P_c. These three marker locations form a non-regular triangle, where

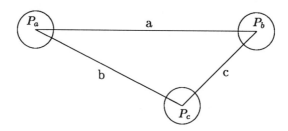

Fig. 4. A predefined triangle

$\|a\| \neq \|b\| \neq \|c\|$. After a unique definition of the used triangle the lengths of the edges a, b and c are used to identify the vertices[3].

The following algorithm is applied to solve this structure identification problem: After applying linear geometry and the epipolar constraint, all calculated 3-d values acquired by the system are used to achieve the best fitting of the known structure of the triangle. The goal of the algorithm is to find the object from a given 3-d point cloud. Therefore, the first step is to calculate the distances d_k between all 3-d points P, which have passed the epipolar constraint within a predefined maximum error. If n is the number of 3-d points, $(n-1)!$ possible distances can be calculated. The following mathematical expression can be read as:

For index k starting from 1 to $(n-1)!$ and index i starting from 1 to $n-1$ and index j starting from index $i+1$ to n the distance d_k is calculated by $\|P_i - P_j\|$.

$$\forall k : 1..(n-1)!. \quad \forall i : 1..n-1. \quad \forall j : (i+1)..n. \quad d_k = \|P_i - P_j\|$$

The second step calculates the differences between a measured distance d_k and the pre-known distances from a, b and c. These differences are stored in ε_{a_k}, ε_{b_k} and ε_{c_k} and denote the errors.

$$\forall k : 1..(n-1)!. \quad \varepsilon_{a_k} = |d_k - \|a\||. \quad \varepsilon_{b_k} = |d_k - \|b\||. \quad \varepsilon_{c_k} = |d_k - \|c\||$$

Thirdly, three sets $\mathcal{A}$, $\mathcal{B}$ and $\mathcal{C}$ include all distances which fulfil an error threshold ϵ.

$$\forall k : 1..(n-1)!. \quad \mathcal{A} = \{d_k | \varepsilon_{a_k} < \epsilon\}. \quad \mathcal{B} = \{d_k | \varepsilon_{b_k} < \epsilon\}. \quad \mathcal{C} = \{d_k | \varepsilon_{c_k} < \epsilon\}$$

Finally, to find a good solution, the following instructions are proofed to de-

---

[3] The interaction device shown in Fig. 1(b) has 7.5cm, 10cm and 5cm side lengths.

termine a structure model. First, each distance of set $\mathcal{A}$ is combined with each distance of set $\mathcal{B}$ and $\mathcal{C}$. For such a combination, a cyclic path from P_a over P_b to P_c and back to P_a has to be found. Second, the error should be the smallest value.

$structure \Rightarrow$

$\forall i : 1..|\mathcal{A}|. \quad d_{a_i} \in \mathcal{A}.$

$\forall j : 1..|\mathcal{B}|. \quad d_{b_j} \in \mathcal{B}.$

$\forall k : 1..|\mathcal{C}|. \quad d_{c_k} \in \mathcal{C}.$

$\exists path : \quad P_a \xmapsto{d_{a_i}} P_b \xmapsto{d_{b_j}} P_c \xmapsto{d_{c_k}} P_a.$

$\exists \varepsilon_{min} : min(|d_{a_i} - \|\boldsymbol{a}\|| + |d_{b_j} - \|\boldsymbol{b}\|| + |d_{c_k} - \|\boldsymbol{c}\||).$

However, if two image points of one camera image plane are lying close to the epipolar plane, our system calculates two 3-d points, whereas only one 3-d point exists. Thus, this structure estimation algorithm has to decide which 3-d point best fits the predefined model. As video-based tracking systems suffer from some measurement errors, the epipolar constraint described above cannot solve the correspondence between left and right image points sufficiently. For example, when all three images of the markers can be seen, the algorithm may select only two image points from the left camera frame and three image points from the right image frame or vice versa. This is because the path with the smallest error is always selected. The problem can be solved if priorities are added to the algorithm. If the whole structure P_a, P_b and P_c is formed by completely different image points, then the priority has the highest value. Otherwise, the priority decreases according to the number of common image points.

After finding the structure of the rigid body, the rotation of the rigid body can be estimated using the vector cross product two times.

4   Experimental Results

The optical tracking system runs on a standard PC with a 300 MHz Pentium II processor. A framegrabber (i.e. ELTEC PCEye2) is required which writes the image data directly into the main memory. A frame rate of 25 frames per second is achieved. Actually we would be able to obtain even higher rates, but due to the limitation of the frame grabber's frequency, we are limited to the given performance. The latency between the creation of an action and the recognition, without regarding the network transmission, depends directly on the latency of the framegrabber. Since the asynchronous grabbing function of the cameras is not used, between a grabbing command and the next available frame, 40 ms have passed. Afterwards the system needs less than one frame for calculating the object position and rotation. The performance of our system allows us to make use of the complete camera sensor plane of 768x484 sensor elements.

As an examination of the pixel accuracy, the determined 3-d position of a reflective marker is projected to the camera plane and compared with the

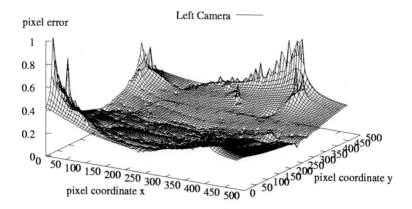

Fig. 5. Pixel accuracy

measurement. In regard to our Augmented Reality setup, two cameras with a distance of 25 cm capture a marker. This marker is moved within a volume of 1.5mx1.5mx1.5m and a distance of 1.5 m, to cover the whole interaction volume. Then a grid, which also shows intermediate values of the left camera's pixel accuracy is drawn (Fig. 5). Considering this figure, a radial lens distortion can be realized and the average pixel accuracy is less than 0.4 pixels.

The resulting absolute precision depends on the camera equipment and the quality of the calibration. Within our setup, an absolute accuracy of 2-6 mm is achieved if the system should report a one meter difference.

In addition, a examination of the rotation accuracy was performed. Therefore, the interaction device was used to effect rotations around the three coordinate axes in regard to the projection plane. Fig. 6 shows an experimental rotation of 90 degrees around the x axis[4].

The experiment starts by pointing towards the y-axis, then pointing to the z-axis and returning to the origin. The second experiment starts by pointing to the y-axis and performing a rotation of 180 degrees around the y-axis[5]. Finally, a rotation of 180 degrees around z is printed in Fig. 6. Considering these plots, the drawn curves are mostly continual. The system fails under specific circumstances, whenever the user moves all three markers of the triangle cursor near the epipolar plane. This situation can be seen in the right plot of Fig. 6, where the interaction device passes the epipolar plane in iteration 170 to 190.

There are different possibilies to solve this problem. One possibility is to use a third camera. Alternatively, the device has to be fitted with a fourth marker. A prediction of the object movement can be used to smooth rotational parametric curves. Hence, the problematic situation given in the plot of Fig. 6 can be solved.

---

[4] The x-axis is given by the width of the projection plane
[5] The y-axis is given by the depth of the projection plane.

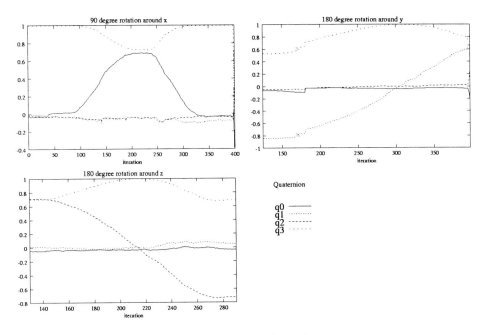

Fig. 6. Experimental rotations

5 Conclusions

In this paper a new optical tracking system was presented, which can be applied in Virtual and Augmented Reality applications. Since the tracking allows to determine both the position as well as the orientation of a distinct device a very flexible interaction technique is provided for Virtual Reality. Since most of the Augmented Reality system make use of a video-based approach, our system allows an easy calculation of the relative orientation between user and scene without the need to cope with the drawbacks in regard to range or interferances of magnetical or ultrasonic tracker.

Acknowledgments

Parts of this work were done in cooperation with BMW, Munich, Germany. I would like to thank R. Grandl for his friendly cooperation. I would also like to thank Prof. J. Encarnação for providing me with the research environment in which this work was carried out. Furthermore, I would like to thank all of our department for their feedback and suggestions with which they came up in many discussions, and Harry Brown for proof reading this paper.

References

[1] A. Azarbayejani and A. P. Pentland *Recursive Estimation of Motion, Structure, and Focal Length*, IEEE PAMI 17(6), June 1995

[2] A. Azarbayejani and A. P. Pentland *Camera Self-Calibration from One Point Correspondence*, Media Lab Technical Report 341, 1995

[3] S. Birchfield *Elliptical Head Tracking Using Intensity Gradients and Color Histograms*, IEEE Conference on Computer Vision and Pattern Recognition, Santa Barbara, California, June 1998

[4] D.F. DeMenthon and L.S. Davis *Model-Based Object Pose in 25 Lines of Code*, International Journal of Coputer Vision (IJVC), Vol. 15, No. 1-2, June 1995, pp. 123-141

[5] K. Dorfmüller and H. Wirth *Real-Time Hand and Head Tracking for Virtual Environments Using Infrared Beacons* In: N. Magnenat-Thalmann, D. Thalmann (Eds.) "Modelling and Motion Capture Techniques for Virtual Environments", International Workshop, CAPTECH'98, Geneva, Switzerland, November 1998, Proceedings LNAI 1537, Heidelberg: Springer Verl., 1998

[6] T. Heap and D. Hogg *Towards 3-D Hand Tracking using a Deformable Model*, 2nd International Face and Gesture Recognition Conference, 1996

[7] D. Koller, G. Klinker, E. Rose, D. Breen, R. Whitaker and M.Tuceryan *Real-time Vision-Based Camera Tracking for Augmented Reality Applications*, In Proc. of the ACM Symposium on Virtual Reality Software and Technology (VRST-97), Lausanne, Switzerland, September 15-17, 1997, pp. 87-94

[8] K.J. Kutulakos and J. Vallino *Affine Object Representations for Calibration-Free Augmented Reality*, IEEE Virtual Reality Ann. Int'l Symposium (VRAIS'96), 1996, pp.25-36

[9] F.Madritsch and M. Gervautz. *CCD-Camera Based Optical Beacon Tracking for Virtual and Augmented Reality*, Eurographics 15(3), 1996

[10] J. Rehg and T. Kanade *Digiteyes: Vision-based Human Hand Tracking*, Technical Report CMU-CS-TR-93-220, Carnegie Mellon University, 1993

[11] J. Rehg and T. Kanade *Visual Tracking of Self-occluding Articulated Objects*, Technical Report CMU-CS-94-224, Carnegie Mellon University, 1994

[12] F. Seibert and M. Wolf *Tracking Faces for Virtual Holography*, Proc. 3D Image Analysis and Synthesis'97, 1997

[13] F. Seibert *Stereo based Augmented Reality in Medicine*, The Third Korea-Germany Joint Workshop on Advanced Medical Image Processing, Seoul, Korea, August 13-16, 1998

[14] A. State, G. Hirota, D.T. Chen, W.F. Garrett and M.A. Livingston *Superior Augmented Reality Registration by Integrating Landmark Tracking and Magnetic Tracking*, SIGGRAPH'96 (New Orleans, LA), August 1996, pp. 429-438

[15] R. T. Tsai *An Efficient and Accurate Camera Calibration Technique for 3-D Machine Vision* , Proccedings of the IEEE Conference on Computer Vision and Pattern Recognition, 1986

[16] J. Weng, T.S. Huang and Ahuja *3D Motion Estimation, Understanding, and Prediction from Noisy Image Sequences* , IEEE Transactions on Pattern Recognition and Machine Intelligence, Vol. PAMI-9, No. 3, May, 1987

[17] C. Wren, A. Azarbayejani, T. Darrell and A. Pentland. *Pfinder: Real-time Tracking of the Human Body*, Integration Issues in Large Commercial Media Delivery Systems. A. G. Tescher and V. M. Bove, 1996

[18] Z. Zhang and O. Faugeras *3-D Dynamic Scene Analysis*, Springer Series in Information Sciences, Springer-Verlag, Berlin 1992

The integration of optical and magnetic tracking for multi-user augmented reality

Thomas Auer, Stefan Brantner, and Axel Pinz

Computer Graphics and Vision, TU Graz,
Münzgrabenstr. 11, A-8010 Graz, Austria
tom@icg.tu-graz.ac.at,
http://www.icg.tu-graz.ac.at/~tom/stube/stube.html

Abstract. Multi-user augmented reality requires excellent registration for all users, which cannot be achieved by magnetic trackers *alone*. This paper presents a new approach combining magnetic and optical tracking. The magnetic tracker is used to coarsely predict the positions of landmarks in the camera image. This restricts the search area to a size which can be managed close to real-time. This new hybrid tracking system outperforms a calibrated magnetic tracker in terms of position, orientation, and jitter.

1 Introduction

In augmented reality applications precise registration is important [1]. If the position or orientation of the user cannot be determined precisely, the augmentation will be unsatisfactory: virtual objects will be displaced or even worse, they will float around freely in the space surrounding the user. Thus, precise registration is needed to avoid these symptoms. Further stress on precise registration is put in a multi-user environment: interactions become difficult at best if not impossible if augmented objects appear at different physical locations for each user.

In this paper we present the tracking system developed for our multi-user augmented reality system "Studierstube" [4], combining both optical and magnetic tracking. We further describe the experimental setup for determining the precision of our system and present results on the accuracy of the optical tracking system for both position and orientation. In addition, the jitter inherent in the system is quantified. All these measurements are set in relation to the precision that can be achieved with a carefully calibrated magnetic tracking system, cf. [7].

2 System Overview

As stated above, multi-user augmented reality systems are requiring precise registration. In order to serve this demand, both optical and magnetic tracking are combined in the "Studierstube". Magnetic tracking has the benefit of being rather robust (i.e., no outliers), but it does not offer the required accuracy. In contrast, optical tracking is not as reliable as magnetic tracking, but if the results are correct, they are more precise than data from magnetic tracking. Thus, by integrating both methods one expects a system both robust and precise.

In order to combine both systems, we built an augmented reality helmet (similar to [6]) that integrates a magnetic sensor, stereo cameras and a see-through display used for augmentation. The helmet is depicted in Fig. 1

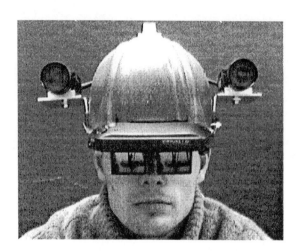 

Fig. 1. AR helmet with *stereo cameras*, *magnetic sensor* and *HMD*.

Our tracking system consists of three components, namely *magnetic tracking*, *optical tracking*, and *integration of magnetic and optical tracking*. We will now briefly describe each of these components.

2.1 Magnetic tracking

The magnetic tracking system consists of a standard Ascension *Flock of Birds* magnetic tracker attached to a PC running Linux. Data are distributed through a multicast channel. In difference to other systems, the magnetic tracker has only been slightly calibrated. We determined the offset between the origin of the magnetic coordinate system and the world coordinate system, as well as the transformation between the axes of both coordinate systems. (Note that this transformation is not simply a rotation due to the fact that the axes of the magnetic tracker are not perfectly perpendicular!)

2.2 Optical tracking

The optical tracking system presented in this paper works with a monocular setup: Only one of the two cameras mounted on the helmet is actually used. The system consists of the following two components:

- 2D tracking: features are tracked in the camera image.
- 3D computation: based on feature locations in 2D and corresponding 3D locations, position and orientation of the camera are computed.

Tracking in 2D is done using "signaled" landmarks, i.e., (artificial) features whose locations have been determined by some external calibration procedure (we used a theodolite). Currently, we are tracking the corners of black rectangles on a white background, cf. Fig. 2. The actual tracking process is performed with XVision (a real-time 2D tracking library developed at Yale University [5]). For increased precision (XVision is only accurate up to a pixel) we have adopted a sub-pixel tracking method [10] for edges (corners are composed of two edges) while still maintaining the real-time capability of the library. It takes approximately 5 msecs to track a single feature.

Among all features visible, ten to sixteen features are selected[1] and tracked. Four of these tracked features (note that all features are coplanar) are used for the computation of an initial camera pose [3]. This initial pose is further optimized using the Gauss-Newton method [8] by minimizing the sum of square distances between real feature positions (as determined by 2D optical tracking) on one hand and positions implied by the initial pose on the other hand.

Fig. 2 depicts the optical tracking system: black triangles indicate feature positions as predicted by the magnetic tracker, red lines indicate tracked corners, green circles mark the features selected for pose computation, and blue crosses denote the projection of all visible features with the computed pose.

2.3 Integration of magnetic and optical tracking

Detection and tracking of the features in the camera image plane is crucial to the time-consumption of the tracker: the larger the (initial) search area, the longer the computation takes. In order to allow for comparatively small search areas, we use the data from the magnetic tracker to predict the location of features in the image. Based on this prediction, features are located and tracked in 2D, and position and orientation of the camera are computed. The result from optical tracking is accepted if the difference to the data from the magnetic tracker (recall that the magnetic tracker is more robust than the optical system) is small enough.

On one hand, the number of features tracked has a direct influence on the cycle time of the system, as each feature takes approximately 5 msecs to track. On the other hand, more tracked features lead to better results in the optimization process. In practice, tracking ten to twelve features is an acceptable solution: the whole tracking cycle (including pose computation and optimization) takes approximately 100 msecs, but there are still sufficient features for optimization.

---

[1] Selected features are spread as much as possible [2].

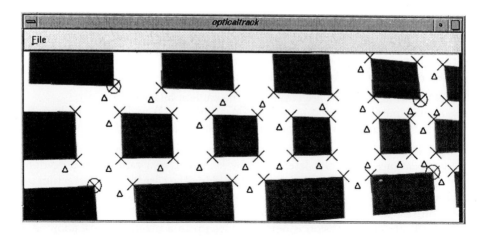

Fig. 2. Optical tracker: magnetic prediction (triangles), tracked corners (gray lines), selected features (circles) and projected feature position (crosses).

3 Experimental Setup

In order to evaluate the quality of a tracking system, two different properties have to be determined:

accuracy describes whether the result obtained by a certain method accurately matches the physical location and orientation of the system, and

jitter describes variations in the measurements for a stationary system.

In the following experiments, the AR helmet is facing a white wall with 28 black rectangular tracking targets whose world coordinates have been determined by theodolite measurements and are thus known to the tracking algorithm. The rectangles are mounted on a wall approximately 1.7 m from the magnetic tracker and their height varies from 0.75 m to 2.0 m. Side lengths of the rectangles range from 9 cm to 19 cm. The features actually tracked are the corners of these rectangles; their location is predicted using the pose of the virtual camera. Obviously, the camera has always to be oriented in a way such that some features are visible to the camera.

In addition to the tracking algorithm described above (selection of ten to twelve features) we also obtained results with a minimum configuration of four features (and optimizing over only these four features) and results with optimization over all visible features.

4 Jitter

In our optical system, 3D jitter originates from jitter in the 2D tracking methods: Due to a known control loop cycle in XVision [5], the position of the tracked edges will vary by about 1.0 pixel with the original tracking method and about 0.1 pixel with our improved sub-pixel tracking algorithm.

In order to determine the amount of jitter we took 50 samples for both the magnetic and optical tracking system at nine different locations. For each of the optical methods mentioned above we computed the standard deviation σ. The deviation obtained when using only four features is denoted by σ_4, the deviation for optimizing over all features is denoted by σ_n, and the deviation of the tracking system (10-12 features) is denoted by σ_t. Finally, σ_m denotes the deviation of the magnetic tracker.

Position jitter, as depicted in Table 1, is computed as the Euclidean distance to the mean vector. Orientation is represented by three independent rotations around the x- (denoted by α), y- (β) and z-axis (γ). For each of these three rotations the standard deviation has been computed and is listed in Table 2.

For the magnetic tracker, it is significant that the amount of jitter increases with distance from the transmitter: compare the positions close to the transmitter (positions 1, 4, and 7) with medium range (positions 2, 5, and 8) and the positions (3, 6, and 9) furthest from the transmitter.

	Position								
	1	2	3	4	5	6	7	8	9
$\sigma_4[mm]$	2.083	1.762	1.155	5.316	3.478	3.590	0.733	3.542	0.931
$\sigma_t[mm]$	0.634	1.987	0.892	2.724	1.832	1.736	0.512	1.767	0.731
$\sigma_n[mm]$	0.760	1.096	0.673	1.614	2.020	1.560	0.382	1.204	0.516
$\sigma_m[mm]$	0.279	1.230	9.218	0.355	1.532	5.164	0.994	3.687	10.713

Table 1. Standard deviation of position data for optical and magnetic tracking.

First, let us consider position jitter: Optical tracking exhibits about the same amount of jitter as the magnetic tracker at medium range. By comparing σ_n and σ_t it can be seen that the addition of all features to the optimization process does not yield a significant reduce in jitter. σ_n lies between 0.38 mm and 2.1 mm, σ_t lies in the range from 0.51 mm to 2.8 mm. On the other hand, using only four features, the amount of jitter will increase significantly (except for position 2): σ_4 lies between 0.74 mm and 5.4 mm. For the magnetic tracker, the deviation is less than 1 mm for close positions, lies between 1.2 mm and 3.6 mm for medium range and lies between 5.1 mm and 10.7 mm for distant positions. Thus, the magnetic tracker has less jitter for close locations, in the medium range the amount of jitter is approximately the same for both methods, and with increasing distance optical tracking exhibits less jitter than the magnetic tracker.

Similar to position jitter, orientation jitter of the magnetic tracker increases with increasing distance: for positions close to the transmitter (1, 4, 7) jitter lies in the range from 0.0008 rad to 0.0032 rad, at a medium range (positions 2, 5, 8)

		\multicolumn{9}{c}{Position}
		1	2	3	4	5	6	7	8	9
σ_4	α	0.00103	0.00046	0.00039	0.00207	0.00052	0.00143	0.00040	0.00070	0.00069
	β	0.00011	0.00009	0.00010	0.00013	0.00030	0.00018	0.00012	0.00039	0.00021
	γ	0.00043	0.00080	0.00040	0.00079	0.00126	0.00066	0.00054	0.00299	0.00070
σ_t	α	0.00024	0.00080	0.00039	0.00086	0.00055	0.00045	0.00027	0.00036	0.00021
	β	0.00004	0.00013	0.00008	0.00021	0.00010	0.00013	0.00007	0.00016	0.00010
	γ	0.00019	0.00069	0.00022	0.00067	0.00052	0.00062	0.00039	0.00153	0.00070
σ_n	α	0.00037	0.00043	0.00026	0.00055	0.00080	0.00059	0.00028	0.00083	0.00043
	β	0.00005	0.00007	0.00004	0.00009	0.00009	0.00008	0.00004	0.00013	0.00011
	γ	0.00018	0.00042	0.00023	0.00036	0.00033	0.00035	0.00027	0.00074	0.00033
σ_m	α	0.00088	0.00206	0.00624	0.00104	0.00228	0.00416	0.00023	0.00086	0.00563
	β	0.00070	0.00153	0.00670	0.00064	0.00170	0.00483	0.00032	0.00145	0.00986
	γ	0.00082	0.00154	0.00549	0.00185	0.00222	0.00442	0.00025	0.00172	0.00534

Table 2. Standard deviation of orientation data for optical and magnetic tracking [rad].

between 0.0008 rad and 0.0023 rad, and for distant positions jitter lies between 0.004 rad and 0.01 rad. Note that an error of 0.01 rad will lead to a displacement of 14 mm at a distance of 1.5 m.

For optical tracking, all measurements lie below 0.003 rad, and again, increasing the number of features will decrease the amount of jitter. The standard deviation of the tracking system is less than 0.0015 rad, and optimization over all visible features reduces the standard deviation to less than 0.001 rad. Thus, the amount of orientation jitter with optical tracking is less for our tracking system and smaller by an order of magnitude than that of the magnetic tracker in the worst cast.

5   Accuracy

In addition to low jitter good registration is also characterized by precise position and orientation measurements. Thus, having obtained satisfying results regarding jitter, the next step was to determine the accuracy of computed position and orientation for the optical tracking system.

Due to limitations in the room where the "Studierstube" is located we were not able to obtain ground truth by using a theodolite. Hence, we are using a "virtual camera" similar to [9] for obtaining ground truth: We rendered the features with the model parameters of the camera at chosen virtual locations. Thus, the results obtained from the optical tracking could be compared to the virtual locations used for rendering.

On one hand, simulated camera image data can be quickly obtained and the simulation can be easily adapted to new feature or environment configurations. In addition, the accurate camera's center of perspective is known (theodolite measurements can only deliver a reference position and orientation). On the other hand, simulated data do not allow the inclusion of the magnetic tracker and the camera is not accurately simulated (e.g., distortions can not be adequately modeled and anti-aliasing does not reproduce edges in real images correctly). Note however, that we obtained similar experiments for 2D optical tracking on both real and simulated image data. In addition, the prediction from the magnetic tracker is good enough to locate and track optical features.

Despite these drawbacks we think that the use of a virtual camera is justified in order to obtain measurements on the accuracy of position and orientation data computed by the optical tracker. Due to the fact that we did not calibrate the magnetic tracker we will compare accuracy measurements of our system obtained with data from [7].

In order to determine the accuracy of the optical tracking system the virtual camera is located on arcs which are centered one meter behind the center of the features. The radius of the arcs ranges from 1.75 m to 2.95 m (with steps of 0.1 m), and the angle between the feature plane and the camera[2] covers the range from 55° to 125° in steps of 5°.

Fig. 3 depicts the average error in relation to the radius of the arc. As expected, the accuracy increases with the number of features: optimization over all visible features shows the lowest average (denoted by E_n), and using only four features has the highest average (E_4). The average error for our optical tracker (E_t) lies between the other two error curves. In addition, Fig. 4 depicts the average position error in relation to the angle between the camera and the feature plane. As can be easily seen, the error increases when image and feature plane become parallel.

In order to compare these results with magnetic tracking, we listed average, minimum and maximum error in Table 3 (results for optimization with four features are denoted by E_4, results for full optimization by E_n, results for the optical tracker by E_t). Compared to the error of a carefully calibrated magnetic tracker (E_m cf. [7]), optical tracking shows good results for position accuracy.

	E_4	E_t	E_n	E_m
max	13.812	8.636	6.423	23.1
min	0.459	0.093	0.140	—
average	3.187	2.106	1.292	6.1

Table 3. Position error (maximum, minimum and average) for optical and magnetic tracking.

In addition to only minor position errors, small orientation errors are also important to achieve precise registration. As for jitter, orientation is described by three independent rotations around the x-, y- and z-axis, respectively. Table 4

---

[2] an angle of 90° indicates that feature plane and image plane are parallel.

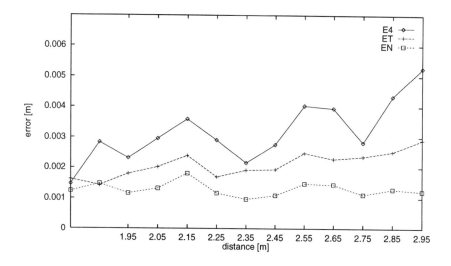

Fig. 3. Optical tracker: position error versus distance.

depicts the errors for the optical tracker, optimization over four features and full optimization. Similar to the position error, the error decreases with an increasing number of features. The average rotation error of optical tracking is less than 0.002 rad which is excellent when compared to the average rotation error for the magnetic tracker (cf. [7]) of 2.1° ($\approx$ 0.037 rad). Even the "worst" result from optical tracking (using only four features) is significantly better than the calibrated magnetic tracker.

Similar results for both position and orientation have been obtained in other experiments, cf. [2].

	E_4			E_t			E_n		
	α	β	γ	α	β	γ	α	β	γ
max.	0.00857	0.00159	0.00743	0.00496	0.00107	0.00300	0.00399	0.00124	0.00266
min.	$< 10^{-5}$	$< 10^{-5}$	$< 10^{-5}$	$< 10^{-5}$	$< 10^{-5}$	$< 10^{-5}$	0.00001	$< 10^{-5}$	$< 10^{-5}$
average	0.00156	0.00027	0.00137	0.00122	0.00019	0.00075	0.00087	0.00015	0.00042

Table 4. Rotation error (maximum, minimum, and average) for optical tracking [rad].

6 Conclusion

We have presented a hybrid tracker integrating both optical and magnetic tracking. By using the robustness of the magnetic tracker (to predict optical features)

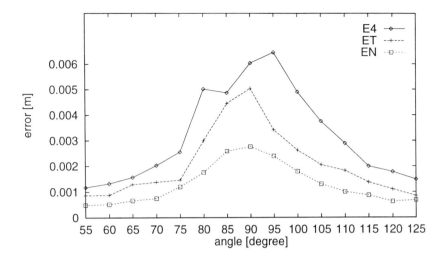

Fig. 4. Optical tracker: position error versus angle.

and the precision of the optical system we obtain results which are superior to either of the single systems:

- accuracy and jitter are better than a standalone magnetic tracker could provide;
- the system is faster than a standalone optical tracker: we are able to track ten to twelve features in real-time (meaning a framerate of ten frames per second);
- accuracy (due to optical tracking) is improved, while robustness (due to magnetic tracking) is maintained.

In order to determine the precision of the system, both accuracy and jitter have been determined. For position data, optical tracking improves the result from magnetic tracking (at least for greater distances), but for orientation data the improvement is significant: Jitter is reduced significantly and precision even gains one order of magnitude. In addition, the optical tracker does not degrade as much as the magnetic tracker with increasing distance.

7 Future Work

Based on the results presented in this paper we think that our method is well suited for tracking in an augmented reality environment. Note however, that the results obtained in this paper have been taken at "static" locations. Our optical tracker does not use any prediction at the moment, and is thus very sensitive to head motion, allowing only slow motions. The next step is the integration of prediction, and thus lowering the restriction on head motion.

52

In addition, all data presented in this paper have been determined by using a single camera, although we have mounted stereo cameras on the AR helmet. Thus, further research has to be directed towards the influence of using the second camera. From photogrammetry we expect that stereo will significantly improve position accuracy. Note however, the computational cost will be approximately twice as much compared to the monocular setup.

Acknowledgments

This work has been supported by the Austrian Science Fund (FWF) under contract number P-12074-MAT. The "Studierstube" is a joint project with the Vienna University of Technology.

References

1. Ronald Azuma and Gary Bishop. Improving static and dynamic registration in an optical see-Through HMD. In *Proceedings of SIGGRAPH'94, Orlando, Florida*, pages 197–204, July 1994.
2. S. Brantner. A vision-based tracking technique for augmented reality. Master's thesis, Computer Graphics and Vision, Graz University of Technology, Münzgrabenstr. 11, 8010 Graz, Austria, 1998. ftp://ftp.icg.tu-graz.ac.at/pub/publications/tom/papers/brantner.ps.gz.
3. M. A. Fischler and R. C. Bolles. Random sample consensus: a paradigm for model fitting with applications to image analysis and automated cartography. *Communications of the ACM*, 24(6):381–395, June 1981.
4. M. Gervautz, D. Schmalstieg, Z. Szalavári, K. Karner, F. Madritsch, and A. Pinz. "Studierstube" - A multi-user augmented reality environment for visualization and education. Technical report TR-186-2-96-10, Institute of Computer Graphics, Technical University Vienna, 1996.
5. G.D. Hager and K. Toyama. Xvision: A portable substrate for real-time vision applications. *Computer Vision and Image Understanding*, 69(1):23–37, January 1998.
6. W.A. Hoff, T. Lyon, and K. Nguyen. Computer-vision-based registration techniques for augmented reality. In *Intelligent Robots and Computer Vision XV, Boston*, pages 538–548, November 1996.
7. M.A. Livingston and A. State. Magnetic tracker calibration for improved augmented reality registration. Technical report, Department of Computer Science, University of North Carolina - Chapel Hill, January 1996.
8. David G. Lowe. Three-dimensional object recognition from single two-dimensional images. *Artifical Intelligence*, pages 355–395, 1987.
9. A. State, G. Hirota, D.T. Chen, W.F. Garrett, and M.A. Livingston. Superior augmented reality registration by integrating landmark tracking and magnetic tracking. In *Proceedings of SIGGRAPH'96, New Orleans, Louisiana*, pages 429–438. ACM SIGGRAPH, August 4-9 1996.
10. J. Steinwendner and W. Schneider. Algorithmic improvements in spatial subpixel analysis of remote sensing images. In *Pattern Recognition and Medical Computer Vision, 22nd Workshop of the Austrian Association for Pattern Recognition*, pages 205–214, May 1998.

An Optically Based Direct Manipulation Interface for Human-Computer Interaction in an Augmented World

G. Klinker[1], D. Stricker[2], and D. Reiners[2]

[1]Moos 2, 85614 Kirchseeon, Germany, klinker@in.tum.de

[2]Fraunhofer Institute for Computer Graphics (FhG-IGD), Rundeturmstr. 6, 64283 Darmstadt, Germany, {stricker, reiners}@igd.fhg.de

Abstract. Augmented reality (AR) constitutes a very powerful three-dimensional user interface for many "hands-on" application scenarios in which users cannot sit at a conventional desktop computer. To fully exploit the AR paradigm, the computer must not only augment the real world, it also has to accept feedback from it. Such feedback is typically collected via gesture languages, 3D pointers, or speech input - all tools which expect users to communicate with the computer about their work at a meta-level rather than just letting them pursue their task. When the computer is capable of deducing progress directly from changes in the real world, the need for special abstract communication interfaces can be reduced or even eliminated. In this paper, we present an optical approach for analyzing and tracking users and the objects they work with. In contrast to emerging workbench and metaDESK approaches, our system can be set up in any room after quickly placing a few known optical targets in the scene. We present three demonstration scenarios to illustrate the overall concept and potential of our approach and then discuss the research issues involved.

1 Introduction

Augmented reality (AR) constitutes a very powerful three-dimensional user interface for many "hands-on" application scenarios in which users cannot sit at a conventional desktop computer. Users can continue their daily work involving the manipulation and examination of real objects, while seeing their surroundings augmented with synthetic information from a computer. These concepts have been demonstrated for construction and manufacturing scenarios like the computer-guided repair of copier machines [3], the installation of aluminum struts in diamond shaped spaceframes [12], for electric wire bundle assembly before their installation in airplanes [1], and for the insertion of a lock into a car door [8].

To fully exploit the AR paradigm, the computer must not only augment the real world but also accept feedback from it. Actions or instructions issued by the computer cause the user to perform actions changing the real world – which, in turn, prompt the computer to generate new, different augmentations. Several prototypes of two-way human-computer interaction have been demonstrated. In the ALIVE project [7], users interact with a virtual dog which follows them and sits down on command. In Feiner et al.'s space frame construction system, selected new struts are recognized via a bar code reader, triggering the computer to update its visualizations. In a mechanical repair demonstration system, Breen et al. use a magnetically tracked pointing device to ask for specific augmentations regarding information on specific components of a motor [9]. Reiners et al. use speech input to control stepping through a sequence of illustrations in a doorlock assembly task [8].

These communication schemes expect users to communicate with the computer at a meta-level about their work rather than just letting them pursue their task. In many real work situations, user actions cause the world to change. When such world changes are captured directly by appropriate computer sensors, the need for abstract communication interfaces can be reduced or even eliminated. The metaDESK system [11] explores such concepts, using graspable objects to manipulate virtual objects like b-splines and digital maps of the MIT campus. It uses an elaborate special arrangement of magnetic trackers, light sources, cameras, and display technology to present the virtual data on a nearly horizontal, planar screen.

In this paper, we present an approach which merges the real-object manipulation paradigm with full three-dimensional AR. Using only optical techniques for analyzing and tracking users or real objects, we do not require elaborate hardware technology. Our demonstrations can be arranged in any room after quickly placing a few known optical targets in the scene, requiring only moderate computing equipment, a miniaturized camera, and a head-mounted display. With such setups, users are then able to control the AR-system simply by manipulating objects or reference symbols in the real world and via simple gestures or spoken commands. With this approach we extend the concepts of the metaDESK towards augmenting more complex realities than planar desktops, arising from a two-dimensional planar desktop reality into a three-dimensional world.

Section 2 presents several demonstrations. Section 3 provides a system overview. Section 4 briefly refers to issues of live camera tracking which are reported in more detail in other papers. Section 5 presents the main focus of this paper, the real-time analysis of real world changes due to user actions. Section 6 proposes schemes for adding 3D GUIs to the real world to support man-machine communication that cannot be automatically deduced from real world changes. Section 7 discusses schemes to automatically account for moving foreground objects, such as users' hands, when merging virtual objects into the scene.

2 Demonstrations

The subsequent three scenarios illustrate the overall concept and potential of optically-based direct manipulation interfaces for AR applications.

2.1 Mixed virtual/real mockups

In many industries (e.g. architecture, automotive design), physical models of a design are built to support the design process and the communication with the customer. Such mockups are time-consuming and expensive to create and thus are typically built only after many of the preliminary decisions have already been made. AR provides the opportunity to build mixed mockups in several stages, using physical models for the already maturing components of the design and inserting virtual models for the currently evolving components. With such mixed prototypes, designers can visualize their progressing models continuously.

Our first demonstration shows a toy house and two virtual buildings. Each virtual house is represented by a special marker in the scene, a black square with an identification label. By moving markers, users can control the position and orientation of individual virtual objects. A similar marker is attached to the toy house. The system can thus track the location of real objects as well. Figure 1a shows an interactively created arrangement of real and virtual houses. Figure 1b shows a VRML-model of St. Paul's Cathedral being manipulated in similar fashion via a piece of cardboard with two markers.

Fig. 1. a) Manipulation of virtual and real objects. b) Manipulation of a model of St. Paul's Cathedral via a piece of card board. (Reprint of Fig. 10b in [10]).

These demonstrations are meant to show that, using our AR-system, preliminary new designs can be combined with existing physical prototypes. Users can analyze a proposed design and move both real and virtual objects about, asking "What if we moved this object overthere?", "What if we exchanged the object with an other one in a different style, color or shape?". The system provides users with intuitive, physical means to manipulate both virtual and real objects without leaving the context of the physical setup. The system keeps track of all virtual and real objects and maintains the occlusion relationships between them.

2.2 Augmented Maps and Cityscapes

Pursuing the interactive city design scenario further, AR can integrate access to many information presentation tools into a reality-based discussion of proposed architectural plans.

56

In the context of the European CICC project we have used AR to visualize how a proposed millennium footbridge across the Thames will integrate into the historical skyline of London close to St. Paul's cathedral (Figure 2a)[5].

Using a map of London, a simple model of the houses along the river shore, and a CAD model of the proposed bridge and St. Paul's cathedral, we have generated a 3D presentation space on a conventional table which pulls all information together, giving viewers the ability to move about to inspect the scene from all sides while interactively moving the bridge (Figure 2b) and choosing between different bridge styles. A hand wave across a 3D camera icon provides access to another information presentation tool: a movie loop with a pre-recorded augmented video clip showing the virtual bridge embedded in the real scene.[1]

Fig. 2. a) Proposed millennium footbridge across the river Thames. b) An augmented map of London including a movie loop with an AR video clip.

2.3 Augmented Tic Tac Toe

We show more elaborate interaction schemes in the context of a Tic Tac Toe game (Figure 3). The user sits in front of a Tic Tac Toe board and some play chips. A camera on his head-mounted display records the scene, allowing the AR-system to track head motions while also maintaining an understanding of the current state of the game, as discussed in sections 4 and 5.

The user and the computer alternate placing real and virtual stones on the board (Figure 3a). When the user has finished a move, he waves his hand past a 3D "Go" button (Figure 3b) or utters a "Go" command into a microphone to inform the computer that he is done. It is important for the computer to wait for such an explicit "Go" command rather than taking its turn as soon as the user has moved a stone. After all, the user might not have finalized his decision. When told to continue, the computer scans the image area containing the board. If it finds a new stone, it plans its own move. It places a virtual cross on the board where the new stone should go and writes a comment on the virtual message panel behind the game. If it could not find a

---

[1] Due to the complexity of the graphical models, this demonstration runs on a high-end graphical workstation (SGI Reality Engine).

new stone or if it found more than one, it asks the user to correct his placement of stones.

The technology presented in these demonstrations forms the basis for many maintenance, construction and repair tasks where users do not have access to conventional computer interfaces, such as a keyboard or mouse.

Fig. 3. Augmented Tic Tac Toe. a) Placement of a new stone. b) Signalling the end of user action.

3 The System

Our AR-system works both in a monitor-based and a HMD-see-through setup. It runs on a low-end graphics workstation (SGI O2). It receives images at video rate either from a minicamera that is attached to a head-mounted display (Virtual IO Glasses) (see Figure 1b) or from a user-independent camera installed on a tripod. The system has been run successfully with a range of cameras including high quality Sony 3CCD Color Video Cameras, color and black-and-white mini cameras and low-end cameras that are typically used for video conferencing applications (e.g., an SGI IndyCam). The resulting augmentations are shown on a workstation monitor, embedded in the video image and/or on a head mounted display. In the HMD, the graphical augmentations can be seen in stereo without the inclusion of the video signal ("see through mode").

At interactive rates, our system receives images and submits them to several processing steps. Beginning with a camera calibration and tracking step, the system determines the current camera position from special targets and other features in the scene. Next, the image is scanned for moving or new objects which are recognized according to predefined object models or special markers. Third, the system checks whether virtual 3D buttons have been activated, initiating the appropriate callbacks to modify the representation or display of virtual information. Finally, visualizations and potential animations of the virtual objects are generated and integrated into the scene as relevant to the current interactive context of the application. (For details, see [8].)

4 Live Optical Tracking of User Motions

The optical tracker operates on live monocular video input. To achieve robust real-time performance, we use simplified, "engineered" scenes, placing black rectangular markers with a white boarder at precisely measured 3D locations (see Figures 1a, 2b, and 3). In order to uniquely identify each square, the squares contain a labeling region with a binary code. Any subset of two targets typically suffices for the system to find and track the squares in order to calibrate the moving camera at approximately 25 Hz. (For details see [5,6,10].)

5 Detection of Scene Changes

Next we search the image for mobile objects using two different approaches. We either search for objects with special markers or we use model-based object recognition principles.

5.1 Detection and tracking of objects with special markers

When unique black squares are attached to all mobile real and virtual objects and if we assume that the markers are manipulated on a set of known surfaces, we can automatically identify the marks and determine their 3D position and orientation by intersecting the rays defined by the positions of the squares in the image with the three-dimensional surfaces on which they lie.

If the markers are manipulated in mid-air rather than on a known surface, more sophisticated approaches are needed, such as stereo vision or the computation of the 3D target location from its projected size and shape.

5.2 Detection of objects using object models

In the Tic Tac Toe game, we use model-based object recognition principles to find new pieces on the board. Due to the image calibration, we know where the game board is located in the image, as well as all nine valid positions for pieces to be placed. Furthermore, the system has maintained a history of the game. It thus knows which positions have already been filled by the user or by its own virtual pieces. It also knows that the game is played on a white board and that the user's stones are red. It thus can check very quickly and robustly which tiles of the board are covered with a stone, i.e. which tiles have a significant number of pixels that are red rather than white. Error handling can consider cases in which users have placed no new stone or more than one new stone – or whether they have placed their stones on top of one of the computer's virtual stones.

This concept extends to other applications requiring more sophisticated object models, such as the modification of a Lego construction or the disassembly of a motor. In an envisioned scenario, the computer will instruct the technician to remove one particular piece at a time, probably even highlighting the image area showing the piece. Thus, it can henceforth check whether the object has been removed, uncovering objects in the back that had been occluded before. This approach is straightforward, if the camera is kept steady during the process. But even for mobile, head-mounted cameras, their calibrated use dynamically provides the correct search area and the appropriate photometric decision criteria for every image due to the fact that a known object model exists.

5.3 Comparison

Both approaches have their merits and problems. Attaching markers to a few real objects is an elegant way of keeping track of objects even when both the camera and the objects move. The objects can have arbitrary textures that don't even have to contrast well against the background – as long as the markers can be easily detected. Yet, the markers take up space in the scene; they must not be occluded by other objects unless the attached object becomes invisible as well. Furthermore, this approach requires a planned modification of the scene which generally cannot be arranged for arbitrarily many objects. Thus it works best when only a few, well-defined objects are expected to move. In a sense the approach is in an equivalence class with other tracking modalities for mobile objects which require special modifications, such as magnetic trackers or barcode readers.

Using a model-based object recognition approach is a more general approach since it does not require scene modifications. Yet, the detection of sophisticated objects with complex shape and texture has been a long standing research problem in computer vision, consuming significant amounts of processing power. Real-time solutions for arbitrarily complex scenes still need to be developed.

Thus, the appropriate choice of algorithm depends on the requirements of an application scenario. In many cases, hybrid approaches including further information sources such as stationary overhead surveillance cameras that track mobile objects are most likely to succeed. Kanade's Z-keying system is a promising start in this direction [4].

6   Virtual GUIs in the Real World

In many application contexts, GUIs such as buttons and menus have proven to be very useful for computers to guide users flexibly through a communication process. Such interfaces should also be available in AR applications. Feiner et al. have demonstrated concepts of superimposing "windows on the world" for head mounted displays [2].

Rather than replicating a 2D interface on a wearable monitor, we suggest embedding GUI widgets into the three-dimensional world. Such approach has a tremendous amount of virtual screen space at its disposal: by turning their head, users can shift their attention to different sets of menus. Furthermore, the interface can be provided in the three-dimensional context of tasks to be performed. Users may thus remember their location more easily than by pulling down several levels of 2D menus.

As a first step, we demonstrate the use of 3D buttons and message boards. For example, we use such buttons to indicate the vantage points of pre-recorded camera clips of the river Thames. The virtual GO-button and a message board for the Tic Tac Toe game use similar means. Virtual buttons are part of the scene augmentations when users turn their head in the right direction.

When virtual 3D buttons become visible in an image, the associated image area becomes sensitive to user interaction. By comparison with a reference image, the system determines whether major pixel changes in the area have occurred due to a user waving a hand across the sensitive image area. Such an approach works best for stationary cameras or small amounts of camera motion, if the button is displayed in a relatively homogenous image area.

3D GUIs are complementary to the use of other input modalities, such as spoken commands and gestures. Sophisticated user interfaces will offer combinations of all user input schemes.

7 Scene Augmentation Accounting for Occlusions due to Dynamic User Hand Motions

After successful user and object tracking, the scene is augmented with virtual objects according to the current interaction state. To integrate the virtual objects correctly into the scene, occlusions between real and virtual objects must be considered. To this end, we use a 3D model of the real objects in the scene, rendering them invisibly at their current location to initialize the z-buffer of the renderer.

During user interactions, the hands and arms of a user are often visible in the images, covering up part of the scene. Such foreground objects must be recognized because some virtual objects could be located behind them and are thus occluded by them. It is extremely disconcerting to users, if this occlusion relationship is ignored in the augmentations, making it very difficult to position objects precisely. We currently use a simple change detection approach to determine foreground objects. While the camera doesn't move, we compare the current image to a reference image determining which pixels have changed significantly. Looking for compact, large areas of change, we discount singular pixel changes as well as thin linear streaks of pixel changes which can be the result of camera noise and jitter. Z-buffer entries of foreground pixels are then set to a fixed foreground value. In the Tic Tac Toe game, this algorithm allows users to occlude the virtual "Go"-button during a hand waving gesture (Figure 3b).

The change detection approach currently is still rather basic. It has problems dealing with some aspects of live interaction in a real scene, such as proper handling of the shadows cast by the users' hands. Furthermore, the current scheme only works for monitor-based AR setups using a stationary camera. Another current limitation is the lack of a full three-dimensional analysis of the position of foreground objects. Such analysis requires a depth recovery vision approach, such as stereo vision [4] performing in real-time. Nevertheless, even the use of basic change detection heuristics yields significant improvements to the immersive impression during user.

8 Discussion

How will AR actually be used in real applications once the most basic technological issues regarding high-precision tracking, fast rendering and mobile computing have been solved? In this paper, we have presented a set of demonstrations illustrating the need for a new set of three-dimensional user interface concepts which require that computers be able to track changes in the real world and react to them appropriately.

We have presented approaches addressing problems such as tracking mobile real objects in the scene, providing three-dimensional means for users to manipulate virtual objects, and also to present three-dimensional sets of GUIs. Furthermore, we have discussed the need to detect foreground objects such as a user's hands.

We have focused on optical scene analysis approaches. We expect computer vision techniques to play a strong role in many AR solutions due to their close relationship to the visual world we are trying to augment and due to people's strongly developed visual and spatial skills to communicate in the real world. Furthermore, the technical effort to set up a scene for an optically-based AR system is minimal and relatively unintrusive since little special equipment and cabling has to be installed in the environment. Thus, the system is easily portable to new places.

Our current technical solutions are just the beginning of a new direction of research activities further addressing the problem of tracking changes in the real world. We have developed and tested several algorithmic variations to address the issues, resulting in a toolbox of approaches geared towards the fast analysis of video data for the current set of demonstrations. In most cases, different approaches each come with their own set of advantages and drawbacks. More sophisticated approaches will become available as the processor performance increases, including more sophisticated multi-camera approaches that currently run only on special-purpose hardware at reasonable speeds.

Yet, even though the current algorithms need to be generalized, they have been able to illustrate the overall 3D human-computer interaction issues that need to be addressed. Building upon these approaches towards more complete solutions will generate the basis for exciting AR applications.

ACKNOWLEDGMENTS

The research is financially supported by the European CICC project (ACTS-017) in the framework of the ACTS programme. The laboratory space and the equipment is provided by the European Computer-industry Research Center (ECRC). The CAD Model of the bridge (Figure 2a) was provided by Sir Norman Foster and OveArup and Partners. We retrieved the virtual model of St. Paul's cathedral from Platinum Pictures' 3D Cafe (http://www.3dcafe.com).

REFERENCES

1. D. Curtis, D. Mizell, P. Gruenbaum, and A. Janin. Several Devils in the Details: Making an AR App Work in the Airplane Factory. 1rst International Workshop on Augmented Reality (IWAR'98), San Francisco, 1998.

2. S. Feiner, B. MacIntyre, M. Haupt, and E. Solomon. Windows on the world: 2D windows for 3D augmented reality. UIST'93, pages 145-155, Atlanta, GA, 1993.

3. S. Feiner, B. MacIntyre, and D. Seligmann. Knowledge-based augmented reality. Communications of the ACM (CACM), 30(7):53-62, July 1993.

4. T. Kanade, A. Yoshida, K. Oda, H. Kano, and M. Tanaka. A stereo machine for video-rate dense depth mapping and its new applications. 15th IEEE Computer Vision and Pattern Recognition Conference (CVPR), 1996.

5. G. Klinker, D. Stricker, and D. Reiners. Augmented reality for exterior construction applications. In W.   Barfield and T. Caudell, eds., Augmented Reality and Wearable Computers. Lawrence Erlbaum Press, 1999.

6. G. Klinker, D. Stricker, and D. Reiners. Augmented Reality: A Balance Act between High Quality and Real-Time Constraints. 1. International Symposium on Mixed Reality (ISMR'99), Y. Ohta and H. Tamura, eds., "Mixed Reality – Merging Real and Virtual Worlds", March 9-11, 1999.

7. P. Maes, T. Darrell, B. Blumberg, and A. Pentland. The ALIVE system: Full-body interaction with autonomous agents. Computer Animation '95, 1995.

8. D. Reiners, D. Stricker, G. Klinker, and S. Müller. Augmented Reality for Construction Tasks: Doorlock Assembly. 1rst International Workshop on Augmented Reality (IWAR'98), San Francisco, 1998.

9. E. Rose, D. Breen, K.H. Ahlers, C. Crampton, M. Tuceryan, R. Whitaker, and D. Greer. Annotating real-world objects using augmented reality. Computer Graphics: Developments in Virtual Environments. Academic Press, 1995.

10. D. Stricker, G. Klinker, and D. Reiners. A fast and robust line-based optical tracker for augmented reality applications. 1rst International Workshop on Augmented Reality (IWAR'98), San Francisco, 1998.

11. B. Ullmer and H. Ishii. The metaDESK: Models and prototypes for tangible user interfaces. UIST'97, pages 223-232, Banff, Alberta, Canada, 1997.

12. A. Webster, S. Feiner, B. MacIntyre, W. Massie, and T. Krueger. Augmented reality in architectural construction, inspection, and renovation. ASCE 3. Congress on Computing in Civil Engineering, pp. 913-919, Anaheim, CA, 1996.

Improving The Illumination Quality Of VRML 97 Walkthrough Via Intensive Texture Usage

Cyril Kardassevitch , Jean Pierre Jessel , Mathias Paulin , and René Caubet

IRIT, 118 route de Narbonne,
31062 Toulouse cedex, France.
{kardasse, jessel, paulin, caubet}@irit.fr

Abstract: In this paper, we introduce a pipeline, dedicated to global illumination and walkthrough of a VRML 97 scene. This pipeline use intensively and exclusively textures to represent light, and is entirely guided by them. We will show how reversing the classic rendering pipeline, allows to privilege high frequency information (direct illumination), and to accelerate the complete lighting process (global illumination). Finally, we will present the filtering and reconstruction methods used to improve the rendering visual quality.

Key words: rendering, walkthrough, VRML 97, texture, light map, global illumination, radiosity, filtering, reconstruction.

1 Introduction And Previous Works

VRML allows to easily transfer 3D environments across the Internet. It gives us a platform and an open language, powerful enough to describe sophisticated environments. Current Internet browsers allow to visualize them via a classic rendering API (OpenGL, Direct3D). Nevertheless, today rendering quality of these scenes depends on VRML 97 ability to manage interactive environments. For example, the use of VRML in the architectural domain is restricted to the manipulation of simple lighting models and prototypes. Because interactivity in this kind of models is often restricted to walk in a static or slightly dynamic scene, we think that it is necessary to develop a better viewer, able to manage correctly lights and materials. We have defined two goals: to evaluate a realistic global illumination model which can be used to represent VRML 97 3D environments, and to privilege high frequency luminous information. Light maps are used to store these luminous data, and to drive the quality of the illumination process. Using light maps allows to directly implement filtering and reconstruction methods, and therefore, to improve the rendering visual quality and accuracy. On the other hand, light maps enhance interactions between the illumination process and the rendering API (OpenGL). They communicate immediately via textures, and do not overload the vertex and quad processors. Our VRML scenes are restricted to contain models described by quads only, without any dynamic information. Some of our current researches are dedicated to overcome these limitations [8].

The use of textures during the rendering process has been introduced to improve the speed and the quality of rendering. Thus, each method of illumination visualization has been treated to be processed with textures. More recently, global illumination models were converted. Arvo proposes in [1] to use of textures (illumination maps) to store the diffuse surface radiosity. Heckbert proposes in [5] to use textures rather than subdividing polygons in radiosity methods. Radiosity textures (rexes) store in each texel the energy arriving on surfaces, calculated using Monte-Carlo ray tracing. Myszowski and Kunii in [7] have developed a model that lightens the visualization process by storing temporarily in textures, and according to the available memory, rectangular zones of the screen buffer, rendered beforehand by Gouraud interpolation. Bastos in [3] reconstructs the photometric information in the light maps by using Hermite bicubic interpolation. We insist on the fact that these models are essentially conversion and visualization models, and that the light maps are partially used in the illumination process. Thus, the pipeline introduced by Bastos ([3]), converts classic radiosity structures (quad trees) in light maps.

2 Our Approach

Our works essentially exploit works concerning the utilization of textures in global illumination process (RAT) to improve the quality and the speed of rendered scenes with complex lighting. We also use classic indirect multi-resolution illumination models introduced by Hanrahan ([4]). Our works focus on the evaluation of a productive model, able to evaluate quickly essential illumination information. This approach can not be done exclusively by using classic progressive radiosity methods. These methods allow to obtain a very general illumination information. However they are less appropriate to calculate high frequency lighting, or only after an important number of expensive iterations. To obtain these high frequency components, It is even often necessary to add a supplementary illumination pass (ray tracing) dependent of the viewpoint. The figure 1 represents a classic illumination pipeline. This secondary and supplementary pass, gives indispensable and essential information for an accurate illumination, especially in an architectural environment. Finally, some information (those participating to the high frequencies) are evaluated twice during the second pass. The aim of our works has been to reverse the illumination pipeline (figure 2), and to correlate the two classic passes. The first stage allows to evaluate quickly high frequency photometric information, and allows to initiate the global illumination process. Moreover, this model allows to lighten the calculation of global illumination by avoiding the direct evaluation redundancy.

Contrary to classic multi-resolution radiosity methods, we make an exclusive and intensive usage of multi-resolution light maps (and not a post-illumination transfers of light elements in textures). These light maps, for a moderate memory cost, allow a permanent and fine control of the illumination rendering quality. Essentially two filtering processes are implemented on our platform: edge filtering to improve visual accuracy of discontinuity zones calculated during the direct illumination stage, and a light map reconstruction stage due to the indirect illumination process.

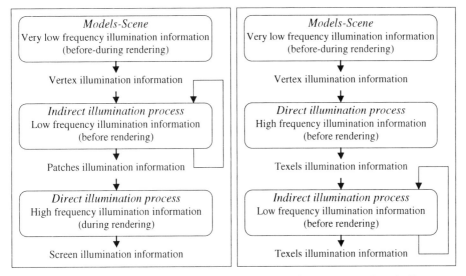

Fig. 1. Classic illumination pipeline   **Fig. 2.** Our illumination pipeline

3 The Light Maps Pipeline

We present here our illumination pipeline. We will try to clearly show the interest to use textures in all stages of the illumination process, and to show that the classic pipeline inversion contributes to decrease times of evaluation and to homogenize classic generation stages.

3.1 General Considerations

Using textures (light maps) to represent the photometric information during the rendering process is not recent. Textures allow to separate shading and geometry, to have a better control on interpolation methods (suppress T vertices and dirty wall), to increase rendering performance with current graphic hardware (better ability to manage textures than vertices), and to allow the manipulation of bigger numbers of elementary photometric cells. The utilization of light maps during the illumination calculation is less common.

The texture representation corresponding to the tree structure used in multi-resolution surfacic global illumination (quad tree) is a mipmap. The quad trees are able to manage only the necessary luminous information. However, the cost induced by the utilization of an isotropic structure is compensated partly by the absence of pointers needed to construct a dynamic representation. In addition, a matrix structure improves the filtering and reconstruction methods, and allows a permanent visualization of the illumination during its evaluation.

66

Finally, the utilization of light maps is decisive during the elaboration of dynamic models, because they are entirely constructed before the illumination process. A tree representation will be constantly modified during this kind of process, requiring to be entirely constructed. Consequently, memory and CPU costs will become more expensive than for a light map.

3.2 The Pipelines

Two possibilities of illumination pipelines can be developed. Each of them affects differently the illumination engine and renderer. These two models diverge by their behavior during the blending operations between the light maps and the surfacic color textures.

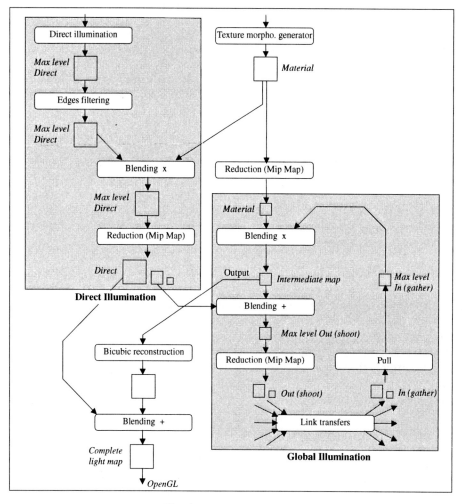

Fig. 3. Illumination pipeline

The first solution is to use the light maps to represent the incident light on surfaces. Blending the terminal light map and the material texture is done "a posteriori", during the rendering process, by the rendering API (multi-pass or multi-texture). Blending the intermediary light map, due to the global illumination process, and the material texture is done on the fly. The advantage of this method is the dissociation of the photometric representation and the surfacic details. Its two most important disadvantages are:

- the overloading of the rendering process with the blending function, and,
- the incorrect representation of the incident light. Indeed the area of validity for the RGB components of the light maps is [0.0,1.0]. Components higher to 1.0 produced by the illumination are clamped to 1.0. Therefore, RGB texel components of the color textures can only decrease.

To correct these last disadvantages, we have chosen another model of pipeline, in which blending is done completely during the illumination process. The most important disadvantage of this method is:

- the need of a morphological texture conversion procedure (resolution, filtering, interpolation and reconstruction) to juxtapose them for the blending function.

The figure 3 represents our illumination pipeline. The illumination engine is divided in two parts (direct and indirect) that communicate via the light map of direct illumination. The complete light map is transferred to the rendering API (OpenGL). Performing the direct illumination first simplifies the global illumination process.

4 Light Map Filtering And Reconstruction

4.1 Shadow Edge Filters

To limit the resolution of the direct illumination evaluation, and to obtain a correct discontinuity zone estimation, it is necessary to make a filtering of the light map luminous information. The figure 4(a) shows an example with aliasing caused by the discretisation of the luminous process. Our objective was to limit CPU resources needed for the calculation of the illumination. In consequence, we have implemented a simple but efficient edge filtering method. The rough application of a Gaussian filter is not satisfactory for the average resolutions of light maps. The figure 4(b) shows the result of the application of a Gaussian discreet filter with a 3x3-sliding window. We can observe some blur effect along the shadow edges. A more efficient model is to use an anisotropic filtering method. Our filter contains three stages, as described below. The first pass does a binary threshold operation of the RGB components taken individually. The result corresponds to a 3x3 matrix with each element set to 1 or 0, and the central element always set to 1. Elements with a value of 1 correspond to elements of a close luminous value to the central texel. A texel with its value set to 0 defines a discontinuous frontier. The second pass, allows to recognize characteristic edge "patterns". The next figure indicates some of these "patterns", currently recognized by our application:

closest components

✓ filtering texels

The third stage makes a 3x3 discreet Gaussian filtering of texels defined by the "pattern" recognized by the second stage. The figure 4(c) shows an example of this kind of filtering methods.

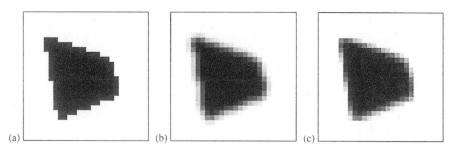

(a) (b) (c)

Fig. 4. Edge filtering: (a) no filtering, (b) Gaussian filtering, (c) anisotropic filtering.

This model allows a better representation of luminous discontinuity zones of direct illumination than with an isotropic filter, and this filtering operation is evaluate with a moderate supplementary cost.

4.2 Global Illumination Light Maps Reconstruction

Another filtering method is necessary: to allow the reconstruction of the photometric information due to the global illumination stage. To not increase the time of evaluation of a more accurate light map during the radiosity process, its size is fixed to a relatively inferior resolution than the light map of the direct illumination process. Therefore, it is necessary to resize the light map given by the indirect stage to the size of the light map given by the direct process. Utilization of a light map without interpolation produces some rectangular discontinuities in appearance. A bilinear interpolation of radiosity components allows to limit the visual impact of these discontinuities, but produces some visual artefacts (star, hexagone). To achieve this reconstruction, Bastos [2] uses Hermite bicubic interpolation functions. He finds necessary elements for the composition of the Hermite matrix by evaluating the tangent plan at each vertex. We have chosen to use another bicubic interpolation, the Lagrange one (1), simpler to use, and especially far more rapid to evaluate:

$$P(x) = \sum_{i=1}^{3} f_i L_i(x) \quad \text{where} \quad L_i(x) = \prod_{k \neq i, k=0}^{3} (x - x_k)/(x_i - x_k) \quad (1)$$

x is the point at which interpolation takes place, f_f are the known values on the grid at points x_i, P(y) represents the desired value, and $L_i(y)$ are the Lagrange polynomials (calculable). However, this method does not allow a reconstruction as precise as the

Hermite one. For a more physical reconstruction of the global illumination, it is recommended to relate to Bastos ([3] and [2]).

Reference (32x32)   Coarse global illumination (4x4)   Bilinear (up) bicubique (down) (32x32)   + OpenGL bilinear filter (32x32)

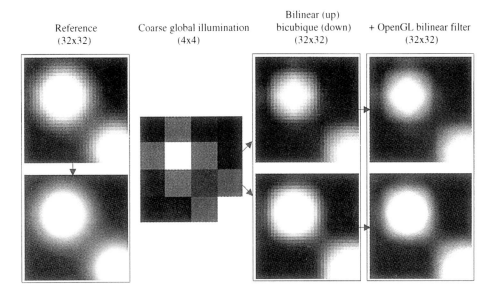

Fig. 5. Light maps reconstruction

The figure 5 represents the light map outputs that comes from a reconstruction process. The reference light maps (32x32) are found on the left (OpenGL bilinear filtered: down). The light map output of a coarse radiosity stage (at the center) gives after reconstruction stages (linear reconstruction: up, bicubic reconstruction: down) the light maps on the right.

5 Illumination Models And Rendering Light Maps

We briefly present in this section some of the methods that we have employed to implement indirect and direct illuminations. We use ray-casting techniques to evaluate the *direct illumination*. The goal is to calculate elements of static illumination (shadows, transparency projection, caustics, perfectly reflective light). We have privileged this model rather than hardware optimization (z-buffer...) to keep the possibility to easily add some characteristics. Thus, managing transparency, normal perturbation (bump mapping), and reflective light (by a perfect mirror) is easy to process by ray-casting. On the other hand, the utilization of a ray tracing in combination with a voxels space, allows us to take advantage from its exploratory character (from source to surface), to illuminate a complex environment. These elements are easily process by our direct illumination pass, avoiding to increase the expensive cost of indirect illumination. For example, the perfectly reflective light is obtained by adding a symmetrical virtual source (to the mirror plan), and whose frustum is constrained by the mirror polygon. To optimize and to keep linear the growth of calculation times, we have implemented a 3D DDA. The picture of the illuminated scene at the end of the paper, shows an example of the obtained effect. Lights from the VRML 97 files, are easy to implement, because they emit from a single point or are directional, and they are not extended. Extended lights are managed directly by the indirect illumination pass.

Indirect illumination is the more expensive stage, in term of CPU resources consumption. Thanks to the first illumination stage, only photometric interactions of second order need to be evaluated. Now, these interactions transport a lesser quantity of energy. Thus, the accuracy of resolution (constraint by the maximum size of the light maps, fixed by the user) is reduced. The model implemented in our platform is the surfacic hierarchical radiosity developed by Hanrahan ([4]). Therefore, the linking cost between surfaces is quadratic. We hope to integrate our former hierarchical radiosity with clustering models ([6]), to decrease the cost of this stage ([9]).

We give here a brief overview on the technique that we use to *render the light maps* generated by the illumination process. We use the OpenGL API for its portability. The version 1.1 allows us to use texture proxies and texture objects, which allow us to transfer textures softly, and to reduce bandwidth consumption. Blending light maps with color textures was done by the illumination process. Rendering requires only one pass (hardware lighting disabled). Mirror effects are created by preliminary rendering of the symmetrical scene and performing a clipping according to the polygon of reflection (using of the stencil buffer). Transparency effects are done by doing an "a posteriori" multi-pass of transparent polygons (a pass for the attenuation, another one for the light maps).

6 First Results And Future Works

Our platform integrates a *VRML 97 interpreter* ([6]). It allows to generate and translate all types of static environments created with the VRML 97 grammar ([10]). However, our current application only exploits quad surfaces (and quad surface compositions). We foresee to exploit all kind of surfaces generated by the language. Thus, it will be necessary to realize a composition module for triangular surfaces able to generate the coordinates for the associated textures.

The illumination session has been processed on a SGI octane station (Mips R10000 processor at 175 Mhz). Results of the appendix show visualizations of the illumination process (4 real + 4 virtual spot lights) at different levels of the evaluation for a minimum texel edge size of 0.05 m for the direct stage, and 0.25 m and 1 pass for the indirect stage. The picture (a) of the appendix results from the visualization of our test scene described in VRML 97 (193 quads) and rendered by CosmoPlayer. The picture (b) shows the output of the first direct illumination stage. The pictures (c) and (d) are representations of the second stage of radiosity (1 pass), respectively not filtered and reconstructed. The final image represents the complete process. The following table illustrates the resources required by our application for various minimum edge sizes of texels:

Direct minimum texel edge length (m)	0.4	0.2	0.1	0.05
Direct texels number (higher level)	3 478	7 615	21 680	72 846
Direct hit test number	104 267	372 208	1 427 983	5 591 130
Direct CPU resources (sec.)	2.04	7.36	28.46	110.88
Indirect minimum texel edge length (m)	0.5		0.25	
Indirect texels number (higher level)	1 737		7 615	
Indirect Links number.	74 112		81 394	
Indirect CPU resources (sec.)	59.37		63.02	
Hardware texture memory requirement (ko)	21.7	50.1	134	417.8
Main texture memory requirement (ko)	255.3	482.8	1 592.6	3 863.4
Total CPU resources (sec.)	61.41	66.73	91.48	173.9

The rendering session has been processed on the same graphic station with a "Solid Impact with option texture" 3D card. The frame rate during the walkthrough is superior to 30 frames/s for the scene with a texel minimum edge size of 0.05 m, without mirror effects, and approximately 20 frame/s with mirror effects.

We envisage to extend our application in several directions. Some of our current works concern the combination of this application and the virtual reality platform developed in our laboratory (VIPER). Research concerning the integration of a dynamic model are one of our preoccupations. Some other works concerns the utilization of light buffers, to increase the performances of our system. It is also envisaged to evaluate an automatic and simple parameterization model.

References

1. Arvo, J., Backward Ray Tracing, *Developments in Ray Tracing SIGGRAPH '86 Course Notes*, Volume 12, August 1986.
2. Bastos, R. M., De Sousa, A. A., Ferreira, F. N., Reconstruction of Illumination Functions using Bicubic Hermite Interpolation, *4th Workshop on Rendering (Eurographics)*, july 1993, Paris, 317-318.
3. Bastos, R. M., Goslin, M., Zhang, H., Efficient Rendering of Radiosity using Textures and Higher Order Reconstruction, *UNC-CH Technical Report*, 1996.
4. Hanrahan, P., Salzman, D., Aupperle, L., A rapid hierarchical radiosity algorithm. *Proceedings of SIGGRAPH'91*, 4 (July 1991), 197-206.
5. Heckbert, P., Adaptative Radiosity Textures for Bidirectional Ray Tracing, *Computer Graphics Proceeding, August 1990*, 145-154.
6. Kardassevitch, C., Paulin, M., Jessel, J. P., Caubet, R., A Hierarchical Radiosity Platform Using Efficient Data Structures And VRML 97, *Compugraphics'97*, December 1997.
7. Myszowski, K., Kunni, T. L., Texture Mapping as an Alternative for Meshing During Walkthrough Animation, *5th Eurographics Workshop on Rendering (Proceedings)*, Darmstadt, June 1994.
8. Paulin, M., Balet O., Rendu Réaliste et Prototypage Virtuel Interactif, *TSI (Technique et Science Informatique, Hermes)*, 1999.
9. Smits, B., Arvo, J., Greenberg, D., A clustering algorithm for radiosity in complex environments, *Proceedings of SIGGRAPH '94*, 4 (July 1994), 435-442.
10. The Virtual Reality Modeling Language, ISO/IEC DIS 14772-1, 4 (April 1997), (http://vrml.sgi.com/developer/index/index .html)

72

(a) VRML 97 Visualization (CosmoPlayer)

(b) Direct illumination

(c) Indirect illumination

(d) Filtered indirect illumination

(e) Direct illumination + reconstructed indirect illumination

Fast Walkthroughs with Image Caches and Ray Casting

Michael Wimmer[1], Markus Giegl[2], Dieter Schmalstieg[1]

[1] Vienna University of Technology
{wimmer I schmalstieg}@cg.tuwien.ac.at
[2] Ars Creat Game Development
m.giegl@magnet.at

Abstract. We present an output-sensitive rendering algorithm for accelerating walkthroughs of large, densely occluded virtual environments using a multi-stage Image Based Rendering Pipeline. In the first stage, objects within a certain distance are rendered using the traditional graphics pipeline, whereas the remaining scene is rendered by a pixel-based approach using an Image Cache, horizon estimation to avoid calculating sky pixels, and finally, ray casting. The time complexity of this approach does not depend on the total number of primitives in the scene. We have measured speedups of up to one order of magnitude.

1 Introduction

In this paper, we present a new approach to the problem of interactively rendering large virtual environments, where the geometric complexity exceeds what modern graphics hardware can render interactively and the user has control over camera position and orientation. This is also commonly referred to as the 'walkthrough-scenario'.

Different solutions have been proposed for various types of virtual environments: Indoor scenes can be efficiently handled using portal rendering [12]. For sparsely populated outdoor scenes, the level of detail approach is viable, providing a number of representations for the same object with different rendering costs. Image Based Rendering has been proposed for very general, complex scenes. More recently, methods have been investigated to handle densely occluded, yet unrestricted scenes, for example urban environments. They are commonly referred to as 'Occlusion Culling'.

Especially in the case of densely occluded outdoor environments, the following basic observations can be made:

- A large part of the screen is covered by a small set of polygons that are very near to the observer (in the 'Near Field').
- Another large part of the screen is covered by sky.
- Pixels that do not fall into one of these two categories are usually covered by very small polygons, or even by more than one polygon.

- The number of polygons that fall outside a certain 'Area of Interest' is usually much larger than a polygonal renderer can handle - but they still contribute to the final image.

The main contribution of this paper is a new algorithm for accelerated rendering of such environments that exploits the observations listed above: the scene is partitioned into a 'Near Field' and a 'Far Field'. Following the ideas of Occlusion Culling, the Near Field is rendered using traditional graphics hardware, covering many pixels with polygons, whereas the Far Field is rendered using an alternative method: every remaining pixel undergoes a multi-stage Image Based Rendering Pipeline in which it is either culled early or sent to the last stage, a ray casting algorithm.

After reviewing previous work relevant to this paper, an overview of the system architecture is given and the various stages of and acceleration methods used in the algorithm are explained. This is followed by a discussion of the behavior of the system and the possible hardware setups where the algorithm works and a summary of the results we obtained in our implementation. Finally, conclusions and future avenues of research in this field are given.

2   Previous Work

Ray tracing is a well-known area of Computer Graphics. A good overview can be found in [7]. The regular grid approach we use has been first introduced in [6]. Later, [2] have introduced a different incremental traversal algorithm which proved to be the fastest for our purpose. On a theoretical analysis of the complexity of regular grids see [5]. Interesting extensions to grids for non-uniform scenes are discussed in [11].

Image Based Rendering and Level of Detail rendering has been a hot research topic in recent time. One of the most well known commercial IBR systems is Quicktime VR [4]. It is capable of displaying a panoramic view of an image acquired by a camera or by synthetic rendering. Different methods are used to interpolate between adjacent images to allow arbitrary viewpoints. Especially the problem of avoiding gaps and overlaps in the final image has received much attention in this area ([13, 18]).

[9] gives a good survey of current geometric Level of Detail algorithms. Hybrid traditional / Image Based Rendering algorithms have been proposed by [17], [16] and [15]: they use graphics hardware to calculate Image Caches for objects on the fly. A similar idea, but taken further to allow affine transforms on the images done in special purpose hardware, is exploited by [21].

[20] describes a consistent way to precalculate 'Potentially Visible Sets' to accelerate architectural walkthroughs. [12] introduces portal rendering, where those PVS are calculated on the fly. More general scenes are made possible by the hierarchical z-buffer method [8], where a hierarchical z-buffer is used to cull occluded geometry. An alternative occlusion culling method, Hierarchical Occlusion Maps, that does not use depth information, is shown in [22]. [3] already partitioned the scene into Near and Far Field. They use colored octree nodes to render the Far Field.

3   Overview of the System

We introduce a second stage to the traditional polygonal rendering pipeline, which is not primitive-based, but purely image-based. Each of the two stages is able to render the whole scene alone, but both would be equally overloaded by the whole database. Thus, rendering of the scene is distributed to the two stages by partitioning the scene into a Near- and Far Field. All primitives within a distance less than a certain threshold are sent to the polygonal renderer. The second stage passes over all the pixels and fills those that have not yet been covered by polygons in the Near Field with the appropriate color.

In the pixel stage, various mechanism exist to allow early exits before a ray is cast to obtain the color information:

- Pixels already covered by polygons are recognized by an opacity buffer that is created during the first stage.
- Pixels that fall into an area covered by sky are recognized by a Horizon Map created before the second stage.
- If a pixel fails those two tests, but its value is still within a valid error range, the pixel color is looked up in an Image Cache.

Only if all these three tests fail, a pixel is sent to the final step in the pipeline, the raycaster. It is important to note that, while ray casting is a very costly technique in itself because it has to be done purely in software, the time complexity of the raycaster is still less than linear in the number of objects. Also, by restricting the number of polygons sent to the graphics hardware, the time spent in the polygonal graphics pipeline is bounded as well (given a reasonably uniform distribution of primitives in the scene). Thus, the overall algorithm can be said to be output-sensitive, i.e., its time complexity is linear in the number of *visible* primitives only, but less than linear in the *total* number of primitives.

4   Ray Casting for Image Based Rendering

4.1   Near Field / Far Field

When rendering a large scene, a huge number of objects can reside in the area defined by the viewing frustrum, but only a small amount of those objects actually contribute to the appearance of the image. Large, near objects usually have much more impact on appearance than small and far away objects. We call all objects within a maximum distance of the viewer to be in the 'Near Field'. Obviously, culling away all objects that do not belong to the Near Field introduces severe visual artifacts. We call 'Far Field' the space of objects beyond the Near Field, but not so far away as to be totally indiscernible. An important property of the Far Field is that it usually

- consists of much more polygons than the graphics hardware can render, but
- contributes to only very few pixels on the screen, because most of the pixels have already been covered by Near Field polygons.

To take advantage of this fact, a separate memory buffer, the 'opacity buffer', is used that records which pixels have already been covered by the Near Field for every frame. This is what has been demonstrated to work already in the 'Hierarchical Z-Buffer'-method, or for 'Hierarchical Occlusion Maps'.

The basic algorithm for our Image Based Rendering technique using ray casting is as follows:

1. Find Objects in the Near Field using the regular grid
2. Render those objects with graphics hardware
3. Rasterize them into the opacity buffer
4. Go through the opacity buffer and cast a ray for each uncovered pixel (enter the resulting color in a separate buffer)
5. Copy the pixels gained by ray casting to the framebuffer

4.2 Ray casting

We claim that ray casting is an appropriate technique for acquiring images for Image Based Rendering on the fly. This might seem strange at first glance, because ray casting (ray tracing) is known to be a notoriously slow technique. The reason for that is the high complexity: in a naive approach every object has to be intersected with a ray for every pixel, so the complexity is O(pixels * objects). In our approach, we want to cast rays into the scene through individual pixels and find the 'first hit', i.e., the first intersection with an object in the Far Field. This means no secondary rays have to be cast, and we are interested in so-called 'first hit' acceleration techniques.

It has been shown ([14, 6]) that theoretically, using an appropriate acceleration structure, the time complexity of ray tracing can be reduced to O(1), i.e., constant, in the number of objects (although this constant may be very large). In our experiments we have observed a sublinear rise in the time to cast rays into a very large scene.

For our purpose, we use a regular grid, because of its speed. Also, given a more or less uniform distribution of objects, which we can safely assume for many types of virtual environments, the memory overhead of a regular grid is very low. Tracing through a grid is fast, using for example Woo's incremental algorithm [2] which only requires few floating point operations per grid cell. If more objects are added, runtime behavior can even improve because rays will collide earlier with objects than if there were huge empty spaces in the grid.

For certain scenes, ray casting alone might already be sufficient and moderate gains can be observed. But generally, this still leaves too many pixels which have to be raycast, and while ray casting is relatively independent of scene complexity, casting a single ray is expensive compared to polygonal rendering and thus only tractable for a moderate number of pixels. The following sections explain how Image Caching and Horizon Tracing can be used to drastically reduce the number of rays that have to be cast.

5   Image Caching

5.1   Panoramic Image Cache

Usually, walkthrough sequences exhibit a considerable amount of temporal coherence, which we exploit in our system: instead of tracing every Far Field pixel every frame, we retain all the color values of the previous frame and try to retrace only those pixels that are outdated according to some error metrics. The validity of pixels depends strongly on the type of viewpoint motion:

Forward/Backward motion. This makes up for a very large amount of motions in a walkthrough sequence. The farther away an object is, the smaller the amount of pixels it moves on the screen due to forward/backward motion. Many pixels will even remain at the same location, so just reusing the pixels from the previous frame is already a good first approximation.

Rotation. Rotation is quite different from forward/backward motion: reusing the contents of the framebuffer would indeed be a very bad solution, because all pixels would be wrong. But actually, many pixels are still valid, they have just moved to a different position. So what is needed is a method to store traced pixels that does not depend on the orientation of the viewer.

Panning (left/right, up/down). This type of movement is similar to rotation in that most pixels move to a different place.

Our assumption is that forward/backward motion and rotation will be the major types of motion in a walkthrough sequence. We therefore choose a representation which is independent of viewpoint rotation: a panoramic image cache.

Panoramic Images have been demonstrated to be a very efficient tool to store full views of a scene where rotation is allowed. We use the panoramic image cache not for presenting a precomputed panorama as for example in the Quicktime VR system [4], but we use it as a rotation-independent Image Cache.

When a ray is cast through a pixel on the (flat) screen, its position on the (curved) map is calculated and the color value obtained by the ray is entered in this position. If, at a later time, another screen pixel projects to the same position in the curved map, its value can be reused if it is still good enough. With respect to rotation, the Image Cache is always up to date for directions in which the viewer has already looked.

In the case of forward/backward movement, the behavior of the map resembles that of a normal, flat image map: reusing the previous panoramic map will be a good approximation to the image and many pixels will be in the correct location. Panning causes more pixels to be invalidated if no costly reprojection is used.

5.2   Cache Update Strategy

Assuming that pixels which have been traced in a previous frame are retained in an Image Cache, the algorithm has to decide which pixels are considered good enough according to a certain error metric, and which pixels have to be retraced. In an interactive walkthrough system, the decision can also be based on a given pixel-'budget' instead of an error metric: which pixels are the most important ones to retrace, given a maximum amount of pixels available per frame.

To select an appropriate set of pixels to retrace, we assign a *confidence value* to each pixel in the map. The pixels are then ordered according to their confidence values and tracing starts with the pixels that have the lowest confidence, proceeding to better ones until the pixel budget is exhausted. Finding a good heuristic for the confidence value of a pixel is not trivial. We chose the euclidian distance of the current viewpoint to the viewpoint where the pixel was sampled – this is efficient and rotation-independent like our Image Cache. Each pixel stores a pointer to a table of viewpoints, indexing the one from where it was sampled. The viewpoint table is updated whenever a certain amount of translation has occurred (rotation is not taken into account, as the Image Cache is rotation-independent).

During the polygon rendering stage, a new opacity-buffer is created. The pixels are sorted according to their confidence value (actually, we don't sort the pixels but the viewpoint table which also records how many pixels refer to each viewpoint in this frame) and as many pixels are traced as the pixel budget allows.

The problem with this approach is that it occurs quite often that all pixels have the same confidence value: if the observer stands still for a while and then suddenly moves, all pixels will be assigned the same new confidence value. In this case, the confidence values are not a good indication of where ray casting effort should be spent. We therefore only trace every n-th pixel that has the same distance, such that the pixel budget is met. In the subsequent frame, the remaining pixels will then be selected automatically for retracing.

To sum up, our update strategy makes sure that pixels are retraced in the order of their distances to the current observer position, taking into account a pixel budget that allows for 'graceful degradation' if the demand for pixels to be retraced is too high in a particular frame. Note that on average, the area left for ray casting only covers a small portion of the screen.

6   Horizon Tracing

For indoor-scenarios with a polygonal ceiling, the system as presented so far would already be sufficient, but a problem arises if there are large areas of empty sky. Theoretically, the ray tracing acceleration structure should take care of rays that do not hit any object in the scene. But in fact, even the overhead of just setting up a ray for every background-pixel is much too large as to be acceptable. The usual case in outdoor scenes is that between one third and one half of the pixels are covered by polygons. A very small part is covered by Far Field pixels that do hit objects, but the rest of the screen is covered by sky.

If it were possible to find out where the sky actually starts, most of the sky pixels could be safely ignored and set to a background-color or filled with the contents of a static environment map.

We assume that the viewer only takes upright positions, i.e., there is no head tilt involved. This is a reasonable restriction in a walkthrough situation. Then, we observe that the screen position where the sky starts only depends on the x-coordinate in screenspace, i.e., on the pixel column. So, for every pixel column we have to find out the y-coordinate of the horizon.

This, again, is a problem that can be solved by ray tracing, but in 2-dimensional space. In addition to the 3D regular grid that is used for tracing pixels, a 2D regular grid is created that contains the height value of the highest point in each grid node - a 2-dimensional heightfield.

For every frame, a 2-dimensional ray is traced through this heightfield to find the grid node that projects to the highest value in screenspace (note: this need not be the highest point in absolute coordinates!). All pixels with a height above this value can be ignored and set to the background color.

Our results indicate that the reduction in the number of pixels to trace was so substantial that the total time spent ray casting and the time spent horizon tracing were comparable. We therefore also investigated methods to speed up horizon tracing: using a coarser 2D grid and graceful degradation (subsampling the horizon while moving) provided good results.

7 Implementation and Results

The algorithms described in this paper have been implemented and tested in an application environment for creating professional computer games. The system was tested with a Pentium 233MMX processor, which is moderately fast for a consumer PC. The 3D board used was a 3DFX Voodoo Graphics, a reasonably fast board for PC-standards. Even better speedups might be possible using a faster main processor. The implementation is still very crude, and it is likely that additional performance gains can be achieved by careful optimization of critical per-pixel operations.

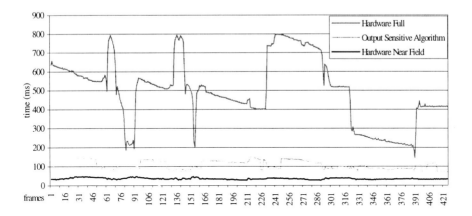

Fig. 1. The chart compares full hardware rendering (backplane set to infinity), our new output sensitive algorithm and hardware rendering (Far Field not rendered) with the backplane at 100m. The image resolution was 640x480 pixels for all tests. The average frame rates were 2.0 fps for full hardware rendering and 9.25 fps for the new algorithm, so the speedup is about 4.6

Because memory transfers from graphics hardware are slow, we create a 1-bit opacity buffer with a very fast software renderer, taking advantage of the fact that neither shading nor depth information is required for the opacity buffer.

Our current implementation is limited to upright viewing positions only. This restriction is inherent to the horizon tracing acceleration, and we believe that it does not severely infringe on the freedom of movement in a walkthrough environment. With respect to the Image Cache, a spherical map could easily be used instead of the cylindrical map that we chose to implement, allowing the viewer to also look up and down.

The first graph (figure 1) shows the time taken to render each frame of a recorded walkthrough sequence (about 400 frames) through a very large environment, a huge city (containing approximately 150000 triangles). Two of the series are for pure hardware rendering only, with the backplane set to infinity in one case and 100m in the other case. The Far Field is not rendered at all, and our algorithm disabled completely (so there is no overhead for tracing horizon pixels, creating or going through the opacity buffer etc.). It shows that up to a certain distance, graphics hardware can render the scene very quickly, but of course misses out on a considerable amount of the background. But if the whole scene is rendered indiscriminately, the hardware simply cannot cope with the amount of triangles, and the framerate drops to an unacceptably low value.

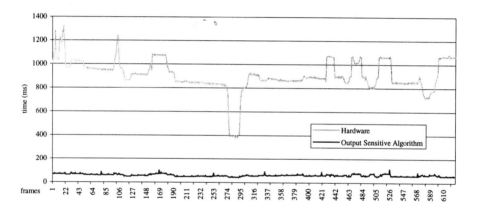

Fig. 2. Frame times for a different walkthrough sequence at a resolution of 320x240 pixels. The average number of polygons in the viewing frustrum was higher than in the first sequence, making hardware rendering even slower. The average frame time for hardware rendering was 1.1 fps, for the new algorithm 16.3 fps, so the speedup is 14.8

Obviously, these are the two extremes between which our algorithm can or should operate. It will certainly not get faster than just rendering the Near Field, but it should be considerably faster than rendering the whole scene with triangles only. The third series shows how our algorithm performs for the same walkthrough sequence with the backplane set at 100m. A speedup of up to one order of magnitude over rendering the full scene in hardware can be observed.

The second graph (figure 2) gives an impression of what the algorithm is capable of if the screen resolution is reduced and the scenery is more complex (in this walkthrough sequence, almost all of the polygons were in the viewing frustrum most of the time, so view frustrum culling is not able to cull geometry). The following chart (figure 3) shows that the performance of the output sensitive algorithm is due to heavy occlusion in the walkthrough sequence (also see the images at the end of the paper for 2 views of the virtual city the walkthroughs were recorded in):

Percentage of pixels...	Min	Average	Max
ray cast and hit an object	0,00%	0,13%	0,49%
ray cast and missed	0,00%	0,10%	0,38%
taken from the image cache	0,00%	0,13%	0,81%
culled by horizon tracing	7,38%	23,76%	39,21%
covered by polygons	60,37%	75,89%	92,62%

Fig. 3. Illustrates that very few pixels have to be calculated using ray casting in a densely occluded environment

8 Discussion

8.1 Scalability

The rendering algorithm described in this paper is applicable to a wide range of environments (see applications). The same is true for the type of platforms it can be used on. Originally, it has been designed with the consumer PC in mind, where almost every new PC is equipped with a 3D accelerator. These accelerators share a common property: they are very good at triangle rasterization, but the transformation step has to be done by the main CPU. Instead of transforming all primitives with the CPU, the algorithm can put this processing power to better use: by using the methods described, the 3D accelerator is used to quickly cover the Near Field with polygons, and the remaining CPU time is used for the pixel based operations.

The algorithm is not restricted to such a platform, though. As the power of the 3D pipeline increases, the size of the Near Field can be increased as well, thus leveraging the additional triangle processing power of the pipeline. More pixels will be covered by polygons, and even fewer pixels will be left to send to the ray casting step. This is especially true if the geometry transformation stage is implemented in hardware, as is the case in higher end PC solutions and midrange 3D workstations.

This means that the approach scales very well with CPU processing power as well as with graphics pipeline speed, and the result is an output-sensitive algorithm that can be used in many different setups.

8.2 Aliasing

No speedup comes without a cost. There are two reasons why aliasing occurs in the algorithm: first, ray casting itself is a source of aliasing because the scene is point sampled with rays. The other reason is the aliasing due to the projection of the flat screen into a curved image map and back. In both cases, antialiasing would theoretically be possible, but it would have a heavy impact on the performance of the algorithm, thus defying the purpose of the algorithm, which is to accelerate interactive walkthroughs.

9 Applications

There is a variety of applications where the algorithms presented in this paper could be applied. Foremost, there is:

9.1 Walkthroughs

Many types of virtual environment walkthroughs fulfill the basic preconditions the algorithm requires. Most and foremost, urban environments are ideal to showcase the points of this paper. Especially in a city, most of the screen is covered by the houses that are near to the viewer. But there are also several viewpoints where objects are visible that are still very far away - imagine looking down a very long street. Polygons cover the right, left and lower part of the image, a good part of the sky is caught by horizon tracing, and the remaining part can be efficiently found by ray casting. Any other scenery which is densely occluded is also suitable. For example, walking through virtual woods is very difficult to do with graphics hardware alone - but with our algorithm, a good number of trees could be rendered in the Near Field, and the remaining pixels traced.

9.2 Computer Games

In recent times, first person 3D computer games have gained immense popularity. Most are set indoors (using portal engines), or outdoors, making use of heavy fogging to reduce the amount of polygons to render. Using the described algorithm, the perceived backplane can be pushed back to the horizon, or at least a considerable distance further away, as the space between the previous backplane and the horizon can be covered by Far Field rendering.

Neither graphics hardware nor processing power will be lacking for computer games in the near future, as both are rapidly catching up with workstation standards. The benchmarks were done on a system whose performance is by no means 'state of the art' even for a PC environment (see results-section) on purpose, to show that good results can be achieved nevertheless.

9.3 Portal Tracing

Previous work [1] has suggested the use of textures as a cache for rendering portals in indoor environments. Those textures are calculated by using the graphics hardware. We propose that under certain circumstances, it might be advantageous to use ray casting to trace through the portals: far away portals cover only a small amount of space on the screen, so there are very few pixels to trace, but the amount of geometry behind a portal can still be quite large, especially if portals have to be traced recursively. Of course in this case, the horizon tracing stage can be omitted.

10 Conclusions and Future Work

We have presented an algorithm which is capable of considerably speeding up rendering of large virtual environments. In scenes where our basic assumptions hold, speedups of an order of magnitude have been measured.

We believe that our way of partitioning the scene into Near Field and Far Field is a sound approach, as we have been able to demonstrate with examples. There is still a lot of work in carefully studying the behavior of the system with respect to scene complexity, overall 'type' of the scene and to the algorithm parameters. We plan to investigate ways to automatically determine such parameters as backplane distance, number of rays to trace per frame and grid resolution, so as to always provide near optimal performance.

The algorithm is not very memory intensive and can easily be integrated with other approaches, like geometric LOD. An interesting avenue of research is the use of graphics hardware for the image-based operations we have introduced. With systems that allow access to frame buffer and texture memory with the same speed as to the system memory, it might be possible to let the hardware do the reprojection of the environment map onto the screen.

11 Acknowledgments

This research is supported in part by the Austrian Science Foundation (FWF) contract no. p-11392-MAT. We would like to thank Ars Creat Game Development for letting us use the 'Ars Machina' framework of their upcoming computer game.

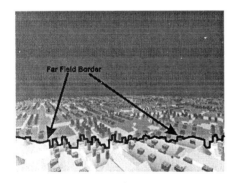 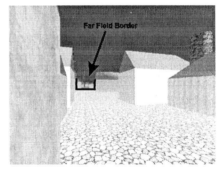

Fig. 4. Left: A view over much of the virtual city that was used for the walkthroughs (the expected framerate would be below 4 fps for this view because the assumption of occlusion does not hold). Right: A typical view from a walkthrough sequence in the city where there is a considerable amount of occlusion

84

References

1. D. G. Aliaga, A. A. Lastra. Architectural Walkthroughs Using Portal Textures. IEEE Visualization '97, pp. 355-362, November 1997.
2. J. Amanatides, A. Woo. A fast voxel traversal algorithm for ray tracing. Eurographics '87, pp. 3-10, North-Holland, August 1987.
3. B. Chamberlain et. al. Fast rendering of complex environments using a spatial hierarchy. Graphics Interface '96, pp. 132-141, May 1996.
4. S. E. Chen. QuickTime VR - An Image-Based Approach to Virtual Environment Navigation. Computer Graphics (Proc. SIGGRAPH'95), pp. 29-38, 1995.
5. J. G. Cleary, Geoff Wyvill. Analysis of an algorithm for fast ray tracing using uniform space subdivision. The Visual Computer, 4(2), pp. 65-83, July 1988.
6. A. Fujimoto, T. Tanaka. ARTS: Accelerated Ray Tracing System. IEEE Computer Graphics and Applications, 6(4), pp. 16-26, 1986.
7. A. S. Glassner (ed.). An Introduction to Ray Tracing. Academic Press, 1989.
8. Hierarchical Z-Buffer Visibility. Computer Graphics (Proc. SIGGARPH'93), 27, pp. 231-238, 1993.
9. P. Heckbert, M. Garland. Survey of Polygonal Surface Simplification Algorithms. Technical Report, CS Dept., Carnegie Mellon U., to appear (draft May'97) (http://www.cs.cmu.edu/~ph/).
10. M. Kilgard. Realizing OpenGL: Two Implementations of One Architecture. 1997 SIGGRAPH / Eurographics Workshop on Graphics Hardware, pp. 45-56, August 1997
11. K. S. Klimaszewski, Thomas W. Sederberg. Faster Ray Tracing Using Adaptive Grids. IEEE Computer Graphics and Applications, 17(1), pp. 42-51, January 1997.
12. D. Luebke, Chris Georges. Portals and Mirrors: Simple, Fast Evaluation of Potentially Visible Sets. Proc. Symp. Interactive 3-D Graphics, ACM Press, April 1995.
13. L. McMillan, G. Bishop. Plenoptic Modeling: An Image-Based Rendering System. Computer Graphics (Proc. SIGGRAPH'95), 29, pp. 39-46, 1995.
14. M. Ohta, M. Maekawa. Ray Coherence Theorem and Constant Time Ray Tracing Algorithm. Computer Graphics 1987 (Proceedings of CG International '87), pp. 303-314, Springer-Verlag, 1987.
15 M. Rafferty, D. Aliaga, A. Lastra. 3D Image Warping in Architectural Walkthroughs. IEEE Virtual Reality Annual International Symposium '98 (Atlanta, GA, 14-18 March 1998), 228-233
16. G. Schaufler, W. Stürzlinger. A Three-Dimensional Image Cache for Virtual Reality. Computer Graphics Forum (Proc. EUROGRAPHICS'96), 15(3), p. C227-C235, C471--C472, September 1996.
17. J. Shade et. al. Hierarchical Image Caching for Accelerated Walkthroughs of Complex Environments. Computer Graphics (Proc. SIGGRAPH'96), 30, pp. 75-82, 1996.
18. J. Shade et. al. Layered Depth Images. Computer Graphics (Proc. SIGGRAPH 98), pp. 231-242, July 1998.
19. Output-Sensitive Visibility Algorithms for Dynamic Scenes with Applications to Virtual Reality. Computer Graphics Forum, 15(3), pp. 249-258, Blackwell Publishers, August 1996.
20. S. J. Teller, Carlo H. Séquin. Visibility preprocessing for interactive walkthroughs. Computer Graphics (Proc. SIGGRAPH '91), 25(4), pp. 61-69, July 1991.
21. Talisman: Commodity Real-time 3D Graphics for the PC. Computer Graphics (Proc. SIGGRAPH 96), pp. 353-364, August 1996.
22. H. Zhang et. al. Visibility Culling Using Hierarchical Occlusion Maps. Computer Graphics (Proc. SIGGRAPH'97), 31(3A), pp. 77-88, August 1997.

Using Virtual Environments to Enhance Visualization

D R S Boyd, J R Gallop, K E V Palmen, R T Platon, C D Seelig

CLRC Rutherford Appleton Laboratory

Chilton, Didcot, Oxon OX11 0QX, United Kingdom

Abstract

Within the EU ESPRIT demonstrator project VIVRE, a commercial virtual environment system has been used to create a user-centred interaction environment for two commercial general-purpose data visualization systems. The project has exploited mechanisms provided by all three systems to incorporate new user-developed functionality. In addition to updating and navigating the visualization scene, this includes user control of the visualization application from within the virtual environment. The project is assessing the degree to which this extended interactive capability results in greater benefits for commercial users.

1. Introduction

1.1 Motivation

Many applications benefit from the use of visualization techniques to more quickly understand the nature of a problem and identify directions to pursue for possible solutions. Often the application data map naturally to a 3D representation and tools are needed to support user investigation of the data in a spatial context.

Commercial data visualization systems, such as AVS/Express [AVS 98] and IRIS Explorer [Explorer 98] provide their users with an essentially data-centred mode of interaction. Having processed the application data through a network of reader, filter, mapper and render modules, the 3D data representation generated is viewed within a 2D window on a monitor screen. The paradigm of holding the data in one's hand and rotating it or pushing and pulling it can be a powerful way of interacting with some forms of data. However, another interaction paradigm may, in some circumstances, offer greater flexibility and seem more intuitive. This is the paradigm of freely navigating through a 3D space while looking around. This user-centred approach is the one often employed within virtual environments.

The work described here applies this user-centred approach to data visualization by using a virtual environment (VE) system to construct a new user interaction environment for two data visualization systems. Users are thus able to "steer" the visualization task to more easily gain the insight they are seeking from their data. In addition, by using a dataflow or object-based visualization system, diverse applications can be flexibly built and existing ones adapted for a VE. This approach is particularly appropriate for the VIVRE project as this is looking at real commercial and industrial application problems with complex visualization requirements. Throughout, the project has been driven by users' requirements and the results are being assessed by the users applying them within their normal commercial working environments.

1.2 Outline of the paper

Section 2 describes some previous work to integrate visualization and virtual environment systems; Section 3 gives an outline of the VIVRE project including the user requirements; Section 4 describes the technical approach taken and Section 5 summarises the results obtained with user data and indicates some of the lessons learnt. Finally there are some brief conclusions.

2. Integrating visualization and virtual environments

There have been several attempts to integrate visualization and VE techniques - see [Gallop 96] for an overall view. A number of approaches have been tried:

- taking an existing visualization system and adding improved navigation and interaction capability [Sherman 93], [Haase 94], [Fuhrmann 98],
- taking a VE system and adding visualization capability [Fruehauf 96], [Sastry 98],
- developing a custom-designed integrated visualization and VE system [Bryson 91], [Cruz-Neira 93], [Haase 96].

Each of these approaches has its strengths and weaknesses. Extending a visualization system exploits existing user expertise in that package but does not solve the problem that real time interaction needs a system architecture designed from first principles to support this capability. Efforts to add visualization functions to a VE system have been able to take advantage of the fast response to user interactions but have tended to focus on the needs of particular application areas where the functionality required is well defined and domain-specific. Custom-designed solutions have demonstrated some of the benefits of closer integration but are not widely available so there is not a large base of experience of using them within industry.

The VIVRE project seeks to take advantage of two existing general purpose visualization systems and to couple each of them to an existing, relatively mature VE system. AVS/Express [AVS 98] and IRIS Explorer [Explorer 98], as well as being leading examples of their type, are already in use in commercial applications and by the end-users in the project in particular, thus taking advantage of existing investment and experience. For the VE system, although not the only system that could have been chosen, dVISE is a relatively mature product, it provides the required extension mechanisms and it supports a wide variety of user I/O configurations. All 3 systems are supported on both SGI/Irix and PC/NT. By coupling these environments, using software developed by the project, it has been possible to provide the user partners with a demonstrator system that will enable them to assess the practical benefits of this approach to highly interactive visualization steering for their applications.

3. The VIVRE project

3.1 Outline of the project

VIVRE (Visualization through an Integrated Virtual Environment) is a demonstrator project in the High Performance Computing and Networking (HPCN) sector of the E.U. 4th Framework Programme [VIVRE 98]. Its objectives comprise demonstrating the integration of data visualization and VE software systems to provide interactive visualization steering for industrial and commercial applications, identifying the resulting business benefits, and disseminating the results into European industry.

To achieve these objectives a generic framework has been designed to achieve this integration and working prototype software developed for both visualization systems.

The partners, in addition to CLRC, are Tessella (UK), Tethys (France), Nag (UK), Air Liquide (France), BSSI (Norway), Labein (Spain), Unilever (UK) and BNFL (UK). 5 of the project partners (those listed last) specify requirements, provide application scenarios and will evaluate the software developed using these scenarios in the context of their own business processes.

The application scenarios provided by the user partners cover a wide range of domain and scale. They include: visualising combustion and gas flow in industrial processes; visualising potential leakage paths surrounding underground storage caverns; visualising the dynamic operation of a flexible fluid control valve; and visualising complex natural microstructures and their properties.

3.2 User requirements

User requirements were captured for each end user and then amalgamated into a single coherent list of prioritised user requirements. These guided the development work and also provided the basis for user evaluation of the integrated environment developed by the project. The user requirements divided into the following categories:

- visualization functions to be provided,
- user control of visualization, user navigation, data display options and data properties all to be available from within the virtual environment,
- operational environment and performance.

The user expects a range of actions to be accessible directly from the VE. The VIVRE implementation provides the necessary communication in both directions. Other actions may require the user to interact directly with the visualization system, such as substituting a different visualization function in the network.

An important requirement which evolved during the project concerned the primary delivery platform for the project software. While this was initially specified to be SGI/Irix, the end users subsequently argued strongly for this to be extended to include PC/NT in recognition of its rapidly growing market share for this type of work.

The hardware configurations in the project range from basic display plus mouse, through intermediate configurations of moderate cost which could include a 6 degree of freedom input device, to stereoscopic projection and immersive head-mounted display. Building on a VE system such as dVISE ensure that all these are supported.

4. Technical approach

4.1 Typical user scenario

Before describing details of the technical approach taken in VIVRE, it may be helpful to outline an example user scenario.

A visualization network is set up, an example of which may include an isosurface calculation for two different thresholds and three planar slices, on each of which an image is calculated.

The resulting geometrical objects, which may constitute a complex scene, are sent to the VE system and the user may control the reception and display of these objects.

Using the navigation facilities of the VE system, the user steers to a position and orientation which enables a region of interest to be inspected. How the user does this critically depends on which interactive hardware is being employed.

The slices are represented as separate objects in the VE. The user selects one of these and manipulates its position and orientation.

When the user releases the slice, the changed position and orientation and the identity of the slice is transmitted to the visualization system, which uses this information to recalculate the image displayed on the slice.

This set of operations could be repeated by the user until a different operation is needed.

Since the application dataset is likely to be complex, it is not productive to recalculate the image on the slice until the slice is released by the user. Also operations local to the VE can be carried out while recalculation takes place. Thus navigation can be carried out concurrently with more expensive visualization operations.

Other operations follow a similar pattern. Float and integer controls in the VE can be associated with parameters in the visualization system under the control of the application developer. Also an object in the VE can be selected for selective execution by the application's visualization network and selective resending to the VE. (Except for a temporary restriction in the NT version), all these operations may take place without the VE user needing to interact directly with the visualization system. An immersed user could remain immersed while controlling such operations.

Other operations in our present design would require direct interaction with the visualization system. For instance, we do not attempt to emulate the visualization network editor in the VE system. Introducing a different visualization operation, such as streamlines of vectors, would therefore require a direct interaction with the visualization network. Similarly, reading a different data file is regarded as a less frequent operation which would be performed directly using the visualization system.

The immersed user needs to emerge to achieve certain controls which with present understanding of immersion is likely to be advantageous.

4.2 Extension mechanisms in underlying systems

The underlying visualization systems and VE system prescribe the mechanisms for adding application software.

A dataflow visualization system, such as IRIS Explorer, allows an application programmer to add modules that each perform a specific processing task in a network consisting of system-defined and application-defined modules. An application-defined module conforms to the rules of the underlying system for receiving and generating data, for communicating with the GUI and for being fired by the underlying system's flow executive. AVS/Express differs in that data is set up as a system of objects, linked by a set of references and interdependencies. Modules fire when their incoming objects change.

Thus, in the visualization system, VIVRE-developed modules are provided for communication each way with the VE system, for sending geometry to the VE system, for maintaining object identity and for responding to user change requests.

The VE system dVISE allows the programmer to associate processing actions with events initiated by the user or by objects in the VE. The actions can be ones that already exist in the dVISE, such as changing the colour of the currently selected object or printing some textual data about this object, or can be new ones developed in VIVRE by making use of the dVISE API. These programmer-supplied action functions can be packaged up together into a single plug-in which is activated by the dVISE run-time system when required.

The dVISE system also provides an interactive, immersive toolbox and a language for programmer-specified toolbox interactions. This allows the user to interact with VIVRE without leaving the VE.

Since the VIVRE software makes use of these standard extension mechanisms (see Figure 1), it can be easily incorporated by users who already have the underlying software.

4.3 Dynamic changes

Although in general the behaviour of a virtual world may be dynamic, responding to user actions, the world is conventionally prepared in advance. However when dealing with data visualization, minor changes to parameters can result in a totally new scene.

In VIVRE therefore, the virtual world read in initially by dVISE is a skeleton. Included is an attachment point for objects to be added or replaced, depending on the multiple objects transmitted from the visualization system.

At present the user is required to explicitly acknowledge the passage of new data into the VE system from the visualization system. This has the benefit that the user is not astonished by the appearance of a totally new scene while navigating around it and does not require the user to leave the VE.

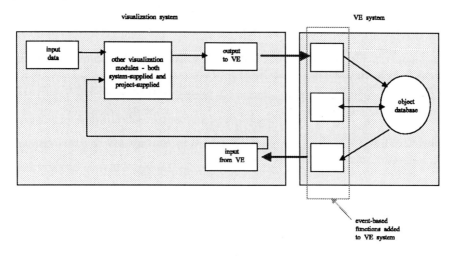

Fig. 1. How system extension mechanisms are used in VIVRE

Paradoxically, although dVISE offers two separate mechanisms, static and dynamic geometry, the dVISE static geometry has been sufficient to allow object replacement and addition when required.

4.4 Multiple objects

In a visualization application, it is common for several different sorts of visualization representations and multiple instances of each to be present in the scene. It is envisaged that can be separately manipulated by the user. It is therefore essential that these be structured in the VE as separate objects.

The structuring of the scene into objects is determined by the visualization network which has parallel strands corresponding to each portion of the network capable of generating geometry. Figure 2 shows this in outline. VIVRE supplies a data preparation module which must be appended to each such strand. One of its functions is to allow the application developer or user to specify the object name which is to be used by the VE system. Since one of the features of the VE system is to display a hierarchical view of the object collection, user-controlled labelling assists user recognition.

VIVRE also attaches a system-defined unique name to the object so that subsequent input may be correctly associated with it, so that for example a user change may be associated with the correct module in the visualization system.

4.5 Geometric conversion

Both visualization systems can write geometry in widely recognised formats and dVISE provides tools that can read these formats. First impressions were that the project would not need to write geometry convertors. An initial version of the VIVRE system was based on these convertors. However, this foundered on vertex colours. Attaching colour to each vertex allows colour to vary over the surface. Conventionally colours on vertices are used to describe the colour of a surface which is then subject to the shading effects due to lighting. This is essential as a tool for understanding the shape of a complex visualization object. However the model for colours on vertices in dVISE is that these are the *result* of shading calculations due to, for example, a radiosity calculation. Therefore shaded, multicolour surfaces were not possible. The solution has been to use texture coordinates on each vertex to encapsulate the colour information. Texture co-ordinates are interpreted in dVISE prior to the shading calculation and the texture map embodies the colour map.

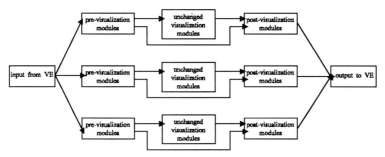

Fig. 2. Managing multiple visualization objects

After conversion, it is possible to use tools supplied by the VE system to optimise the geometry, which is one factor in efficient navigation. The default method in dVISE creates levels of detail which are reduced by specific percentages, which may arbitrarily lose vital detail. A solution to this was to use a criterion based on the projected size of each feature in the scene.

4.6 Support of multi-variate data

The user partners in the project regard multivariate data as vital. One typical CFD example dataset uses 12 variables over a 3 dimensional base. This is just one aspect of complexity in the data that may lead a user to consider VE as a visualization tool. A particular visualization representation (one of the objects in the scene) would use a subset of the variables - in practice commonly one or two. The ability to switch variables is regarded as essential, sufficiently frequently that being able to control this from within the VE is a requirement.

4.7 Interrogation of the visualization scene

In addition to controlling the course of the visualization application, the user also requires information to be presented in the VE to assist the user's decision making,

92

particularly if the user is immersed. An example of this is - what is the current value of the isosurface threshold ?

5. Operational results

The prototype system is still being implemented and although the early version made available to users at this stage allows two way communication, only a subset of the functionality has been provided. Figure 3 shows a screenshot with a network (right) of one of the visualization systems (Explorer), containing VIVRE and application modules, and the dVISE environment (left) on a conventional monitor.

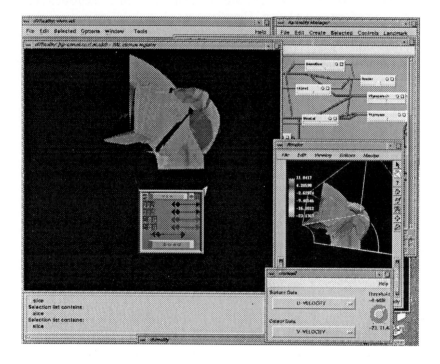

Fig. 3. Example session using Explorer

The project is engaged in a user evaluation which has only just begun. However some early experiences can be outlined at this stage.

5.1 Grouping visualization modules

Several visualization modules have been added to allow for communication with the VE and their firing strategy and ports and parameters need to be correctly incorporated in the network. The implementation therefore relies upon the module grouping facilities in both systems - groups (in Explorer) and macros (in Express).

5.2 Scale

Visualization technology allows users to explore phenomena of any scale. Even within the restricted number of users in the project, one application may be in mm, while another is in km. In a user-centred environment, do we imagine the user is scaled up or down or do we make a virtual scale model? At present our approach is, using the existing VE system GUI, to make a virtual scale model that corresponds approximately to the defaults in the VE system, which is of the order of a few metres. This would need to be evaluated in the light of user experience.

5.3 Adaptability

Because dataflow visualization systems are used as a base, the system is extensible to other visualization modules. By inserting VIVRE modules in the visualization network, toolbox parameters in the VE can be associated with essentially any parameters in the visualization application.

6. Conclusions

The work carried out in the VIVRE project has shown that it is technically feasible to link commercial data visualization and VE software systems to provide users with an integrated environment offering access to the capabilities and strengths of both systems. This new environment can exploit the computational performance and graphics capability of high-end HPC systems while also being accessible to PC users. The project has developed a prototype system, which does provide a sufficient range of visualization functions that users are able to develop useful application scenarios. These scenarios provide the basis for evaluating the degree to which this user-centric experience of navigating and interacting within an immersive VE will offer measurable commercial benefits compared with the data-centric systems used previously.

7. Acknowledgements

The authors wish to thank the European Commission for their support for the VIVRE project and the VIVRE project partners for their co-operation and contribution to the project.

8. References

[AVS 98] AVS/Express, see http://www.avs.com/products/expovr.htm

[Bryson 91] Bryson, S., Levit, C., The Virtual Windtunnel: An Environment for the Exploration of Three Dimensional Unsteady Flows, Proceedings of IEEE Visualization '91, 1991

[Cruz-Neira 93] Cruz-Neira C., Sandin D.J., DeFanti T.A., Surround-Screen Projection-Based Virtual Reality: The Design and Implementation of the CAVE, Computer Graphics, Siggraph 93 Proceedings, pp135-146

[dVISE 98] dVISE, see http://www.division.com/2.sol/a_sw/sol_a.htm

[Explorer 98] IRIS Explorer, see http://www.nag.co.uk/Welcome_IEC.html

[Fruehauf 96] Fruehauf, T., Dai, F., Scientific Visualization and Virtual Prototyping in the Product Development Process, Proceedings of the 3rd Eurographics Virtual Environments Workshop, pp223-233, Springer-Verlag, 1996

[Fuhrmann 98] Fuhrmann, A., Loeffelmann, H., Schmalsteig, D., Gervautz, M., Collaborative Visualization in Augmented Reality, IEEE Computer Graphics and Applications, 18(4), pp54-59, 1998

[Gallop 96] Gallop, J.R., Virtual Reality - its Application to Scientific Visualization, Eurographics 96 Tutorial 3, ISSN 1017-4656, 1996

[Haase 94] Haase, H., Goebel, M., Astheimer, P., Karlsson, K., Shroeder, F., Fruehauf, T., Zeigler, R., How Scientific Visualization Can Benefit from Virtual Environments, CWI Quarterly, 7(2), pp159-174, 1994

[Haase 96] Haase, H., Symbiosis of Virtual Reality and Scientific Visualization System, Proceedings of Eurographics '96, 1996

[Sherman 93] Sherman, W.R., Integrating Virtual Environments into the Dataflow Paradigm, Proceedings of 4th Eurographics Workshop on Visualization in Scientific Computing, 1993

[Sastry 98] Sastry, L., Boyd, D.R.S., Fowler, R.F., Sastry, V.V.S.S., Numerical flow visualization using virtual reality techniques, Proceedings of the 8th International Symposium on Flow Visualization, 1998

[VIVRE 98] VIVRE, see http://www.tessella.co.uk/projects/vivre/vivre.htm

Semantic Behaviours
in Collaborative Virtual Environments[*]

Emmanuel Frécon[1] and Gareth Smith[2]

[1] Swedish Institute of Computer Science, Box 1263, 164 29 Kista, Sweden
emmanuel@sics.se
[2] Computing Department, Lancaster University, Lancaster LA1 4YR, UK
gareth@comp.lancs.ac.uk

Abstract. Scripting facilities within a collaborative virtual environment (CVE) allows animation and behaviour to be added to otherwise static scenes. This paper describes the integration of the TCL scripting language into an existing CVE, and describes the advantages gained by such a marriage. Further, we describe how high-level semantic behaviours can be readily introduced into cooperative applications. They benefit from the scripting language to provide an abstraction over application development and be exploited to drastically reduce network traffic.

1 Introduction

This paper describes enhancements to a Collaborative Virtual Environment (CVE) to ease the development of collaborative applications in distributed virtual worlds. These include integrating an interpreted scripting language and support for semantically identified behaviours.

A CVE scripting language is an interpreted language with a semantic relationship with objects and actions in the virtual environment. Adding scripting facilities to a CVE allows animation and behaviour to be added to otherwise static scenes. The power of a scripting facility relies on the fact that scripts offer easy access to the main functionality of the platform, in a manner that hides complexity by offering simple and coherent commands. Scripts describe how objects react to user interaction and other CVE events such as collisions. Interpreted scripts do not require compiling, which supports tighter prototyping cycles and greatly improves initial application development.

In addition to a general scripting language, we also wish to consider the nature of semantic modelling within virtual environments, the potential role it offers within these environments and the development of an approach to modelling that offers significant advantages to the development of cooperative environments. Semantics are used to convey and represent meaning within virtual environments. Semantic modelling is a means of structuring objects in terms of their "meaning". Conveying semantically enriched information aids scalability as a single semantically enriched message can describe a large amount of semantic free data. In essence, the use of

---

[*] This research was partly funded by the European ACTS programme (COVEN AC040).

semantics allows us to deal with a higher degree of abstraction in terms of conveying instructions and meaning within the virtual environment. The provision of a rich semantic model allows us to express the properties of the world more succinctly.

2 Background and Motivation

Traditional CVE platforms rely on low-level programming interfaces. These interfaces release the underlying power of such systems, enabling developers to utilise the complexity of the platform. However, they also introduce design complexity by typically forcing application programmers to understand the internals of the platform. Little abstraction is offered over the underlying details of the system. Additionally, these interfaces favour compiled languages, such as 'C', in an attempt to offer the highest computing execution speed in order to increase interaction time. Thus, low-level interfaces to CVEs are synonymous with long development times and frequent application restarts during test phases. This factor is not in accord with the fact that CVEs are still a maturing technology that is not yet supported by proven methods of programming and design techniques.

A further drawback of compiled languages is that they are generally platform dependent and produce executable code that will only run on specific computer architectures.[†] This drawback opposes itself to the heterogeneous nature of CVEs.

This is evident in systems such as Massive [8], which does not support behaviour scripting, and enforces developers to construct platform dependant code through a complex programming interface to the system. Use of a scripting language is not in itself novel, and is used in a number of systems. Most notably of these is VRML97 [10], which uses the ECMAScript language to describe behaviour. ECMAScript is based on JavaScript and is platform independent. The scripting language offered by VRML97 provides developers with a rapid means of developing behavioural attributes of a virtual space. However, VRML97 is a limited virtual environment in that it does not support events such as inter-object collisions, and is a single user system. Systems such as Blaxxun [5] offer multi-user extensions to VRML97 based browsers, but require a dedicated server to manage script-enhanced entities, and are obviously limited to the features offered by VRML97.

These systems also offer little support for network traffic bandwidth optimisation. Many numbers of participants in CVEs generate large amounts of update information. Network protocols such as DIS [3] aid in this problem by semantically describing the update information, but are poorly integrated with CVE application development, and support a limited number of event semantics. Little support exists to enable application developers to create their own semantically enriched messaging system. Such a system would enable developers to simply identify application level semantics, and exploit these at a network level.

In this paper, we show that interfacing a scripting language to a CVE provides programmers with a rapid means of developing object behaviours and distributed applications. We also show that application level semantic behaviours can be identified and exploited to ease application development and network bandwidth.

[†] While new technologies such as Java emerge to solve this problem, they still have relatively reduced execution speed.

3 Approach

When integrating a scripting language into a CVE platform, our goal is to achieve a behavioural interface that provides the highest possible interaction while keeping the use of network bandwidth as low as possible. We address network issues by analysing different levels of behaviour and investigating the consequences on network bandwidth. Hence, we propose a behavioural interface that supports all levels of behaviour and promotes synchronisation among connected peers to reduce network throughput.

We demonstrate a programming interface that places the burden of execution on the processes that generates the interaction. This is advantageous over a low-level interface that uses a unique application to describe the behaviour. In this case, it is the specific process, which hosts the application that will endure the execution burden that results from user interaction with these entities. Our approach permits implementation of truly distributed applications. That is, applications that do not rely on the existence of a specific peer, but rather on the will for all connected processes to execute the part of the application that they have triggered by generating events. In the following sections, we describe how categorising types of behaviours can be used to reduce network bandwidth, and how semantic behaviours can be identified, implemented and exploited.

4 Categorising Behaviours

Classifying behaviours and entities enables them to be reasoned about in terms of their complexity and likely activity within the CVE. Any activity within a CVE is distributed to all peers. This distribution can be expensive in terms of network traffic if many activities are taking place. These taxonomies can be used to aid in the reduction of network traffic. We define four levels of behaviour in increasing complexity, based on work described in [1]:

- **Level 0.** *Direct modification of an entity's attributes.* This level simply updates state within an entity, for example: set colour = blue.
- **Level 1.** *Change in an entity's attributes over time.* This allows an entity's state to be updated deterministically, for example: move forwards at 0.1 ms^{-1}.
- **Level 2.** *Series of calls to level 1 behaviours to perform some task.* A single high level command such as: crowd $\Rightarrow$ move towards the door.
- **Level 3.** *Top-level decision making.* This is the highest level of behaviour and encapsulates the highest form of intelligent reasoning. This level will normally choose from a number of level 2 behaviours. For example, decide whether to move crowd to greet a user who has just entered the room; disperse; exit the room; etc.

The level 3 behaviour selects a level 2 behaviour to execute. It sets priorities and does "executive level" decision-making. The level 2 behaviours decompose a task into simpler level 1 actions, which in turn update the actual entity's state.

4.1 Behaviours and Distribution

A high level of behaviour describes more activities than a lower level of behaviour, but requires a greater amount of interpretation. For example, a level 1 call will update the hands of a clock so that they move correctly (this is the approach taken by systems such as DIS [3] and HLA [2]) this requires three network requests (one for each hand). However, this would require many network requests if only level 0 behaviours are used, one every second to update the second hand, and so on. Here, level 0 calls are distributed between two CVE processes, simply maintaining state between them. Level 1 calls however, encapsulate repetitive level 0 calls, and form a virtual link between the processes. A virtual link must be formed because:

- The message sent from A to B, must be executed by B. That is, B must understand the *semantics* of the message.
- The execution of the message at B must be identifiable and should not result in a number of 'feedback' level 0 messages being sent to A. For example, if the message was move forward at 0.51 ms^{-1} the entity will continuously move in the environment held in B. However, as this causes a change in the environment, B will try to communicate the change to A. Hence B must know that the results of the issued behaviour should not be distributed.

Use of level 2 behaviours can aid in network scalability in the same manner that level 1 behaviours have been used over level 0. Although level 2 behaviours can be too complex to compound into an identifiable message, this is not the case for all level 2 behaviours. It is possible to sub-divide level 2 behaviours into categories:

- Encapsulated. This category of level 2 behaviour contains all behaviours that are atomic and pseudo-deterministic. That is, the effects resulting from the executed behaviour can be identified. This allows the executing process to identify which actions are a result of a level 2 behaviour and which are not, preventing the feedback loop described earlier.
- Non-Encapsulated. These are level 2 behaviours, which cannot guarantee outcome of the resultant effects during execution.

For example, consider the case of a complex avatar, which simulates a doorman outside a virtual hotel. Example behaviours may include:

- *Level 3* - Greet closest user; stop a user from entering; help with baggage
- *Level 2* - wave_right_arm; open_door
- *Level 1* – Rotate right arm (joint 1) 0.05° per second for 2 seconds
- *Level 0* – Rotate_fixedxyz [right_forearm] 0 1 0 0.3445

Level 0 and 1 behaviours can be dealt with as described previously. The level 2 behaviour wave_right_arm invokes a deterministic action. The behaviour can be interpreted by each of the distributed processes and executed (i.e. translated into level 1 and 0 behaviours) to perform the desired action. This allows a distributed CVE to have the doorman wave his hand with minimal network traffic. Both behaviours wave_right_arm and open_door are *encapsulated* as they are deterministic; the doorman's arm comes to the same resting position in the two distributed processes.

Consider the two ways to define the case where a proximity sensor controls a door, using both level 0 calls, and level 1 & 2 calls. The message from the proximity sensor to the door is similar in both cases, a simple update/notification message. However, the main difference is in the execution of the message by the door. In the case of level 0 behaviours, the door will animate so that it opens, each angle of opening is distributed throughout the CVE. However, in the other case, the single level 1/2 message is simply distributed throughout the CVE, the network bandwidth saved in this manner can be substantial, see Figure 2.

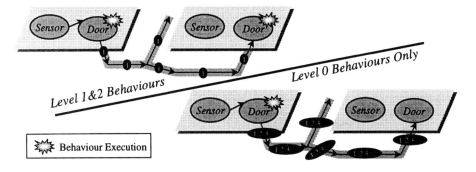

Fig. 1. Effect on network when using different levels of behaviours to distribute state.

5 Semantic Behaviours

In this section, we describe a scripting language that supports all the different levels of behaviours described in the previous section and allows flexible application development with the DIVE environment.

The Distributed Interactive Virtual Environment (DIVE) is an experimental platform for the development of virtual environments, user interfaces and applications based on shared 3D synthetic environments. DIVE is especially tuned to multi-user applications, where several networked participants interact over the Internet. Initially developed as a lab tool in 1991, DIVE has evolved into a mature system running on many platforms.[‡] The DIVE architecture is described in [7].

DIVE is based on a peer-to-peer approach with no centralised server, where peers communicate by reliable and non-reliable IP multicast. Conceptually, all peers share a hierarchical database and interact by making concurrent accesses to the database. Consistency and concurrency control are achieved by active replication and reliable multicast protocols. Objects are replicated at several nodes where the replica is kept consistent by being continuously updated. Update messages are sent by multicast so that all nodes perform the same sequence of updates.

DIVE has support for application defined data which can be associated to any entity of the environment. Application defined data, called properties is distributed along with the entities. Properties have a name and a type and specific functions exist to retrieve, change and create properties from the applications. A small number of usual data types such as strings, integers and floating point numbers are pre-defined; new

---

[‡] DIVE runs on many UNIX platforms (SGI, HP, Sun and Linux) and on Windows NT. Binaries are available for free for non-commercial use at http://www.sics.se/dive/.

100

types can be created and smoothly ignored in applications which do not recognise these types. Properties enhance the semantics of virtual environments by allowing applications to expose their parameters and data and other applications to understand these and react according to some logic.

5.1 Design Requirements

The undertaken approach is based on a small set of requirements that were isolated before interfacing a scripting language to DIVE. These requirements are:

- *Clarity of syntax.* As the scripting language is intended for use by a wide range of programmers, its syntax should not be cumbersome.
- *Flexibility.* As the language is intended for use by a variety of applications, it should be sufficiently flexible to support a diverse range of requirements.
- *Compact.* If the integration of a scripting language is successful, it is foreseen that the behaviour language will be used in many applications and at different levels of the VR platform. Thus, one requirement is then to have a scripting language that executes in a small kernel, as quickly as possible.
- *Windowing extensions.* The scripting language should have extensions to open usual two-dimensional windows on a user's screen.
- *Ready for distribution.* It should be easy to distribute scripts between the different application processes participating to the virtual environment, i.e. scripts should be compact in size and should be adapted to run under different platforms.

There are several scripting languages that partially or totally satisfy these criteria. The Tool Command Language (TCL) is one of them. It was chosen for reasons summarised in the next section.

5.2 DIVE/TCL

The TCL programming system [4] was originally developed at the University of California, Berkeley. TCL originates from the idea of offering a common scripting language to different applications. As such, it offers a set of standard features and is easy to extend to fit the needs of a specific application. Extensions are made by adding new commands to the core TCL facilities. TCL supports many of the features of conventional procedural languages, including variable assignment and scoping, procedure calls and control structures.

Integrating TCL with DIVE

TCL scripts are used to describe how DIVE objects react to user interaction and other external events. Scripts are associated to the objects themselves so that execution can be run in parallel on different hosts and in different scripts. Given the extension facilities offered by TCL, a straightforward approach is to add a new set of commands, which will interface DIVE specific capabilities. Scripts will then be able to call these commands to modify the state of the virtual environment at any time, or to be notified when changes are applied. Notification to scripts will be done upon registration when events are occurring within the environment. The commands interface the level 0 and

1 operations that are built in the DIVE platform. The following commands exist in DIVE/TCL, a complete list can be found in [6]. Their existence is application driven:

- Bind a procedure to an event of the simulation, e.g. user interaction, collision between objects, entity creation/deletion, geometry modifications, and so on. When an event occurs, the procedure is called with the arguments carried by the event.
- Register commands to be executed on a regular basis and unregister them.
- Get information from the entities and their hierarchy. Modify their properties and attributes including position, orientation, velocity, material, texture and so on.
- Add and remove entities, additions may be done programmatically or by reading files and uniform resource locators.
- Communicate between scripts associated to entities,[§] i.e. call a command in the context of another entity and (possibly) get back the result in the calling entity.
- Visualise external documents by interfacing the DIVE multimedia and WWW facilities and execute authorised external programs.
- Generate high-level application events, together with application specific data, and react to these events.

Core Execution Principles

Scripts are associated with entities, but not with any peer. Associating a script with a peer would excessively load this peer and would not fit with DIVE's general distribution philosophy. Furthermore, this would lengthen reaction time. For example, a script reacting on user interaction would only start reacting when the interaction event has reached the peer associated to this script, which might happen hundreds of milliseconds after the interaction was generated, when running on a long-distance network.

Typically, a peer generating an event will execute the script that it triggers. Results of the executed commands within the script are then distributed to all other connected peers. For example, consider an object associated with a script that moves the object forward on user interaction. User interaction is a system event that will trigger the script at the peer where the interaction is generated. Consequently, the script will move the object forward in the local database, ensuring optimal reaction time. Moving the object will itself generate a network message which will end up at all connected peers and move the object forward in their own local databases. Thus, all connected peers will have reached an identical state.

An additional mechanism consists of windowing system extensions. Users are represented in the virtual simulation by process bound entities called 'actors'. These actors are enhanced with TK, the TCL windowing system companion. Thus, adding TCL/TK commands to a script, enables application developers to communicate with the user through a two-dimensional user interface.

Parallel Script Execution

The design model detailed above offers several key advantages. It places the burden of script execution onto the responsible peer. Consequently, computing intensive

---

[§] Script communication allows an object-oriented approach to application development by defining precisely the different types of services that objects offer.

scripts will only affect the process that triggers their execution. Furthermore, the model guarantees high interaction since the database modifications resulting from script execution are applied at the interacting peer first.

However, this model presents a major drawback: Even if the logic of the entity behaviour is distributed at all connected peers, when an event occurs, only one peer will react. It is the results of script execution that are distributed in the form of database modifications, i.e. generating level 0 and 1 operations. While this implementation model fits with the general DIVE philosophy, it can be argued to be cumbersome. In this section, we describe two solutions that seek to avoid distributing database changes as much as possible by executing the script logic at all peers in parallel.

In order to describe object movements that are a predictive function of time, DIVE allows binding the position and orientation of an object to a TCL procedure. Each time an application requires the transformation matrix of such an object, the TCL script will be called back and return the value at that time. This mechanism is useful for describing object animations that follow complex mathematical paths or kinematics equations that are not built in the system. Thus, it represents a high-level implementation of level 1 behaviours. However, it directly depends on TCL execution speed.

Another technique to achieve parallel script execution is based on local 'holders'. Holders encapsulate a branch of the hierarchy under a multicast group. Parallel execution can be achieved by creating local holders that encapsulate objects with scripts. Using a reference node, all connected peers will be initiated with the same visual and logical database construction. Since holders are shared entities, they can be used to send and distribute high-level semantically rich events and synchronisation events. The low-level events that result from the logic contained in the scripts, usually database modifications, will *not* generate network traffic since they occur below a local holder.

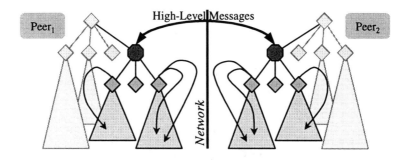

Fig. 2. Parallel script execution can be achieved by encapsulating objects and scripts under local holders.

Figure 2 exemplifies these mechanisms in-between two peers sharing the same environment. The picture shows the database as seen from $Peer_1$ to the left and as seen from $Peer_2$ to the right. Entities of the hierarchy are depicted as diamonds, while entire sub-trees are simplified as triangles. The local holder is represented as an octagon. The entity tree under the holder is read separately at both peers, it results in an identical structure that is *not* shared between the processes. Consequently, database modifications that occur according to script logic do not generate any network traffic. However, since the structure is identical, the results are visually and logically identical. Since it is shared between both peers, the holder is used to transport semantic-rich events that will trigger the logic of the scripts beneath. Additionally, the scripts have to contain some logic that allows new incoming peers to loosely catch on with the current state. This can be achieved using synchronisation events that are sent to the holder at a low frequency.

6 Visual Semantic Editing

To ease development of applications that exploit the mechanisms detailed in this document, a visual development tool (figure 3) has been built. This enables application developers to more easily assign high level behaviours between objects in the virtual world. A key abstraction offered by the tool is that level 1 and 2 behaviours have been merged and categorised as external *functions* and *events*:

- **Functions** identify level 1 or 2 behaviours that may be invoked on that entity.
- **Events** are invoked by the entity when a particular condition occurs. These are a means of an entity promoting its activities to other entities. Events may be linked to functions in other entities in a "callback" fashion.

The only types of link allowed are variables to variables and events to functions. That is, events will fire and invoke functions. Links may be easily assigned using the visual editor. Any element present within the editor may also be edited, including geometry manipulation through the AC3D editor [9]. This enables the geometry to be updated independently of its behaviour. All underlying event distribution mechanisms to support the communication links specified in the editor are created by the editor when the DIVE code is generated.

In Figure 3, it can be seen that two objects from a simple hierarchy have been expanded, depicting a sensor linked to a door. The sensor monitors a space for movement, and is configured so that it maintains a local variable 'Door_state' and generates an event based on activity within the spatial proximity. This event also dispatches the contents of the 'Door-state' variable. In the editor the event from the sensor is linked to the 'Set_door_state' function of the door. This defines the event sequence to control the state of the door through a sensor object. A counter depicting the number events is also kept and updated by the door object. This variable is also mirrored, through the link defined in the editor, in the sensor object, providing it with local access to the counter state. Each of the elements can also be assigned as 'encapsulated', this notes them as deterministic, and places them in a DIVE holder (see above). This stops any non-high level behaviour events from being distributed.

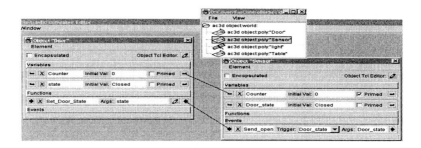

Fig. 3. The visual behaviour editor. (Note: figure distorted for space reasons).

7 Conclusions

This paper has described an integration of an interpreted language into a CVE. This marriage supports rapid prototyping and development of multi-user applications. Identification of semantic behaviours provides a higher level of abstraction over application development and can drastically reduce network bandwidth.

The DIVE/TCL interface has been widely used to develop a range of different applications and extensions. Its flexibility, power and simplicity enable developers to quickly generate distributed applications. Notable examples include WebPath, an interactive Web history visualisation tool. WebPath [11] exploits the windowing extensions of DIVE/TCL to present users with common 2D interaction techniques. Additionally, a suite of virtual collaborative tools, described in [12], has been developed using scripts. The suite supports common meeting functions within any DIVE world.

References

1. Roehl B.: Behaviour in VR. http://ece.uwaterloo.ca/~broehl/behav.html (1995).
2. Defense Modeling and Simulation Office: Department of Defense High Level Architecture for Simulations Version 0.4 Interface Specification (1996).
3. DIS Steering Committee: The DIS Vision, A Map to the Future of Distributed Simulation Version 1, Institute for Simulation & Training, Orlando, FL, USA, IST-SP-94-01 (1994)
4. Ousterhout J.: TCL and the TK toolkit, Addison-Wesley, (1994) ISBN 0-201-63337-X
5. Blaxxun Interactive. http://www.blaxxun.de/.
6. Frécon E. (ed.): DIVE/TCL Ref. Manual (1997), http://www.sics.se/dive/manual/tclref.html.
7. Frécon E., Stenius M.: DIVE: A scaleable network architecture for distributed virtual environments, Distributed Systems Engineering Journal, Bristol, UK, Institute of Physics Publishing, Vol. 5, No. 3 (1998) 91-100.
8. Greenhalgh C., Benford S.: MASSIVE: A Virtual Reality System for Tele-conferencing, ACM Transactions on Computer Human Interfaces, Vol. 2, No. 3 (1995) 239-261.
9. Colebourne A.: AC3D. http://www.comp.lancs.ac.uk/computing/users/andy/ac3d.html.
10. VRML 1997. The Virtual Reality Modelling Language, http://www.vrml.org/.
11. Frécon E., Smith G.: WebPath - A three-dimensional Web History, IEEE Symposium on Information Visualisation (InfoVis '98), Research Triangle Park, NC, USA (1998) 3-10.
12. Frécon E., Avatare-Nöu A.: Building Distributed Virtual Environments to Support Collaborative Work, VRST'98 ACM Press (1998) 105-114.

A Distributed Device Diagnostics System Utilizing Augmented Reality and 3D Audio

Reinhold Behringer, Steven Chen, Venkataraman Sundareswaran, Kenneth Wang, and Marius Vassiliou

Rockwell Science Center, Thousand Oaks, CA 91360, USA
phone ++1-805-373-4435, fax ++1-805-373-4862
{reinhold,slchen,vsundar,kkwang,msvassiliou}@rsc.rockwell.com
WWW home page: http://hci.rsc.rockwell.com

Abstract. Augmented Reality brings technology developed for virtual environments into the real world. This approach can be used to provide instructions for routine maintenance and error diagnostics of technical devices. The Rockwell Science Center is developing a system that utilizes Augmented Reality techniques to provide the user with a form of "X-Ray Vision" into real objects. The system can overlay 3D rendered objects, animations, and text annotations onto the video image of a known object, registered to the object during camera motion. This allows the user to localize problems of the device with the actual device in his view. The user can query the status of device components using a speech recognition system. The response is given as an animation of the relevant device module and/or as auditory cues using spatialized 3D audio. The diagnostics system also allows the user to leave spoken annotations attached to device modules for other users to retrieve. The position of the user/camera relative to the device is tracked by a computer-vision-based tracking system especially developed for this purpose. The system is implemented on a distributed network of PCs, utilizing standard commercial off-the-shelf components (COTS).

1 Context and Related Work

During the past few years, technology developed for Virtual Environments (VE) has become a valuable tool for providing an intuitive human-computer interface. In the domain known as *Augmented Reality* (AR), this technology is being applied in the integration of the virtual environment with the real world [11].

1.1 Augmented Reality

Rapid progress in several key areas (wearable computing, virtual reality rendering) has focused significant attention on *Augmented Reality* research in recent years [3]. Although AR is often associated with visualization (starting with the first head-mounted display by Sutherland [20]), augmentation is also possible in the aural [4] [13] and other domains. AR technology provides means of intuitive information presentation for enhancing situational awareness and perception by exploiting the natural and familiar human interaction modalities with the environment, e.g., augmenting paper drawings [10], a desk environment [16], or familiar collaborative modalities [21].

The concepts of AR have been demonstrated in many applications [1]. AR systems can provide navigational aid in an unknown environment, e.g., in an urban setting [7]. Industrial applications of AR techniques include airplane manufacturing [12], guided assembly [17], improving machine maintenance procedures, and a number of applications in the area of *virtual prototyping*.

1.2 Registration for AR

In applications that utilize the concept of virtual environments, various methods have been developed to track the user's head in order to provide a view which is consistent with the user's sensory information. Such systems include magnetic tracking and attitude sensors. However, visual AR applications require a much higher registration precision, because the human eye is very sensitive to a mismatch between virtual and real objects [1].

Vision-based tracking can potentially provide a very high tracking accuracy. Video-based observer pose estimation methods attempt to compute the position and orientation of the camera from the position of landmarks in the images. The general problem of reliable 3D motion estimation from image features is largely an unsolved problem in computer vision. However, by restricting to the sub-problem of easily identifiable landmarks, the motion estimation problem can be solved (e.g., [9]).

1.3 The RSC Distributed Device Diagnostics System

The Rockwell Science Center (RSC) is developing and integrating components for a system using AR techniques for visualization and auralization during maintenance and error diagnostics procedures. This system is based on an Augmented Reality (AR) approach by overlaying textual information, registered 3D rendered objects, and animations onto a live video of the actual device to be diagnosed, and ultimately by directly overlaying this display into the field of view of the user. 3D audio rendering techniques are used to indicate the location of objects which are currently not in the user's field of view. To employ a non-tethered human-computer interface, the system is operated by speaker-independent speech recognition. To achieve the registration necessary for a well-aligned visual overlay, we have developed a visual tracking module, which relies on tracking of visual fiducial markers and on the mathematical formalism of *visual servoing*. One of the novel features of our concept is the integration of computer vision, speech recognition, AR visualization, and 3D audio in a distributed networked PC environment.

In this paper we describe the system components and the tracking algorithms as well as the status of the system integration.

2   System Components

2.1   Head Tracking: Visual Servoing with Fiducial Markers

The fiducial markers used by the visual tracking system have been designed for
easy detectability in clutter and under a wide range of viewing angles. Each
marker has a unique ID. Circular markers with concentric rings have a high
degree of symmetry, which allows the application of a simple viewpoint-invariant
detection algorithm. Similar markers are used by Neumann [14] who developed
a color-code scheme for ring marker identification, and Sharma [17] who uses the
configuration pattern of a set of markers for detecting ID and orientation of the
marker set.

Fig. 1. Left two circles: Schematics of fiducial ring marker. The left marker shows the
ring fields i_j which correspond to a binary number. The middle marker, for example,
denotes the ID=2. The right marker is distorted to an ellipse when seen under a large
viewing angle.

Visual servoing is controlling a system – typically a robot end-effector – based
on processing visual information. It is a well-developed theory for robotic vision
([5], [6], [15], [19], [22]). Our application of the visual servoing approach has been
outlined in [18], but for completeness, it will briefly be summarized below.

Visual servoing is carried out in a closed-loop fashion, as shown in Fig. 2.
We would like the set of system states **s** to attain certain target values $\mathbf{s}_r$. The
current values of the states **s** are measured by a camera looking at the scene. The
system uses the error (difference between the target values and current values)
to determine the motion parameters T and Ω to move the camera in order to
reduce the error. We adopt the standard coordinate systems shown in Fig. 2.
The translational velocity T has components U, V, and W. The components of
the rotational velocity Ω are A, B and C.

To do this, we need to know the analytical relationship between the motion
parameters and the state **s**. Usually, the forward relationship, namely the change
in **s** due to parameters T and Ω is known. The goal is to minimize $\|\mathbf{s} - \mathbf{s}_r\|$. Let
us define the error function

$$\mathbf{e} = \mathbf{s} - \mathbf{s}_r \qquad (1)$$

We would like the error function to decay exponentially:

$$\dot{\mathbf{e}} = -\lambda \cdot \mathbf{e},$$

108

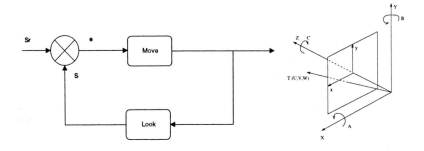

Fig. 2. Schematic of the visual servoing approach (left) and the coordinate system (right).

where λ, the constant in the exponential, controls the decay rate (i.e., speed of convergence). Therefore $\dot{s} = -\lambda \cdot (s - s_r)$. From standard optic flow equations (see for e.g. [8]), we know that we can write the 2D displacement of an image feature at (x_p, y_p) as:

$$\dot{x}_p = \frac{1}{Z(x_p, y_p)} [-U + x_p W] + A x_p y_p - B [1 + x_p^2] + C y_p,$$
$$\dot{y}_p = \frac{1}{Z(x_p, y_p)} [-V + y_p W] + A [1 + y_p^2] - B x_p y_p - C x_p. \tag{2}$$

We assume that the images are planar, obtained by the pin-hole perspective approximation with a focal length of unity (see Fig. 2). This relationship between change in 2D projection of a point and the motion parameters is of the form

$$\dot{s} = L \begin{pmatrix} T \\ \Omega \end{pmatrix}, \tag{3}$$

where L is the "interaction matrix" consisting of 2D coordinates (x_p, y_p) and the depth Z of the 3D point projected at (x_p, y_p), T is the translation vector and Ω is the rotation vector. We would like to determine T and Ω. Assuming that the motion of features s is due to the motion T and Ω, we obtain:

$$L \begin{pmatrix} T \\ \Omega \end{pmatrix} = -\lambda \mathbf{e}. \tag{4}$$

Inverting Eqn. 4, we get the control law

$$\begin{pmatrix} T \\ \Omega \end{pmatrix} = -\lambda L^+ \mathbf{e}, \tag{5}$$

where L^+ is the pseudo-inverse of L.

This allows us to compute the motion of the camera required to minimize the error $\mathbf{e}$. When performed in closed-loop, the value s will reach s_r when error $\mathbf{e}$ is reduced to zero.

2.2 The Automatic Speech Recognition (ASR) Server

Rockwell Science Center's Automatic Speech Recognition (ASR) Server software provides an easy way to rapidly prototype speech-enabled applications, regardless of the computing platform(s) on which they execute. It provides both automatic speech recognition and text-to-speech synthesis (TTS) capabilities.

The ASR capability is obtained through abstraction of a commercially available off-the-shelf speech recognition technology, IBM ViaVoice^{TM}. Using the ViaVoice engine, speaker-independent continuous phonetic recognition constrained by finite state grammars is possible, as well as speaker-adapted continuous dictation using an American English language model. The TTS functionality provided with the ViaVoice engine is likewise abstracted and exposed to client applications. The ASR Server's architecture provides for the future addition of other vendors' speech recognition technologies as needed.

A client application connects to the ASR Server over an IP network using TCP sockets. Although the ASR Server runs on a Windows 95/Intel Architecture PC, the client application may be running on MS-Windows, Solaris, IRIX, or any other operating system that supports TCP/IP networking. Using a serial-like ASCII command protocol, the client application indicates its identity to the server, as well as any contextual data of relevance to the speech recognition task, such as the currently selected object in the graphical portion of the client application's user interface. Speech recognition is requested and activated by the client, and asynchronous speech recognition results are sent from the ASR Server to the client. Both of these interactions occur using a vendor-independent protocol.

Speech is currently acquired locally through a sound card installed in the PC on which the ASR Server executes, although an add-on option for uncompressed streaming audio over IP networks has been developed to allow the microphone to reside on another computer. Recognition results are reported to the client application immediately (per word) and/or upon the completion of a whole utterance (sentence).

If the client application's user interface can wait for whole utterance results, an application-specific text parser in the ASR Server may be exploited to relieve the client application of the burden of parsing the recognition results. This provides an advantage in the application design phase when rapidly iterating through grammar and vocabulary designs. Per-word confidence scores can be reported to the client application if requested; in addition, reporting of word timing hypotheses is being developed – this capability will enable concurrent gesture and speech interfaces.

In the device diagnostics system, described in this paper, speech is used both to control the operation (initialization, mode switching), and to ask questions about device modules, such as the query "Where is the Power Supply?". Moreover, the dictation recognition mode is exploited to attach textual "virtual notes" to selected objects in the virtual environment. The recognition is started by a trigger button pressed by the user.

2.3 AR Visualization

The AR visualization provides visual rendering of the device which is to be diagnosed, and its components. The following items can be overlaid in real-time in the live video image:

− A CAD wireframe model of the outer device shape.
− CAD models of the interior components of the device.
− Textual annotations, attached to components of the device.

The CAD models are overlaid onto the video image of the device and, therefore, provide a kind of "X-ray vision" into the interior of the device. They can be animated to blink between *shaded* and *wireframe* display rendering in order to highlight the corresponding module of the device. In Fig. 3 (right) the two rendering modes are shown. The rendering engine used for creating the 3D overlay is the Sense8 World-Toolkit library.

2.4 3D Audio Auralization

A three-dimensional (3D) audio system provides an auditory experience in which sounds appear to emanate from locations in 3D space. 3D audio can be used to indicate spatial locations as well as increase the differentiability of multiple audio communication channels. Thus, both visual display clutter and message comprehension time may be reduced through the use of 3D audio. Head-Related Transfer Functions (HRTF) [2] are basically filters incorporating the effects of the sound signal reflecting off the listener's head, shoulders, and pinnae (outer ears). These HRTFs are usually different for each listener. However, it has been shown that the HRTFs of a "good localizer" are suitable for a large group of users [23]. A good localizer is defined as a human who localizes real sound sources with high accuracy and precision.

In our device diagnostics system, we use the commercial Aureal Semiconductor off-the-shelf (COTS) 3D audio system. This comprises a software application programming interface (API) based on the Microsoft DirectSound/DirectSound3D standard as well as a PC sound card including a chip designed and manufactured by Aureal. The inputs of an HRTF-based 3D audio system include the monaural sound source signal(s) (one signal per sound source), the user position and orientation, and the positions of the sound source(s). The 3D audio is output over a pair of headphones or two speakers. In order to provide 3D audio capability to non-platform-specific applications, a TCP/IP sockets server (the RSC 3DA Server) was developed. This allows application developers to simply exploit the Aureal 3D audio services by establishing a socket connection to the RSC 3DA Server and providing real-time user position and orientation and sound source position data. The sound source signals are stored as wave files on the 3DA Server host PC. The 3DA Server operates at 30 fps, and current COTS 3D audio sound cards support up to three 44.1 kHz-sampled sound sources.

3   System Integration

The system components of the AR device diagnosis system were implemented on a PC. We also used a standard tower PC as the example *device* which was to be "diagnosed". A CAD model was hand-coded to describe the outer geometry and a few inner components of the PC: CD ROM drive, network card, power supply, and structural components. The AR visualization is implemented on a 200 Mhz PC, running under Windows NT. The rendering algorithms are based on the Sense8 WorldToolkit library, which provides functionality for the display of 3D worlds. The implementing PC is equipped with a Imaging Technology color framegrabber, which digitizes the video signal from a Cohu 2200 CCD camera. In order to illustrate potential diagnosis capabilities, we introduced the following simulated device errors in the PC being "diagnosed": CD ROM failure, power supply overheating, and network card failure. The spatial interpretation for the 3D auralization is obtained solely from the visual servoing algorithm.

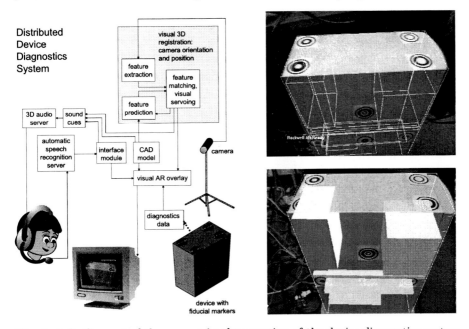

Fig. 3. Left: Concept of the current implementation of the device diagnostics system. Right: Registered wireframe and shaded overlay onto the video image.

The speech recognition server (ASR server) and the 3D audio server are both running on another PC (166 Mhz) under Windows 95. The user can query by voice command the location of the CD ROM drive, network card, and power supply. A flashing animation, overlaid on the video, visualizes the location. The user can also query the location of printer and UPS. Their location is indicated by a 3D audio cue: spatialized sounds "move" in the direction of the location and guide the user.

4   Experimental Results

The visual AR overlay is rendered with a framerate between 6-10 fps, depending on the system load. The framerate is slowed down by the image transfer implementation in Windows, which is currently not optimized for speed.

Fig. 4 to Fig. 6 show various display modalities of the visual overlay on the video image. Fig. 4 shows the wireframe overlay from two different directions. The overlay matches very well with the real object under a wide viewing angle range. Not surprisingly, the registration error depends on the number (and the location) of the recognized fiducial markers. The alignment/registration is slightly off for more extreme viewing angles where only markers in one plane are well visible. The markers in the other plane are too slanted for robust recognition. However, the range for acceptable registration is quite large, and the error is acceptable.

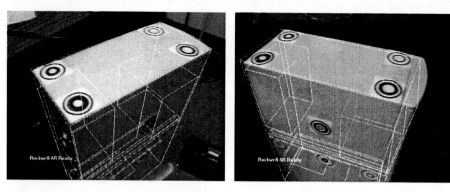

Fig. 4. Overlay of wireframe onto video stream from different directions.

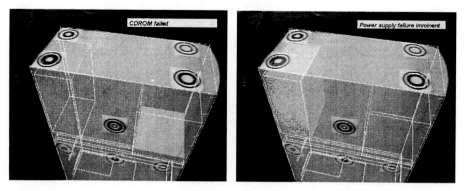

Fig. 5. Overlay of error indication onto video image: CD ROM and power supply.

In Fig. 5 the error indication is shown by a flashing volumetric rendering of the relevant PC components. In Fig. 6 two examples of annotations are shown.

These notes have been left by a previous user who attached these notes to components of the PC. They are spoken and translated by the ASR text-to-speech (TTS) system into ASCII text.

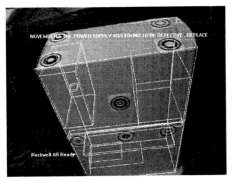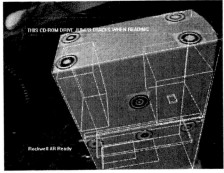

Fig. 6. Retrieval of textual annotations.

5 Summary and Conclusion

We have demonstrated the capability of a distributed, networked system for device diagnostics as a novel, tetherless interface for human-computer interaction. The distributed architecture of the system ultimately allows for scalability and enables the user to be equipped with only a light, wearable computer system that provides wearable display capabilities. Such a system can one day replace service manuals by providing direct overlay of maintenance instructions or error diagnosis onto the real object.

References

[1] AZUMA, R. T. A survey of Augmented Reality. *Presence: Teleoperators and Virtual Environments 6*, 4 (1997), 355–385.

[2] BLAUERT, J. *Spatial Hearing: The Psychophysics of Human Sound Localization*. MIT Press, 1997.

[3] CAUDELL, T. P. Introduction to Augmented and Virtual Reality. In *Proc. of SPIE Conf. on Telemanipulator and Telepresence Technologies* (Boston, MA, Oct. 1994), SPIE, pp. 272–281.

[4] COHEN, M., AOKI, S., AND KOIZUMI, N. Augmented audio reality: Telepresence/VR hybrid acoustic environments. In *Proc. of Workshop on Robot and Human Communication* (Tokyo, Japan, Nov. 1993), IEEE Press, pp. 361–4.

[5] ESPIAH, B., CHAUMETTE, F., AND RIVES, P. A new approach to visual servoing in robotics. *IEEE Transactions on Robotics and Automation 8*, 3 (1992), 313–326.

[6] FEDDEMA, J., AND MITCHELL, O. Vision-guided servoing with feature-based trajectory generation. *IEEE Transactions on Robotics and Automation 5*, 5 (1989), 691–700.

[7] FEINER, S., MACINTYRE, B., HÖLLERER, T., AND WEBSTER, A. A touring machine: prototyping 3D mobile Augmented Reality systems for exploring the urban environment. In *Proc. of 1st In. Symp. on Wearable Computers* (Cambridge, MA, Oct. 1997), pp. 74–81.

[8] HORN, B. K. P. *Robot Vision.* MIT Press, Cambridge, 1987.

[9] KOLLER, D., KLINKER, G., ROSE, E., BREEN, D., WHITAKER, R., AND TUCERYAN, M. Real-time vision-based camera tracking for Augmented Reality applications. In *Proc. of VRST '97* (Lausanne, Switzerland, Sept. 1997).

[10] MACKAY, W., PAGANI, D., FABER, L., INWOOD, B., LAUNIAINEN, P., BRENTA, L., AND POUZOL, V. ARIEL: Augmenting paper engineering drawings. In *Proc. of Conf. on Human Factors in Computing Systems (CHI)* (Denver, CO, May 1995), IEEE Press, pp. 421–422.

[11] MILGRAM, P., TAKEMURA, H., UTSUMI, A., AND KISHINO, F. Augmented Reality: a class of displays on the reality-virtuality continuum. In *Proc. of SPIE Conf. on Telemanipulator and Telepresence Technologies* (Boston, MA, Oct. 1994), SPIE, pp. 282–292.

[12] MIZELL, D. Virtual reality and Augmented Reality in aircraft design and manufacturing. In *Proc. of Wescon Conference* (Anaheim, CA, Sept. 1994), p. 91ff.

[13] MYNATT, E. D., BACK, M., WANT, R., AND FREDERICK, R. Audio Aura: lightweight audio Augmented Reality. In *Proc. of ACM UIST '97* (Banff, Canada, Oct. 1997), ACM, pp. 211–12.

[14] NEUMANN, U., AND CHO, Y. Multi-ring fiducial systems for scalable fiducial Augmented Reality. In *Proc. of VRAIS '98* (Atlanta, Mar. 1998).

[15] PAPANIKOLOPOLOUS, N., KHOSLA, P., AND KANADE, T. Visual tracking of a moving target by a camera mounted on a robot: a combination of control and vision. *IEEE Transactions on Robotics and Aautomation 9*, 1 (1993), 14–35.

[16] RAUTERBERG, M., MAUCH, T., AND STEBLER, R. Digital playing desk: A case study for Augmented Reality. In *Proc. of IEEE Workshop on Robot and Human Communication* (Tsukuba, Japan, Nov. 1996), IEEE Press, pp. 410–415.

[17] SHARMA, R., AND MOLINEROS, J. Computer vision-based Augmented Reality for guiding manual assembly. *PRESENCE: Teleoperators and Virtual Environments 6*, 3 (June 1997), 292–317.

[18] SUNDARESWARAN, V., AND BEHRINGER, R. Visual servoing-based Augmented Reality. In *Proc. of First Int. Workshop on Augmented Reality (IWAR) '98* (San Francisco, CA, Nov. 1998).

[19] SUNDARESWARAN, V., BOUTHEMY, P., AND CHAUMETTE, F. Exploiting image motion for active vision in a visual servoing framework. *International Journal of Robotics Research 15*, 6 (1996), 629–645.

[20] SUTHERLAND, I. E. A head-mounted three dimensional display. In *Proc. of Fall Joint Computer Conference* (Washington, DC, 1968), Thompson Books, pp. 757–764.

[21] SZALAVARI, Z., GERVAUTZ, M., FUHRMANN, A., AND SCHMALSTIEG, D. Augmented Reality enabled colaborative work in "Studierstube". In *Proc. of EUROVR '97* (Amsterdam, The Netherlands, 1997).

[22] WEISS, L., SANDERSON, A., AND NEUMANN, C. Dynamic sensor-based control of robots with visual feedback. *IEEE Transactions on Robotics and Automation 3*, 5 (1987), 404–417.

[23] WENZEL, E. M., ARRUDA, M., KISTLER, D. J., AND WIGHTMAN, F. L. Localization using non-individualized head-related transfer functions. *Journal of the Acoustical Society of America* (1993), 111–123.

Texture-based Volume Visualization for Multiple Users on the World Wide Web

Klaus Engel and Thomas Ertl

Computer Graphics Group (IMMD9)
University of Erlangen-Nürnberg
Computer Science Department (IMMD)
Am Weichselgarten 9
91058 Erlangen, Germany
Email: {engel,ertl}@informatik.uni-erlangen.de
URL: http://www9.informatik.uni-erlangen.de

Abstract. We present a texture-based volume visualization tool, which permits remote access to radiological data and supports multi-user environments. The application uses JAVA and the Virtual Reality Modeling Language (VRML), thus it is platform-independent and able to use fast 3D graphics acceleration hardware of client machines. The application allows the shared viewing and manipulation of three-dimensional medical volume datasets in a heterogeneous network. Volume datasets are transferred from a server to different client machines and locally visualized using a JAVA-enabled web-browser. In order to reduce network traffic, a data reduction and compression scheme is proposed. The application allows view dependent and orthogonal clipping planes, which can be moved interactively. On the client side, the users are able to join a visualization session and to get the same view onto the volume dataset by synchronizing the viewpoint and any other visualization parameter. Interesting parts of the dataset are marked for other users by placing a tag into the visualization. In order to support collaborative work users communicate with a chat applet, which we provide, or by using any existing video conferencing tool.

1 Introduction

The hypermedia structure of the Web offers the possibility for global distribution of medical datasets, such as radiological patient databases. A multi-user system for the visualization of computer tomography (CT) data, magnetic resonance imaging (MRI) data and positron emission tomography (PET) data will offer new perspectives. The use of telemedical applications improves medical care and allows experts from all over the world to participate in the discussion of diagnoses by joining a multi-user volume visualization session.

A possible approach for the visualization of volume datatsets on the WWW consists in rendering an image on a server and sending the images to a client system. Changes of visualization parameter are sent from the client to the server, a new image is rendered and displayed on the client after transmission. The limited bandwidth and latency of the network would be the limiting factor for the interactivity of such an application.

As we are interested in providing fast response times, we propose a web-based volume visualization applications with rendering on local client systems. However, such an application requires fast 3D graphics hardware [10, 2]. High quality volume visualization by maens of 3D texture mapping is still restricted to expensive high-end graphics workstations. Driven mainly by the game industry, the cost of 3D graphics hardware with 2D texture mapping support is continuously decreasing over the past few years. In the near future this development will enable every standard personal computer to visualize 3D volume datasets by using two dimensional texture mapping - an important aspect, because doctors are normally using only a standard PC with internet access in their office.

We developed a new web-based, multi-user visualization tool for medical volume datasets (Fig. 1). Since it is completely written in JAVA, it can be executed on a standard web-browser. The Virtual Reality Modeling Language (VRML) [13, 6, 3] is used to visualize medical volume datasets using 2D texture mapping , which enables the use of fast 3D graphics acceleration hardware of client systems - especially 2D texture mapping hardware.

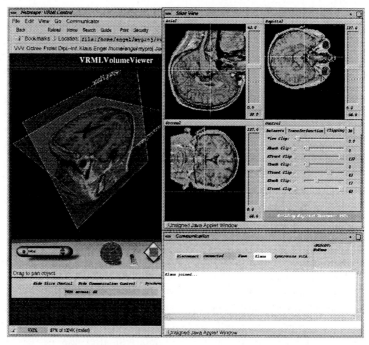

Fig. 1. The VRML Volume Visualization Application

A possible scenario for our application is a computer network connecting the computers in hospitals and other medical sites. A dedicated server stores radiological patient data which can be accessed and visualized by radiologists using a standard PC in their office. Experts from other locations all over the world can be consulted in order to discuss the diagnostic findings. To join the discussion only a standard PC with a HTML-browser and a installed VRML-plugin is needed. The users are able to share the view onto the dataset, while manipulating any visualization parameter and marking parts of the dataset.

The techniques we build on were introduced by Ofer Hendin [7]. We add some important extensions to this approach. First, we developed a fast volume clipping algorithm, which does not require per-voxel operations. The second extension is the ability for multiple users to join a visualization session and to share the view and manipulation of the volume dataset. Another extension we add is the reduction of the data to be transferred to the client machines. This is achieved by a cutting and compression scheme. The combination and close linkage of a 2D slice control panel and the 3D volume visualization offers a better spatial impression for the user. We also implemented a client-side java-based iso-surface extraction algorithm, which allows the combination of volume visualization with reconstructed surfaces.

In the following section we will discuss related work in the field of distributed web-based volume visualization applications. The techniques we used to develop our application are described in Section 3. Section 4 explains fast volume clipping using VRML. Our application enables multiple users to share the viewpoint, manipulate the visualization and mark interesting details of the volume dataset, which is discussed in Section 5. As volume datasets must be transferred to client machines in our application, data reduction is a very important subject. We will go into details on this subject in Section 6. In Section 7 we present some results regarding visualization speed and quality. We will conclude the paper with some remarks on future activities.

2   Related Work

In the past years several approaches for scientific visualization on the web were investigated. One of the first progressive applications for volume visualization was presented by Lippert et. al [14]. Their system is based on the local reconstruction of wavelet-compressed data, but since it works in the Fourier domain it is restricted to X-ray like images.

Trapp and Pagendarm presented a prototype of a WWW-based flow visualization service [9]. They allow arbitrary user data to be sent to a visualization server by a copy-and-paste operation from a data producer application into a HTML form. The server generates a VRML model of the visualization of the data, which is requested by a JAVA applet and visualized by the browser VRML plug-in. The data transfer between client and server is done using plain ASCII text, which requires a very high network throughput and processing time. The major drawback , however, is that the geometric data produced by the server has to be transmitted to the client, before it can be visualized, thus limiting the possibilities of the user to control the data visualization interactively.

Another interesting approach is the VisWiz [4] platform independent visualization tool for iso-surfaces, cutting planes and elevation plots for 2D and 3D datasets. The system is completely written as a JAVA applet. Due to the JAVA software renderer, no graphics hardware can be used, even if available.

Kwan-Lui Ma and James Patten introduced a web based volume visualization system called DiVision, which allows the user to explore remote volumetric datasets using a web browser [17]. The system computes images on a visualization server, which are transferred to the client and inserted into a graph. The graph represents the relation-ship of all images which the user has rendered so far. The edges of the graph show the change of rendering parameters between two images.

While Kwan-Lui Ma and James Patten focus on showing the entire process of vol-ume visualization, we are mainly interested in allowing the user to interactively inspect-ing datasets by fast local volume rendering. Our application is based on previous work by Ofer Hendin. We will discuss the techniques, he introduced in the next chapter.

3   Technical Background

Ofer Hendin introduced a VRML-based volume visualization tool, which uses three stacks of perpendicular slices. The VRML-plugin is controlled by a JAVA applet using the External Authoring Interface (EAI) [16].

VRML plug-ins are available for nearly every computer hardware architecture. They are able to visualize polygonal data very fast, since they are often written in optimized native code and use available 3D graphics hardware. Moreover if 2D texture mapping hardware is available, VRML is able to display bilinear interpolated texture maps. An external JAVA applet, which is embedded into a HTML page with a VRML plug-in, can access it through the External Authoring Interface (EAI). Since JAVA and VRML are defined platform independently, this combination can be applied to any computer architecture.

For each volume three stacks of planes in orthogonal orientations (XY, XZ and YZ) are built up in the VRML scenegraph. The volume slices for the corresponding stacks are texture mapped onto these planes (Fig. 2).

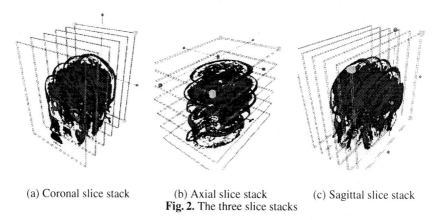

(a) Coronal slice stack   (b) Axial slice stack   (c) Sagittal slice stack
Fig. 2. The three slice stacks

From a given viewpoint only the most perpendicular slice stack is rendered back-to-front. The texture maps are interpolated bi-linearly across each projected polygon and blended into the frame buffer using the over-operator.

When the VRML scene for a volume dataset is created, three stacks of rectangu-lar faces are built using `IndexedFaceSet` nodes (Fig. 3). Each `IndexedFaceSet` represents one slice of the volume. A `PixelTexture` node is used to texture map

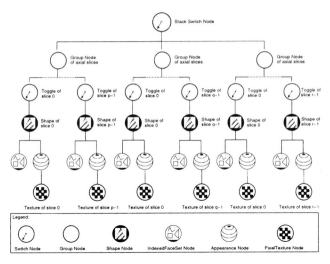

Fig. 3. VRML Scenegraph

one slice image of the volume data onto one face. The lookup-table is used to produce RGBA texture data, which is then sent to the `PixelTexture` node using the `eventIn` field `image`.

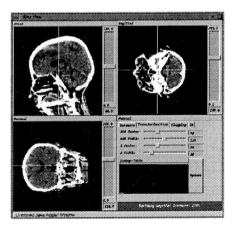

(a) The slice panel with the transfer function control

(b) Combination of iso-surface with direct volume visualization

Fig. 4.

If the transfer function is changed, the textures have to be completely rebuilt. This time consuming operation is necessary, because VRML does not allow to define lookup-tables. In order to find an interesting transfer function it is often necessary to adjust the transfer function several times and to get the results immediately. To decrease to number of VRML texture builtups, we have added a two-dimensional slice control panel (Figs. 4(a)). It's used to preview the result of lookup-table changes immediately. If a new transfer function is found, the new textures are produced and sent to the VRML plugin.

The combination of a 2D slice control panel and the 3D volume visualization offers new possibilities for radiologists. The 3D volume visualization and the 2D slice control are linked to each other. If the user selects a slice of the volume dataset using the slice control panel the position of the slice is displayed in the 3D volume visualization. On the other hand, the user is able to move a probe plane in the 3D volume visualization and the corresponding slice can be viewed in the slice control panel. The close linkage of 2D and 3D visualization will give radiologists a better spatial impression of volume datasets.

The combination of the direct volume visualization using two-dimensional texture mapping and iso-surfaces [15] is another interesting capability of our application. The user is able to select a subvolume using the 2D slice view and to compute an iso-surface for a given iso-value in this part of the volume. The surface is computed on the client by a JAVA class, consequently no additional network transfer is needed. Figure 4(b) shows the volume visualization of a CT dataset with an iso-surface that was generated by selecting the front part of the skull for iso-surface generation.

4 Fast VRML Volume Clipping

VRML does not allow to define arbitrary clipping planes. Hendin proposed to use the z-far clipping plane for view dependent clipping of volumes in VRML. We implemented a fast orthogonal volume clipping algorithm, which does not require per-voxel operations.

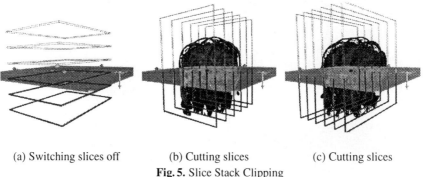

(a) Switching slices off   (b) Cutting slices   (c) Cutting slices

Fig. 5. Slice Stack Clipping

The main idea of our algorithm is to clip the volume data by omitting slices of the volume data which are ordered parallel to the clipping plane. Slices that are orthogonal to the clipping plane are cut off and the corresponding texture coordinates are adjusted.

Figure 5 shows the situation for a given clipping plane. For the first slice stack it is sufficient to switch of slices that lie beyond the clipping plane. The slices of the second and third slice stack have to be cut and the texture coordinates have to be adjusted.

Since every slice is the only child of a `Switch` node, it can be toggled on and off by using the `whichChoice` `eventIn` field of the switch node, which selects the child node to be rendered. The slices are cut by sending new dimensions to the `coord` `eventIn` field of the `IndexedFaceSet` node. The texture coordinates are adjusted using the `texCoord` `eventIn` field of the corresponding `PixelTexture` node.

This scheme permits interactive creation and movement of orthogonal clipping planes.

5 Multi-User Interaction

An essential feature of our web-based teleradiology system is the possibility for different users to share the viewpoint, to manipulate the visualization and to mark interesting details of the volume dataset.

The design of our web application shown in Figure 6 is particularly suitable for providing collaborative diagnosis among multiple users. A server synchronizes the visualization of the patient data by broadcasting events about changes of the view, clipping planes, transfer function, etc. from one user to all other interested users. Each user is able to synchronize his local visualization with any other user.

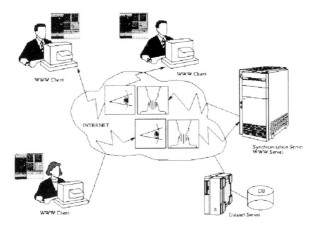

Fig. 6. Shared view on a dataset in a visualization session

From a list of all users which are logged, each user is able to select a user for synchronization. If a user changes the view, transfer-function, clipping planes or any other parameter, the changes are sent to synchronization server, which forwards the information to the synchronized clients. The parameters on these clients are changed and the visualization is updated.

Interesting parts of the volume dataset can be marked by clicking onto a part of the volume using the mouse or any other pointing device. A small marker (red ball) is added into the visualization (Fig. 7(a)). The position of the marker is broadcasted and the markers are updated for all synchronized users.

To support collaborative work users must be able to talk to each other in some way. For this purpose any existing video conferencing tool can be used. Alternatively we provide a chat applet (Fig. 7(b)) with basic communication features.

6 Data Reduction

One major drawback of direct volume visualization on local clients is the need to transfer volume datasets to the client system. Due to the large size of medical volume

(a) Marked aneurysm   (b) Communication panel

Fig. 7.

datasets, we propose several filter and data reduction steps to reduce the overall amount
of data to be transferred (Fig. 8).

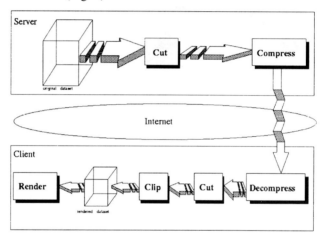

Fig. 8. Data reduction from original dataset to rendered dataset

Quite often experts are only interested in a certain smaller part of a volume dataset.
So the first filter operation is the cutting of a sub-volume out of the volume dataset. For
orientation purposes three slices in the XY, XZ and YZ directions are requested from
the dataset server. These slices are used to mark a rectangular part of the dataset, which
is transferred to the client.

All volume data is transferred in compressed format using the GZIP format. JAVA
1.1 supports this format directly in the *java.util.zip* package.

After transferring the data it is decompressed and visualized in the slice view window of our application. Now the user is able to inspect the dataset by navigating through
the slices using the slice view window. Again a rectangular part of the transferred volume can be selected. This part is cut and visualized by the VRML visualization module.

The final possibility to reduce the amount of data shown, is the placement of clipping planes.

7 Results

In this section we show some results regarding visualization performance and data reduction.

We used Netscape Communicator 4.04 and CosmoPlayer 1.1 on the IRIX clients systems and Netscape Communicator 4.07 and Blaxxun Contact 4.0 on the PC for our tests.

For a 256 x 256 x 128 volume a performance of 2 frames per second was achieved on a SGI O2 with a R10000 Processor (Table 1). The Voodoo Banshee graphics adapter [1], performed very well for the low resolution volume. Since the adapter is limited to 16 MB it was not able to visualize the high resolution volume [2].

machine / dataset	128 x 128 x 64	256 x 256 x 128
SGI O2 (R1000)	7 fps	2 fps
SGI OCTANE MXE	20 fps	4 fps
Pentium 200/Voodoo Banshee	15 fps	- fps[a]

Table 1. Performance of the application (frames per second)

[a] no result due to 16MB memory limit

Our fast orthogonal clipping algorithm allows the interactive composition and movement of clipping planes with the same frame rate as achieved when rotating, scaling or translating the volume. This is due to the fact that only little changes in the VRML scene-graph are needed by our volume clipping algorithm. The switching and cutting of slices can be done efficiently using the event mechanism of VRML.

dataset / format	uncompressed	compressed	compression factor
128 x 128 x 64 x 1 byte	1 048 576	397 868	2.64
256 x 256 x 128 x 1 byte	8 388 608	1 170 860	7.16
512 x 512 x 106 x 1 byte	27 787 264	4 720 204	5.89

Table 2. Data sizes of uncompressed, compressed datatsets in bytes and compression factors

We achieved compression rates between 2 and 10 by using the GZIP compression (Table 2). As this format is a JAVA 1.1 standard feature, that is implemented in native code, the compression and decompression times do not significantly influence the dataset transfer time.

8 Conclusions and Future Work

A prototyped application for volume visualization using VRML and JAVA has been proposed. It permits the platform-independent, fast and interactive visualization of volume datasets for multiple user on the world wide web. As the hardware requirements for the application are very low, a standard PC with two-dimensional texture mapping and alpha blending hardware can be used.

[1] less than 90 $
[2] 256 x 256 x 128 = 8MB x 3 = 24 MB

Currently we are computing iso-surfaces on the client system. Another possibility, however, would be to integrate techniques for progressive generation and transmission of iso-surfaces [5]. The iso-surface could be either progressively generated on the client system or computed on the server and then progressively transferred to the client.

Security of patient data is a very important requirement of a web-based teleradiology system [1]. We will evaluate the applicability of the new JAVA security mechanisms in the future.

Currently we are evaluating JAVA3D, JAVA OpenGL bindings and JAVA Cosmo3D bindings for the possible use in our application. A shear-warp, based on OpenGL bindings, has already been developed.

References

1. Andrea Abrardo and A.L. Casini. Embedded JAVA in a Web-based Teleradiology System. *IEEE Internet Computing*, pages 60–68, May - June 1998.
2. B. Cabral, N. Cam, and J. Foran. Accelerated Volume Rendering and Tomographic Reconstruction Using Texture Mapping Hardware. *ACM Symp. on Vol. Vis.*, pages 91–98, 1994.
3. Rikk Carey and Gavin Bell. *The Annotated VRML 2.0 Reference Manual*. Addison-Wesley Developer Press, 1997.
4. Michael Bailey Cherilyn Michaels. VizWiz: A Java Applet for Interactive 3D Scientific Visualization on the Web. In *Proceedings IEEE Visualization '97*, pages 261–267, 1997.
5. K. Engel, R. Grosso, and T. Ertl. Progressive Iso–surfaces on the Web. In *accepted for publ.: Proc. Visualization 98*. IEEE Comp. Soc. Press, 1998.
6. Jed Hartman and Josie Wernecke. *The VRML 2.0 Handbook*. Addison Wesley Developers Press, 1996.
7. Ofer Hendin, Nigel John, and Ofer Shochet. Medical Volume Rendering Over the WWW using VRML and JAVA. In *Proceedings of MMVR*, 1997.
8. ISO/IEC 14772-1:1997. The Virtual Reality Modeling Language. http://www.vrml.org/Specifications/VRML97/, 1997.
9. Hans-Georg Pagendarm Jens Trapp. A Prototype for a WWW-based Visualization Service. In *Proceedings Eurographics '97*, pages 23–30, 1997.
10. T. Kulick. Building an OpenGL Volume Renderer. http://reality.sgi.com/kulick/devnews/volren/article.html, 1995.
11. P. Lacroute. Real-Time Volume Rendering on Shared Memory Multiprocessors Using the Shear-Warp Factorization. In *Parallel Rendering Symposium*, pages 15–22, Atlanta GA USA, 1995. ACM.
12. P. Lacroute and M. Levoy. Fast Volume Rendering Using a Shear–Warp Factorization of the Viewing Transform . *Computer Graphics*, 28(4):451–458, 1994.
13. Rodget Lea, Kouichi Matsuda, and Ken Miyashita. *JAVA for 3D and VRML Worlds*. New Riders Publishing, 1996.
14. L. Lippert, M.H. Gross, and C. Kurmann. Compression domain volume rendering for distributed environments. In *Proceedings Eurographics '97*, pages C95–C107, 1997.
15. W.E. Lorensen and H.E. Cline. Marching Cubes: A High Resolution 3D Surface Construction Algorithm. *Computer Graphics*, 21(4):163–169, 1987.
16. Chris Marrin. Proposal for a VRML 2.0 Information Annex. http://cosmosoftware.com/developer/moving-worlds/spec/ExternalInterface.html, 1997.
17. James Patten and Kwan-Liu Ma. A Graph Based Approach for Visualizing Volume Rendering Results. In *Proceedings of GI'98 Conference on Computer Graphics and Interactive Techniques*, 1998.

PVR
An Architecture for Portable VR Applications

Robert van Liere and Jurriaan D. Mulder

Center for Mathematics and Computer Science CWI,
P.O. Box 94097, 1090 GB Amsterdam, Netherlands
{robertl,mullie}@cwi.nl

Abstract. Virtual reality shows great promise as a research tool in computational science and engineering. However, since VR involves new interface styles, a great deal of implementation effort is required to develop VR applications.

In this paper we present PVR; an event-based architecture for portable VR applications. The goal of PVR is to provide a programming environment which facilitates the development of VR applications. PVR differentiates itself from other VR toolkits in two ways: First, it decouples the coordination and management of multiple data streams from actual data processing. This simplifies the programmer's task of managing and synchronizing the data streams. Second, PVR strives for portability by shielding low-level device specific details. Application programmers can take full advantage of the underlying hardware while maintaining a single code base spanning a variety of input and output device configurations.

1 Introduction.

Virtual reality shows great promise as a research tool in computational science and engineering. The analysis of 3D data sets (read from disk or computed on the fly) may benefit from the interface styles provided by virtual reality. By providing additional depth and viewing cues, the virtual reality interface can aid the unambiguous display of 3D structures. In addition, virtual reality input interfaces allow the direct and intuitive exploration of the data, as well as providing control over the application through widgets integrated into the interface.

However, the development of VR applications is not easy. In order to fulfill the real-time requirements posed on VR applications, programmers must learn many new and non-standard methods. Technical issues that make these methods more difficult than traditional 3D graphics methods are mostly related to: (i) the management of multiple I/O data streams at predictable and time critical intervals, (ii) 3D interaction with the virtual world, and (iii) the large variety of display and input devices with each device having individual characteristics and constraints. Virtual reality development environments will need to provide high-level support for each of these issues, as well as support found in traditional 3D graphics toolkits, such as for modeling and rendering.

Event-driven programming models are well known to graphical user interface programmers. Instead of explicitly polling and responding to user actions, applications register event handlers and the underlying user interface toolkit will call the handler when a particular event occurs. Event-driven models can ease the programmer's task since the control and coordination of the user interface objects is left to the underlying toolkit.

In this paper we present the design and implementation of a portable virtual reality architecture, PVR. The architecture was inspired by our work on distributed computational steering [1]. The motivation for designing and implementing PVR was to provide an application programmer an easy to use and portable development environment. Ease of usage is accomplished by decoupling the coordination of multiple data streams from actual data processing. This simplifies the programmer's task of managing, synchronizing and processing multiple I/O streams. Portability is realized by allowing the programmer to abstract from specific input and output devices.

The format of the paper is as follows: First, in section 2, we briefly survey related work. In section 3 we present the underlying concepts of the PVR architecture and discuss design considerations. In section 4 we discuss implementation aspects of the PVR architecture. Finally, we provide two examples on how the environment is used: a molecular dynamics visualization and the analysis of nuclear division.

2   Related Work.

Bryson has extensively studied the application of virtual reality interfaces in scientific visualization. Although the work has mostly been related to studies in the virtual windtunnel, the lessons have lead to generalized requirements with regard to implementation issues concerning computation, graphics and data management (eg. [2,3]). Requirements related to real-time performance and natural "anthropomorphic" VR interfaces are discussed in some detail.

Numerous academic and commercial efforts have focussed on the development of distributed virtual reality applications. Often these efforts have resulted in generic toolkits; many of these have similar objectives and motivations as PVR. For example, a non-exhaustive list of widely used VR toolkits is: Alice [4], AVOCADO [5], Bamboo [6], COVISE [7], DIVE [8], Lightning [9], and World Toolkit [10]. It is beyond the scope of this paper to give an exhaustive overview of each of these toolkits.

The MR toolkit was one of the first toolkits to decouple the simulation from the rendering in order to achieve the real-time requirements of VR user interfaces [11]. MR provides many high-level features that are needed in the development of VR applications: support for distributed computing, workspace management, performance monitoring, input devices abstractions, data sharing, etc.

Researchers at IBM have used multiple workstations to support the real-time requirements of VR user interfaces [12,13]. Their virtual world architecture addresses the requirements of virtual reality for high performance computing, concurrency and synchronization of multiple events, and flexibility. Processes communicate through a central event-driven user interface management system (UIMS). The UIMS uses a collection of rules to synchronize concurrent input/output events. It also provides flexibility by clearly separating the interaction techniques from the virtual world application.

The CAVE library is an API of C functions and macros to control the operation of the CAVE [14]. The CAVE library takes care of all the tasks that have to be performed to correctly operate the CAVE. CAVE functions keep all the devices synchronized, produce the correct perspective for each wall and provide applications with the current state of all CAVE elements.

Despite similar objectives and functionality, PVR differs from these toolkits in many ways. First and foremost is the emphasis of PVR on the ease of usage for the VR application programmer. PVR provides a modular architecture that shields the management and synchronization of multiple data streams. This is achieved by decoupling the coordination and management of multiple data streams from actual data processing. Programmers need only to supply the processing modules, while the coordination of the data streams is maintained by PVR. Second, PVR strives for portable applications. Portability goes beyond portability of low-level input devices. The PVR architecture allows flexible mapping from high-level interaction abstractions onto lower-level device abstractions. Also, although not unique, PVR allows for the flexible mapping of logical to physical output devices.

3   PVR Architecture.

3.1   Internal Structure of PVR

An overview of the PVR architecture is given in figure 1. The architecture consists of one or more processes attached to a bus. Processes communicate using an event-based mechanism. This mechanism is conceptually easy to understand: after a process attaches to the bus, it registers patterns with the bus that describe the events it is interested in. This allows each process to set an *event filter*. When an event is posted on the bus, it is redistributed to the interested processes. Each process is parameterized with a user supplied callback. The bus will invoke the callback whenever an event occurs that the process is subscribed to.

PVR supports a small number of predefined events, such as PVR_REDRAW, PVR_MOTION, PVR_PRESS, etc. In addition, applications may define events to denote any application specific action.

Processes are categorized in one of four types:

1. Render processes are responsible for rendering. The application defined callback will be executed when a redraw is necessary. Often, particular output device configurations will require more than one render process; i.e. the CAVE will use one process per wall whereas a HMD might have two.

128

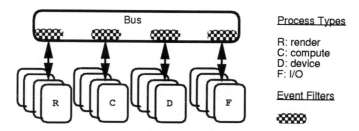

Fig. 1. The PVR architecture consists of one or more processes attached to a bus. Each process registers event filters that describe events that the process is interested in. A process posts events to the bus to signal the completion of an action. The bus redistributes events to processes according to their event filters.

2. Device processes are responsible for device handling. An event will be posted each time the state of a device changes (i.e. button press, sensor motion, etc). The event report will contain the information of the device.

3. File processes are responsible for all file I/O. Having designated file processes is useful, since I/O tends to be very slow. File processes are also responsible for I/O transactions with external services. For example, performing transactions with data base management systems, CORBA servers, or external simulations.

4. Compute processes are responsible for all other required computation. This may be the complete simulation itself, or the computation of visualization techniques (streamlines, iso-surfaces, etc). It is the programmer's choice to determine the granularity of the compute processes.

A shared data facility allows multiple processes to share data structures. This facility allows processes to allocate and lock shared data structures in a simple and flexible way. Pointers to shared data structures can be stored in events.

3.2 PVR's Mechanisms

Rather than discussing the architecture in detail, we highlight three mechanisms unique to PVR.

1. Device independence.
   Virtual reality environments may have a plethora of display, tracking, and input devices, each operating in their own physical coordinate space. PVR is designed to be portable, allowing applications to take full advantage of the underlying hardware while maintaining a single code base spanning multiple device configurations. For example, applications are developed independently of the tracker geometry, room geometry and device configurations.
   PVR uses the notion of a workspace that removes the application's dependency on the physical location of the devices that it uses. Workspace management functionality provides two sets of transformation mappings; a mapping between application workspace and standard workspace and a mapping

between standard workspace and device workspace. These two mappings allow applications to use device independent input and output spaces. The mapping between standard workspace and device workspace is defined in a configuration file. The application can define the mapping between application workspace and standard workspace. PVR events encapsulate device information, so processes that register device events are device independent.

2. Synchronization and Data Ordering.

Events are used by a process to signal the end of an action. In this way a sequence of processes can be set up; each process sends an event to the next process in the sequence. However, when processes operate on one data set in parallel, additional mechanisms must be provided. For example, consider the case that one process computes iso-surfaces and a second process computes streamlines in a time dependent data set. Both geometries must be rendered in the same frame.

PVR provides a data framing mechanism to order data from parallel processes. Applications may define a frame structure which consists of an number of data slots and an event. Processes may put data in a slot. As soon as all slots are filled the bus will distribute the event. This signals that the frame is complete. The familiar notion of a barrier can be implemented with the framing mechanism.

A time line for a frame with four slots is diagrammed in figure 2. Processes may fill data into a slot at any time and in any order. Only when the last slot is filled will the bus invoke the callback of those processes that have registered EVENT.

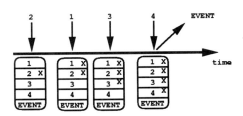

Fig. 2. A frame with four slots and event EVENT. Processes add data to a slot. The bus will distribute EVENT as soon as all slots have new data, signaling a new frame.

The bus can also manage a stack of frames. If a process refills a slot before the frame is filled, the bus will place the data in the next frame in the stack. In this way processes do not need to wait until a frame is complete, but can continue to process new data.

3. Distributed Virtual Reality.

In addition to the single user virtual reality, multi-user distributed virtual reality can provide added value in those cases where collaboration is needed. Two cases are distinguished: First, multiple remote environments are linked together to form one single distributed environment in which users have the ability to manipulate a common data set. Second, multiple users can participate in a single environment.

PVR includes a mechanism for distributed applications, whereby several users on different machines can share a virtual environment. This is achieved by connecting remote busses together. A posted event will be redistributed to a remote bus, according to event registration patterns on the remote bus (see figure 3).

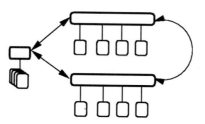

Fig. 3. Multiple busses are connected to form a distributed architecture. Events are redistributed according to event filters on the remote bus.

From the perspective of a process, it makes no difference whether the application is distributed. The bus will invoke the process's callback whenever an event occurs that is designated for the process, irrespective of whether the event was posted from a process on the local or remote bus.

4 Implementation.

The PVR architecture sketched in the previous section can be implemented in a number of ways. The current implementation uses a number of portable supporting software packages (see figure 4). The implementation relies on POSIX threads for process support, the X11 window system and OpenGL for windowing and rendering support, and the University of North Carolina's tracker library for a portable tracking interface. Applications may make use of higher level rendering packages can be used on top of OpenGL; for example: Inventor, OpenGL Optimizer or OpenGL Volumizer can be used within the rendering thread. However, packages like Inventor can only be used in configurations with one render thread.

The current implementation supports an Electrohome Retrographics Display and the CAVE as output devices. The Electrohome is driven by one render thread, while the CAVE is driven by four render threads. Tracking and input devices include Polhemus Fastrak and Ascension Flock of Birds tracking systems flying joysticks for spatial input, and keyboard. The current implementation has been ported to SGI/IRIX6.5 and Intel/Linux platforms.

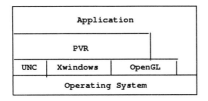

Fig. 4. The layered implementation of the PVR architecture.

5 Applications.

5.1 Molecular Dynamics Visualization.

The application is a molecular dynamics simulation of a mixture of molten lithium and potassium carbonates at 1200 Kelvin[1]. The movements of 158 Li^+ ions, 98 K^+ ions and 128 CO_3^{2-} ions in a cubic box are calculated during 2500 time steps. Of particular interest is the study of the coordination number; this is the number of CO_3^{2-} ions in a neighborhood of a Li^+ or K^+ ion. Typically, Li^+ ions are enclosed by 4 carbonates, and the K^+ ions by 6 carbonates.

Figure 5 shows two snapshots of the interface. Small spheres are used to display Li^+ions, triangles are used display the carbonate ions. A convex hull is used to visualize the coordination between a Li^+ ion and related CO_3^{2-} ions. The dashed line shows a measuring tape (each line segment represents 0.25 nm.), which is used to monitor distances between ions.

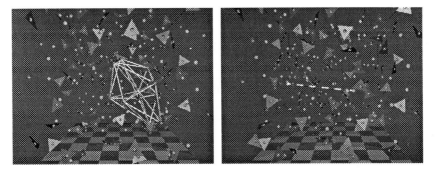

Fig. 5. Molecular dynamics of a mixture of molten lithium and potassium carbonates. Left uses a convex hull to visualize a coordination of a selected Li^+ ion. Right uses a measuring tape to monitor distances between two selected ions.

---

[1] Thanks to Jos Tissen (Unilever) and Jack van Wijk (TU Eindhoven) for providing the data. The 3D visualization techniques and their implementation are discussed in [15].

132

Virtual reality techniques are used to study the structure and the dynamics of the simulated molten carbonates. Immersive environments are very suited to perceive valuable spatial information from the displayed data. For example, in what pattern the ions are diffusing, the dynamic nature of a coordination, in what way are carbonate ions oriented towards the metal ions, etc. In addition, immersive environments can provide added functionality to directly manipulate the data, such as direct manipulation of ions for selection and direct manipulation for measuring distances and angles between ions.

The bus configuration for the molecular dynamics visualization is shown in figure 6. It consists of 6 processes: one file, one render, two compute and two device processes. The file process reads in a sequence of data sets from disk. Every time step a data set is read, the file process will send an application specific event (TIME_STEP) to the bus. One device process manages head movements and posts a HEAD_TRACK event when applicable. The second device process manages the spatial joystick and posts a JOYSTICK event when the position, orientation or button state of the joystick has changed. One compute process computes the convex hull (triggered by the TIME_STEP and JOYSTICK events). The second compute process computes distances between atoms (triggered by the TIME_STEP and JOYSTICK events). Both compute processes post a REDRAW event. The render process redraws the scene (triggered by the REDRAW event). If appropriate, multiple redraw requests will automatically be collapsed into a single redraw.

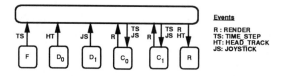

Fig. 6. PVR Molecular Dynamics Visualization configuration. The flow of incoming and outgoing events is shown.

PVR programmers can improve application performance by interleaving (eg reading the next data set while rendering the previous one) and parallelism (executing multiple techniques simultaneously). When necessary, the programmer can change the process granularity by joining/splitting callback procedures. For the molecular dynamics application, the following typescript is a profiling synopsis that has been collected on a 2 CPU SGI Onyx2 system:

```
Total time: 48.41
Total number of events: 16171
Event latency: avg_latency= 0.01, max_latency= 0.05
Total time per thread: <D0+D1, 0.43><R, 47.6><C0+C1, 0.71><F, 6.25>
```

Given times are in seconds. PVR latencies are defined as the time interval between sending an event to the bus and receiving the event by a process.

5.2 Nuclear Division.

One of the problems studied by researchers at the E.C. Slater Institute of the University of Amsterdam is that of nuclear division, i.e. *mitosis*. In the process of mitosis, two sets of microtubles interact to form the mitotic spindle. Of particular interest is the monitoring of the microtubles in the spindle over time.

Data sets have been acquired from a confocal light microscope and displayed using PVR[2]. Figure 7 shows two snapshots of the interface. The two spindle poles are clearly shown at 5 and 11 o'clock. The render process uses OpenGL Volumizer for the actual volume rendering. Simple colormap editing operations are available to allow interactive manipulation of the transparency values. Currently there is no interaction other than colormap manipulation and simple viewing transformations. The combination of stereoscopic graphics and head tracking allow the researcher to walk around the spindle, thus effectively perceiving the complex spatial relationships of the microtubules in the spindle.

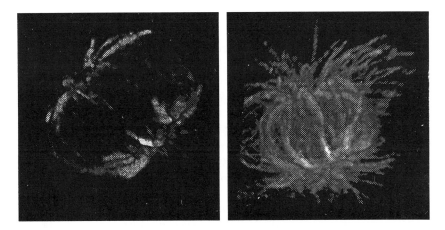

Fig. 7. Microtubules in a spindle during nuclear division. Left uses a blue-yellow color map with high transparency values, right uses a red-yellow color map with lower transparency values. Head tracked stereo display allow researchers to effectively perceive the complex spatial relationships of the microtubules.

The bus configuration for the spindle is shown in figure 8. It consists of 4 processes: one file, one render and two device processes. The file process reads in the data sets from disk (currently, only one data set is read). After a frame is read, the file process will send an application specific TIME_STEP event to the bus. One device process manages the head positions. This is exactly the same callback procedure as in the molecular dynamics application. The second device

---

[2] Thanks to Roel van Driel (ECSI, UvA) and Hans van der Voort (Scientific Volume Imaging B.V.) for providing the data.

process edits a new colormap, and sends the application specific NEW_CMAP event to the bus. The render process redraws the scene (triggered by the REDRAW, or NEW_CMAP events). The NEW_CMAP event indicates that a new colormap must be used by the rendering process.

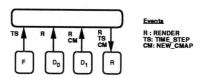

Fig. 8. PVR Nuclear Division configuration.

6 Conclusion.

In this paper we introduced PVR, an architecture for portable VR applications. PVR facilitates the development of highly concurrent yet synchronized virtual reality interfaces by decoupling the coordination of the data streams from actual data processing. Two VR applications were used to illustrate PVR's governing ideas.

PVR differentiates itself from other VR toolkits in two ways. First, PVR is completely event driven. Programmers only supply callback routines which are executed whenever necessary. Application specific events can be posted to signal the completion of an application action. Second, PVR strives for portability by shielding low-level device specific details from the programmer. A single code base can be used to span a variety of workspace and input device configurations.

In the future we will extend PVR with a number of new concepts. These will include the usage of the Fahrenheit scene graph for distributed VR applications, composition of higher level virtual input devices and other forms of high-level interaction [16], incorporation of multiple 2D and 3D workspaces in a single application, and event tracing/monitoring tools.

References

1. R. van Liere, J.A. Harkes, and W.C. de Leeuw. A distributed blackboard architecture for interactive data visualization. In R. Yagel and H. Hagen, editors, *Proceedings Visualization '98*, pages 235–244. IEEE Computer Society Press, 1998.
2. S. Bryson. Virtual reality in scientific visualization. *Computers & Graphics*, 17(6):679–685, 1993.
3. S. Bryson. Real-time exploratory scientific visualization and virtual reality. In L.J. Rosenblum et al, editor, *Scientific Visualization: Advances and Challenges*, pages 65–86. Academic press, 1994.

4. R. Deline. Alice: A rapid prototyping system for three-dimensional interactive graphical environments. Technical report, Computer Science Department, University of Virginia, 1993.

5. F. Hasenbink. Avocado system. Technical report, GMD Department of Visualization and Media Systems Design, Bonn St. Augustin, 1997.

6. K. Watson and M. Zyda. Bamboo - a portable system for dynamically extensible, real time, networked, virtual environments. In *1998 IEEE Virtual Reality Annual International Symposium*, pages 252–260. IEEE Computer Society Press, March 1998.

7. D. Rantzau and U. Lang. A scalable virtual environment for large scale scientific data analysis. *Future Generation Computer Systems*, 14(4):215–222, 1999.

8. C. Carlsson and O. Hagsand. Dive - a platform for multi-user virtual environments. *Computers & Graphics*, 17(6):663–669, 1993.

9. J. Landauer, R. Blach, M. Bues, A. Rosch, and A. Simon. Towards next generation virtual reality systems. In *Proceedings of the IEEE Conference on Multimedia Computing and System*, Ottawa, 1997. IEEE Computer Society Press.

10. World toolkit. Technical report, Sense8, 1997. http: // www.sense8.com/ products/ worldtoolkit.html.

11. C. Shaw, J. Liang, M. Green, and Y. Sun. The decoupled simulation model for virtual reality systems. In *Proceedings of the CHI 92 Conference on Human Factors and Computing Systems*, pages 321–328, 1992.

12. P. Appino, J. Lewis, L. Koved, D. Ling, D. Rabenhorst, and C. Codella. An architecture for virtual worlds. *Presence*, 1(1):1–17, 1992.

13. C. Codella, R. Jalili, L. Koved, and J. Lewis. A toolkit for developing multi-user, distributed environments. In *Virtual Reality Annual International Symposium*, pages 401–407. IEEE Computer Society Press, 1993.

14. D. Pape, C. Cruz-Neira, and M. Czernuszenko. CAVE users guide. Technical report, Electronic Visualization Laboratory, University of Illinois at Chicago, 1996. http: // www.evl.uic.edu /pape / CAVE / prog / CAVEGuide.html.

15. J.J. van Wijk and J.T.W.M. Tissen. Visualization of molecular dynamics. In *Proceedings of the Fourth Eurographics Workshop on Visualization in Scientific Computing*, Abingdon, UK, 1993.

16. J.D. Mulder. Remote object translation methods for immersive virtual environments. Presented at the 1998 Virtual Environments Conference & 4th Eurographics Workshop, June 1998.

Rapid Development of VRML Content via Geometric Programming

A. Paoluzzi, S. Francesi, S. Portuesi and M. Vicentino

Dip. di Informatica e Automazione, Università di Roma Tre
Via della Vasca Navale 79, 00146 Roma, Italy
{paoluzzi, francesi, portuesi, vicenti}@dia.uniroma3.it
http://www.dia.uniroma3.it/~plasm

Abstract. This paper aims to show that a functional design language can be used as a *general-purpose VRML generator*. The PLaSM language, which allows for algebraic computations with geometric shapes and maps, has been recently extended with non geometric attributes like colors, lights and textures. PLaSM is used in the paper both to develop some general-purpose tools, including Bézier manifolds of any dimension and degree, the n-th derivative of any parametric curve and "Bézier stripes" of small width, as well as to quickly implement a quite complex mountain landscape. Customized PLaSM applications may generate fully parameterized virtual worlds starting from small data files or streams.

1 Introduction

One of major problems with the development of VRML [8] content is the lack of primitives for curve and surface generation, as well as the lack of algebraic operators able to generate complex geometric objects by combining simpler objects.

At this purpose the functional design language PLaSM [6] can be used as a *general-purpose automatic VRML generator*. Such a VRML generator is an application that automatically generates VRML based upon user or data file input. With this approach both powerful generative geometric methods [9] can be quickly implemented and complex VRML models can be easily generated.

PLaSM is a functional language for computing with geometry and programming complex shapes and animations [2]. The blending of such interpreted language with the VRML primitives produces a simple and powerful way of rapid prototyping complex worlds. The paper presents the design lines of such an integration, and gives the full implementation of a quite complex mountain landscape example.

In order to show the building of virtual environments via a geometric programming approach, Bèzier manifolds of any dimension and degree are first generated. Then it is shown how to implement the n-th derivative of any parametric curve. Finally curves and derivatives are combined to generate thin stripe surfaces of constant width depending only on a few control points. Such set of tools is used here to generate a virtual world which contains a piece of hillside, a lake, a beach, a mountain hut and a footpath generated as a "Bézier stripe". To remark the position of the control points of such a path, some simplified models of a tree are put on the hillside. Colors, textures, and light sources are added to increase reality. The PLaSM model is finally exported as a VRML file to be experienced on the web.

2 Geometric programming

PLaSM [6] is a geometry-oriented extension of a subset of the functional language FL developed by Backus, Williams and others at IBM Research [1]. In such design language the algebraic approach to programming of FL was combined with a dimension-independent treatment of embedded data structures and geometric algorithms [3, 6, 7].

Among the strong points of PLaSM we cite its functional approach, which allows to compute with geometries as well as with numbers and functions. This feature results in a very natural and powerful approach to parametric geometry. The use of dimension-independent data structures, coupled with the "combinatorial engine" of FL, gives the language a very high descriptive power when algebraically computing with geometry.

The interested reader might either look at the language definition on paper [6] or read the tutorial [4] or access the URL[1]. We like to note that the PLaSM code given in the present paper is a full implementation of the discussed topics. Remember that the names in all caps usually correspond to pre-defined operators.

2.1 Bézier curves and surfaces

Parametric representation of geometric objects is a mapping between two normed vector spaces, say $E^p \to E^q$, where $p = 1, 2$ for either curves or surfaces, respectively, and q is the dimension of the embedding space of the generated point-set, which is usually either 2 or 3.

When using PLaSM, it turns out as natural to adopt a transfinite method for implementing curves, surfaces and higher dimensional manifolds [5]. Transfinite Bézier blending of any degree is given below, by combining coordinate maps which may depend on any number of parameters.

Such a transfinite **Bezier** mapping can be used either by blending points to give curve maps, or by blending curve maps to give surface maps, or by blending surface maps to give solid maps, and so on. The given implementation is independent on the dimensions p and q of domain and range spaces of the mapping, as well on the degree n of the resulting manifold. At this purpose, first a small tool-box of related functions is defined, to compute the factorial $n!$, the binomial coefficients $\binom{n}{i}$, the Bernstein/Bézier polynomials $B_i^n(u)$ and the $\mathbf{B}^n(u)$ polynomial basis of degree n, with

$$\mathbf{B}^n(u) = (B_0^n(u), B_1^n(u), \ldots, B_n^n(u))$$

---

[1] http://www.dia.uniroma3/~plasm, where also the PLaSM engine and the code given here can be found.

```
DEF IsNotNeg = AND~[IsInt, GE:0];
DEF Fact (n::IsNotNeg) = *:(CAT:<<1>, 2..n>);
DEF Choose (n,i::IsNotNeg) = Fact:n / (Fact:i * Fact:(n-i));
DEF Bernstein (u::IsFun)(n::IsNotNeg)(i::IsNotNeg)
  = *~[K:(Choose:<n,i>),**~[ID,K:i], **~[-~[K:1,ID],K:(n-i)]]~u;
DEF BernsteinBase (u::IsFun)(n::IsNotNeg) = AA:(Bernstein:u:n):(0..n);
```

Then the **Bezier** function is given, to be applied on the sequence of **Control-Data**, which may contain either control points or control maps (i.e. vectors of functions, since the method is transfinite). In the former case each control point is firstly transformed into a sequence of constant functions. The body of the **Bezier** function just combines linearly and component-wise the sequence of coordinate functions generated by the expression **(TRANS~fun):ControlData** with the basis sequence generated by **BernsteinBase:u:degree**, where **degree** is the number of geometric handles minus one.

```
DEF Bezier (u::IsFun) (ControlData::IsSeq) = componentWiseLinearCombine:
  < BernsteinBase:u:degree, (TRANS~fun):ControlData >
WHERE
  componentWiseLinearCombine = AA:(+~AA:*~TRANS) ~ DISTL,
  degree = LEN:ControlData - 1,
  fun = (AA~AA):(IF:<IsFun,ID,K>)
END;
DEF Domain (a::IsRealPos)(n::IsIntPos) = (QUOTE~#:n):(a/n);
```

The **Domain** function generates a decomposition with n segments of the interval $[0, a]$, with $a \in \Re$.

It is quite hard to explain in few words what actual argument to pass (and why) for the formal parameter u of the **Bezier** function. As a rule of thumb let pass either the selector **S1** if the function must return a univariate (curve) map, or **S2** to return a bivariate (surface) map, or **S3** to return a three-variate (solid) map, and so on. Several examples of transfinite Bézier are in Section 4.

2.2 Derivatives

The derivative of a parametric curve (vector-valued map) with respect to its parameter is very easy to generate. Let remember the standard definition of the derivative of a function $f : \Re \to \Re$ as the limit, where it exists, of the incremental ratio:

$$f'(x) = \lim_{dx \to 0} \frac{f(x + dx) - f(x)}{dx}.$$

One possible **PLaSM** implementation of the derivative for a real-valued function **f** of a real variable, with a small variable increment **dx**, may directly correspond to the above definition:

```
DEF deriv1(dx::IsReal)(f::IsFun)(x::IsReal) = (f:(x + dx) - f:x) / dx;
```

A slight modification must be introduced for computing the derivative of the first coordinate of a point **a**, being the points represented in **PLaSM** as sequences of numbers, with $f : E^d \to R$.

```
DEF deriv2(dx::IsReal)(f::IsFun)(a::IsSeq) = ((f~LIST):(S1:a+dx)-f:a)/dx;
```

The following **DER1** function can so be applied either to numbers or to 1D points. Finally, the **DER** function is defined to compute the n-th derivative of any parametric curve embedded in any d-dimensional space:

```
DEF DER1 (f::IsFun)(a::OR~[IsReal,IsSeq]) =
   IF:< IsReal, deriv1:1E-4:f, deriv2:1E-4:f >: a;
DEF DD (n::IsIntPos) = (COMP~#:n):DER1;
DEF DER (n::IsIntPos) = AA:(DD:n);
```

2.3   Planar stripe surface

A planar thin surface patch of constant width, later on called *stripe*, may be generated [9] as a ruled planar surface. Such kind of surfaces have a vector equation given by the sum of a parametric curve and a ruled line, defined along the normal unit vector to the curve, times the second parameter:

$$\mathbf{p}(u, v) = \mathbf{q}(u) + v\mathbf{q}^\perp(u)$$

where

$$\mathbf{q}^\perp(u) = \begin{bmatrix} 0 & -1 \\ 1 & 0 \end{bmatrix} \frac{\mathbf{q}'(u)}{||\mathbf{q}'(u)||}$$

and

$$\mathbf{q}'(u) = \frac{d}{du}\mathbf{q}(u).$$

To compute the ruled line we need to normalize the first derivative of the curve.

```
DEF isPairOf (IsType::IsFun) = AND~[IsPair, AND~AA:IsType];
DEF Norm (fun::IsPairOf:IsFun) = <-~y/den, x/den>
WHERE
   x = S1:fun, y = S2:fun,
   den = SQRT~+~AA:sqr~[-~y, x],
   sqr = ID * ID
END;
```

Notice that the above implementation makes large use of algebraic operators over spaces of functions. The type of the output of the following **BezierStripe** function is the hierarchical polyhedral complex [6, 7]. The formal parameter n is used here to specify the number of quadrilaterals in the polyhedral approximation of the curved stripe.

```
DEF BezierStripe (ControlPoints::IsSeq; width::IsReal; n::IsIntPos) =
   MAP:[Xuv,Yuv]:(Domain:1:n * Domain:width:1)
WHERE
   Xuv = S1:curve+(v*S1:(Norm:(DER:1:curve))),
   Yuv = S2:curve+(v*S2:(Norm:(DER:1:curve))),
   curve = Bezier:S1:ControlPoints,
   v = S2
END;
```

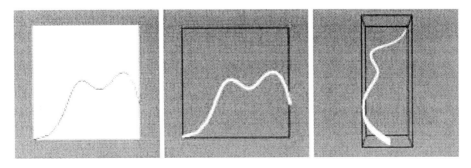

Fig. 1. (a) Image of a Bézier curve in $[0,1]^2$; (b) "stripe" of constant width; (c) previous stripe mapped in 3D via a Bezier's surface mapping.

3 VRML generation

3.1 Hierarchical assemblies

According to the ISO PHIGS standard graphics model, in PLaSM a hierarchical assembly is described as a *structure*, i.e. as the application of a specialized STRUCT operator to a sequence of shape components (in either local or global coordinates) and affine transformations. Subsequent objects in a STRUCT sequence may either inherit or not an affine transformation, depending on the way it is inserted into the sequence, so allowing for maximum programming flexibility.

In VRML a hierarchical assembly is described as a scene graph made by *nodes* and *fields*. A predefined set of nodes is given with basic geometric shapes, face sets and groups. Each node has a specified set of *fields* to define a particular instance of it. A PLaSM hierarchy, internally represented as a *hierarchical polyhedral complex*, can be exported to the equivalent scene graph. PLaSM may export both VRML 1.0 and VRML 2.0 files, as well as the *Open Inventor* file format.

The export function of PLaSM is able to preserve the assembly hierarchies by representing affine transformations with the appropriate rotation, translation and scaling nodes. It also enforces the reusing of geometry by *instancing* data whenever is possible, and in particular by instancing each name associated to a geometric value. The resulting VRML code is quite simple and readable.

3.2 Adding non-geometric properties to polyhedral complexes

The PLaSM language and its underlying representation were recently extended by adding properties to some elements of the Hierarchical Polyhedral Complex. In such a way graphics concepts like appearance, lights, and viewpoints, that do not strictly depend on the geometry, can be inserted in the hierarchy in a simple and non invasive way. Furthermore, such properties are consistently retained after the evaluation of every PLaSM operators, including e.g. mapping, skeleton extraction, product and so on, and without any change in the implementation of the predefined language operators. For the actual implementation of HPC properties and other examples see the dedicated website [2].

Appearance: Colors and Textures According to the VRML approach, the *appearance* of an object is the result of the blending of a *color* and a *texture*. A color is specified by giving a sequence of parameters which express the light behavior of the object surfaces. A more complex appearance can be obtained in VRML by applying a *texture* to an object. Textures are GIF, JPEG or PNG images that may add an higher degree of realism to the scene when mapped to the surfaces of scene objects. An appearance can be assigned in PLaSM to a polyhedral complex via the following functions:

```
ASSIGNCOLOR:<pol_complex,color> -> pol_complex
ASSIGNTEXTURE:<polyhedral_complex, texture> -> pol_complex
ASSIGNAPPEARANCE:<polyhedral_complex,color,texture> ->  pol_complex
<<diffuse_R,diffuse_G,diffuse_B>,
 <specular_R,specular_G,specular_B>,
 <ambient_intensity>,
 <emissive_R,emissive_G,emissive_B>,
 <shininess>,
 <transparency>> -> color
<'url',
 <repeatS, repeatT>,
 <translationS, translationT>,
 <rotation>,
 <scaleS, scaleT>,
 <centerS, centerT>> -> texture
```

Let us remember that each binary operator can be applied in PLaSM also in infix form, often increasing the code readability. PLaSM also offers two utility functions providing common use parameters, where the user may specify just the filename for the texture and the RGB triplet for the color.

```
RGBCOLOR:<Red,Green,Blue> -> color
SIMPLETEXTURE:'url' -> texture
```

Lights and Cameras Lights can be assigned the scene by three slightly different functions that allow the user to specify, besides a type, both the color and geometry:

```
ASSIGNSPOTLIGHT: <pol_complex, <appearance, geometry>> -> pol_complex
ASSIGNPOINTLIGHT:<pol_complex, <appearance, geometry>> -> pol_complex
ASSIGNDIRLIGHT:  <pol_complex, <appearance, geometry>> -> pol_complex
<color,intensity,ambientIntensity,on> -> appearance
<location,direction,attenuation,radius,beamWidth,cutOffAngle> -> geometry
```

Also the viewpoints can be assigned in a similar way:

---

[2] http://www.dia.uniroma3/~plasm/EGVE99.

```
ASSIGNCAMERA:<pol_complex,camera>
ASSIGNORTOCAMERA:<pol_complex,camera>
<position,orientation,fieldOfView,focal-distance,description> -> camera
```

4 Example

Geometric tool-box No predefined basic shapes exist in *plain* PLaSM. The user may import, when needed, packages of definitions as e.g. for Bezier manifolds, derivatives and stripes. We show here the set of geometry generation functions used in this paper, which allow for generating circles, cylinders, cones (even truncated). The function Q allows for generating a 1D polyhedral complex starting from either a number or a sequence of numbers.

```
DEF Q = QUOTE~IF:<IsSeq,ID,LIST>;
DEF cyl (h::IsReal)(r::IsReal)(n::IsInt) = circle:(2*PI):r:n * Q:h;
DEF circle (a::IsReal)(r::IsReal) (n::IsInt)
  = (S:<1,2>:<r,r>~JOIN):(MAP:([cos,sin]~s1): ((Q~#:n):(a/n)));
DEF TrunCone (r1,r2,h::IsReal)(n::IsInt) =
  MAP:[x*cos~S2,x*sin~S2,z]:(Q:1 * (Q~#:n):(2*PI/n))
WHERE
    x= K:r1 + s1 * (K:r2 - k:r1),
    y= k:0,
    z= s1 * K:h
END;
```

Color definition The set of colors used in a model can be named by using the standard PLaSM definitions. Such names may then be used everywhere useful.

```
DEF grass   = RGBCOLOR:<0.55,0.92,0.14>;
DEF green   = RGBCOLOR:<0.15,0.50,0.25>;
DEF water   = RGBCOLOR:<0.19,0.84,0.79>;
DEF brown   = RGBCOLOR:<0.40,0.25,0.25>;
DEF terrain = RGBCOLOR:<0.88,0.64,0.37>;
```

Details modeling Three sets of definitions are given here to generate a footpath along the mountain side, a set of trees on the path control points and the geometric model of the mountain hut starting from its plan and section. The tree model is defined by stacking a brown cylinder and a green cone. It is interesting to notice that a tree is mapped at each 3D position of the controlpoints generating the path stripe of constant width. Such a path is defined in the unit 2D interval, and then mapped over one of the patches of the mountain side.

```
DEF pathpoints = <<0,0>,<0.5,0>,<0.1,0.8>,<0.6,0.7>,<0.9,0.4>>;
DEF pathstripe = BezierStripe:<pathpoints,0.025,22>;
DEF mapping= T:<1,2,3>~(CONS:sup_c1_c2);
```

144

Fig. 2. Snapshot generated from the presented code

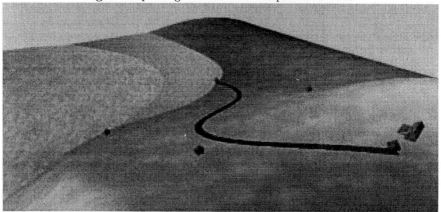

Fig. 3. Snapshot generated with color per vertex and textures and crease angle

```
DEF mytree = STRUCT:< cyl:8:2:5 ASSIGNCOLOR brown,
    T:3:5,  TrunCone:<8,0,12>:5 ASSIGNCOLOR green  >;
DEF controlTrees = (STRUCT~CONS:(AA:mapping:pathpoints)):mytree;
DEF hutPlan = MKPOL:<<<5,-2>,<-5,-2>,<-5,2>,<5,2>,<2,-2>,
            <-2,-2>,<-2,5>,<2,5>>,<1..4,5..8>,<1..2>>;
DEF hutSection= MKPOL:<<<5,2>,<-2,3>,<-2,-1>,<5,-1>,<0,5>>,
            <1..4,<2,4,5>>,<1..2>>;
DEF mountain_hut = hutPlan (<1,2,0> && <0,1,2>) hutSection ASSIGNCOLOR brown;
DEF hutmapped = (mapping:<0.90,0.30>):(S:<1,2,3>:<3,3,3>:(mountain_hut));
```

Bézier curves and surfaces The `Bezier` function is used here both to generate
some curves of various degrees and some surface patches interpolating and/or
approximating such curves.

```
DEF c1 = Bezier:S1:<c1a,<400,300,100>,<400,50,100>,<400,150,200>,c1Last>;
DEF m1 = Bezier:S1:<m1a,<300,200,100>,<300,150,100>,<300,50,200>,
                   <300,-200,200>>;
DEF m2 = Bezier:S1:<m2a,<150,260,100>,<220,150,100>,<180,30,200>,
                   <200,-200,200>>;
DEF c2 = Bezier:S1:<c2a,<0,300,100>,<0,50,100>,<0,150,200>,c2Last >;
DEF c1a = <400,300,0>;        DEF m1a = <300,220,0>;
DEF m2a = <220,330,0>;        DEF c2a = <0,300,0>;
DEF c0a = <400,700,0>;        DEF m0a = <600,220,0>;
DEF c3a = <-300,300,0>;       DEF m3a = <-100,330,0>;
DEF c1Last = <400,-200,200>;  DEF c2Last = <-10,-300,400>;
DEF c0 = Bezier:S1:<c0a,<900,50,100>,<850,150,200>,<900,0,200>>;
DEF c3 = Bezier:S1:<c3a,<-250,300,100>,<-300,50,100>,<-350,0,200>>;
DEF m0 = Bezier:S1:<m0a,<650,200,100>,<1200,50,200>,<600,30,200>>;
DEF m3 = Bezier:S1:<m3a,<-150,150,100>,<-600,30,200>,<-50,40,200>>;
DEF sup_c1_c2 = Bezier:S2:<c1,m1,m2,c2>;
DEF sup_c0_c1 = Bezier:S2:<c0,m0,c1>;
DEF sup_c2_c3 = Bezier:S2:<c2,m3,c3>;
DEF sup_b12_b56 = Bezier:S2:<b12,m0a,b56>;
DEF b12  = Bezier:S1:<c1a,m1a,m2a,c2a>;
DEF b56  = Bezier:S1:<c0a,<300,820,0>,<220,730,0>,b56a>;
DEF b56a = <0,1000,0>;
DEF bLake1 = Bezier:S1:<c2a,m0a,b56a>;
DEF bLakem = Bezier:S1:<m3a,b56a>;
DEF bLake2 = Bezier:S1:<c3a,<-100,800,0>,b56a>;
DEF sup_lake = Bezier:S2:<bLake1,bLakem,bLake2>;
```

High-level assembly The modeled scene is then generated as a hierarchical assembly which contains three surface patches for the mountain side, one patch for the lake and one patch for the beach. The last two components of the assembly define the set of trees associated to the path control points and the house model, placed near the limit point of the path. The VRML model of the scene is finally generated by evaluating the PLaSM expression scene.

```
DEF dom2d = Domain:1:8 * Domain:1:8;
DEF mountains = STRUCT:<
  MAP:(CONS:sup_c1_c2):(dom2d),
  MAP:(CONS:sup_c0_c1):(dom2d),MAP:(CONS:sup_c2_c3):(dom2d) >;

DEF scene = STRUCT:<
  mountains ASSIGNCOLOR grass ,
  T:3:1:( MAP:(CONS:sup_c1_c2):(pathstripe)) ASSIGNCOLOR terrain ,
  MAP:(CONS:sup_b12_b56):(dom2d)  ASSIGNCOLOR terrain ,
  MAP:(CONS:sup_lake):(dom2d)  ASSIGNCOLOR water ,
  controlTrees ,
  hutmapped >;
```

146

5   Conclusions

In this paper we have shown how to define sophisticated generative geometric operators, including Bézier manifolds and stripes, starting from scratch. Then by using simple color functions we rapidly developed a quite complex mountain scene. More realism can be easily added by using textures.

It is easy to notice that the functional style of the **PLaSM** language allows for algorithmic generation of both geometric models and their properties. E.g., we could have algorithmically defined a pre-colored 2D domain and then applied the Bézier mapping to it. For a realistic rendering it is also possible to use the VRML *crease-angle* approach or to explicitly calculate the normals (see Figure 3)[3].

The shown approach can be further extended. We are currently developing functions giving color and normal per vertex. These functions take advantage of the multidimensional nature of **PLaSM** and its underlying representation. In particular we are specializing the export function by properly projecting in 3D geometries which are embedded in any d-dimensional space. An example is Bézier with control points in $\Re^6$. In such a case the first three coordinates may be associated to the geometry and the last three to the color. The normals per vertex can also be smoothed in a similar way.

References

1. BACKUS, J., WILLIAMS, J.H. AND WIMMERS, E.L. "An Introduction to the Programming Language FL". In *Research Topics in Functional Programming*, D.A. Turner (Ed.), Addison-Wesley, Reading, MA, 1990.
2. BAJAJ, C., BALDAZZI, C., CUTCHIN, S., PAOLUZZI, A., PASCUCCI, V. AND VICENTINO, M. "Web-based approach for very complex animations through geometric programming". *Submitted paper*, August 1998.
3. BERNARDINI, F., FERRUCCI, V., PAOLUZZI, A. AND PASCUCCI, V. "A Product Operator on Cell Complexes". *Proc. of the ACM/IEEE 2nd Conf. on Solid Modeling and Appl.*, ACM Press, 43–52, 1993.
4. PAOLUZZI, A. "Generative Geometric Modeling in a Functional Environment", in *Design and Implementation of Symbolic Computation Systems. Lecture Notes in Computer Science*, **1128**, 79–97, Springer & Verlag, 1996
5. PAOLUZZI, A. "Transfinite blending made easy", Tech. Rep. RT-DIA 40-1999, Dip. Informatica e Aut., Univ. Roma Tre, Rome, 1999.
6. PAOLUZZI, A., PASCUCCI, V., AND VICENTINO, M. "Geometric programming: a programming approach to geometric design". *ACM Trans. on Graphics*, **14**(4):266–306, 1995.
7. PASCUCCI, V., PAOLUZZI, A. AND FERRUCCI, V. "Dimension-Independent Convex-Cell Based HPC: Skeletons and Product". *International Journal of Shape Modeling*, **2**(1):37–67, 1996.
8. PESCE, M. *VRML Browsing and Building Cyberspace*. New Riders, London, 1992.
9. SNYDER, J.M. *Generative Modeling for Computer Graphics and CAD*. Academic Press, London, 1992.

[3] For extended examples, including actual implementation, VRML models, and color snapshots, look at http://www.dia.uniroma3/~plasm/EGVE99.

Augmented Reality, the other way around.

Didier Verna and Alain Grumbach

ENST, Département Informatique et Réseaux,
46, rue Barrault
75013 Paris, France
{verna,grumbach}@infres.enst.fr

Abstract. This paper aims at showing that the notion of Augmented Reality has been developed in a biased way: mostly in destination to the *operator*, and at the level of his *perceptions*. This demonstration is achieved through a model describing a situation of tele-operation, on which we represent major cases of Augmented Reality encountered in recent applications. By taking advantage of the symmetry of the model, we are able to show how Augmented Reality can be seen "the other way around", that is, in destination to the *environment*, and at the level of the operator's *actions*.

1   Introduction

As described in [7], we consider that the expression "virtual reality" denotes a situation in which the user is *not* directly in contact with the environment in which he evolves, but rather interacts with it through some artificial device (screen, data glove, network . . .). As a consequence, any real environment can be labeled "virtual", as long as the user does not interact directly with it. Consequently, Tele-Operation belongs to Virtual Reality. The relationship between Tele-Operation and Virtual Reality extends farther than that though. Tele-Operation system designers have been integrating virtual reality concepts in their work for a long time; this is actually the main source of augmented reality examples, namely, enriching a *real* situation with *virtual* components.

Historically speaking, the first solution that roboticians found in order to ease the process of tele-operation was to provide some level of immersion in the distant environment. Consequently, most augmented reality applications were focused on the operator's perceptions. In this paper, we demonstrate that this constitutes a bias in the acceptation of the notion. In a first step, we propose a model that is suitable to describe virtual reality situations and tele-operation ones in particular. In a second step, we use this model to represent several characteristic examples of augmented reality, in terms of localization (where they take place in the model) and semantics [8] (how they influence the conveyed information). After noticing that those examples are indeed biased towards the operator and his perceptions, we take advantage of the symmetry of the model to revert the examples, and see Augmented Reality "the other way around", that is towards the environment and the actions applied to it.

2 A Generic Model for Virtual Reality

Out of [7], we propose on figure 1 a generic model of Virtual Reality, suitable to represent tele-operation situations in particular. This model features a set of **agents** (each box in the model) interacting with each other by exchanging information. According to its orientation, action or perception, this information is noted A or P.

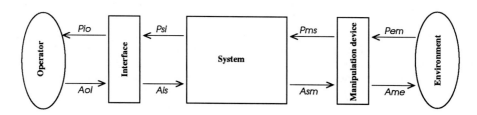

Fig. 1. A Generic representation of Virtual Reality

The **operator** denotes the user of the system. In this paper, we consider a single operator, assuming that other people, possibly part of the situation, belong to the environment[1]. The operator interacts with the rest of the situation through the **interface** in both action and perception sense. The interface (which may contain a screen, a head mounted display, data gloves, a joystick...) generates the A_{is} information from the operator's physical actions A_{oi}, and uses the received P_{si} information to display P_{io} to the operator.

At the other end of the model is the **environment**, which is the one which the operator is working on. As denoted previously, the environment does not include the operator's real world, since we are modeling Virtual Reality. Rather, it represents the distant area in the case of Tele-Operation, or the computer generated scene in the case of a synthetic world. The operator can work on the environment by controlling the **manipulation device**. In the case of immersion in a synthetic world, this manipulation device simply boils down to the computer generated human body avatar. In the case of a real tele-operation situation, the manipulation device represents the remote robot that the operator is controlling. The manipulation device acts upon the environment through A_{me} and perceives it through P_{em}.

The operator/interface and environment/manipulation device duets are separated by the **system**. In the most basic, fully controlled case of Tele-Operation, the system just represents the physical channels used to convey information (e.g. a network). In more complex examples, as when Augmented Reality occurs, the system includes information processing capabilities which allow it to wear an intelligent behavior.

---

[1] This also implies that collaborative virtual environments are regarded from a single participant's point of view.

Before proceeding to the next section, we would like to precise the meaning of some words or expressions that will be used in the subsequent parts of this paper:

- An **information path** crosses at least one of the agents of the model. Information is then subject to processing occuring inside the agent.
- An **action** is a stream of information going from the operator to the environment $(A_{oi} \rightarrow A_{is} \rightarrow A_{sm} \rightarrow A_{me})$.
- A **perception** is a stream of information going from the environment to the operator $(P_{em} \rightarrow P_{ms} \rightarrow P_{si} \rightarrow P_{io})$.
- A **command** designates an action and the corresponding perception it should trigger, thus looping back to the operator.

3 Examples of Augmented Reality

In this section, we propose to consider several typical examples of augmented reality. Those examples are examined in comparison with the model previously described, in terms of their influence on the information conveyed across the virtual reality system.

3.1 Mixing real and virtual perceptions

In [4], Mellor describes an environment for brain surgery, in which virtual images are superimposed on the real view of the patient's head. Those virtual images are aimed at helping the surgeon, by outlining schematically the incision areas, coloring zones which should be avoided, or locating the diseased tissue. This example illustrates the process of mixing virtual and real perceptions, which is perhaps the most widely used application of the concept of Augmented Reality.

Compared with our model, the process corresponding to this example is located inside the system and affects the $P_{ms} \rightarrow P_{si}$ information path: the system needs P_{ms} in order to acquire the current position of the patient's head and alters P_{si} in order to add the synthetic drawings superimposed on the original image. Semantically speaking, the original perception is preserved (transmitted as-is), and *enriched* with some artificially generated one. Reality is then *augmented* with a virtual perception. This particular process can be formalized in the following statement:

Perception Enrichment

Given a goal of a perceptual nature (e.g. the operator being able to localize the diseased tissue), the system adds additional information of the same perceptual nature (e.g. a schema), in order to help achieving this goal.

150

3.2 Reconstructing a missing perception

In [1], a tele-operated submarine is used for underwater dam inspection and maintenance. However, the environment is very dark, which makes it impossible for the operator to receive any usable underwater video stream from the dam. To cope with this problem, a computer model of the dam is implemented, and position captors are used on the submarine and on the dam real structure. Thanks to the captors, the submarine can compute at anytime its position relatively to the dam, and a synthetic image with the proper viewpoint is generated for the operator.

Compared with our model, the process corresponding to this example is located on both $P_{em} \rightarrow P_{ms}$ (generation of the position information) and $P_{si} \rightarrow P_{io}$ (generation of the virtual visual perception). Semantically speaking, this process does not just enrich a particular perception, but completely reconstructs it. Moreover, it is interesting to notice that the final perception (the visual feedback) is generated from an original perception of a completely different modality (e.g. electro-magnetic signal from the captors). This process can be formalized as follows:

Perception Reconstruction

Given that a particular perception is originally missing (e.g. the visual feedback), some substitute information (e.g. from position captors) is used in order to recreate this perception in a synthetic way.

3.3 Restricting the command field

Still in the surgical field, another well-known example of augmented reality is described in [2]: a surgeon controls a micro-camera and some surgery tools that must go inside the patient's body. To prevent any damage on the patient's tissues and to help the surgeon find his way inside the body, a system applies some force feedback on the control device, limiting its degrees of freedom and thus indicating to the surgeon that he might be trying to move the camera in the wrong direction.

Compared with our model, the information path affected by this process is located at $A_{oi} \rightarrow P_{io}$, and possibly at $A_{is} \rightarrow P_{si}$ for intelligent processing. Semantically speaking, what this process does is restricting the operator's field of control. While it can appear surprising to talk of "augmented" reality whereas the operator's control is actually "diminished", his perceptions are still augmented, since the force feedback is an *additional* perceptive information (something forbidden was tried). This process can be formalized as follows:

Command Restriction

Given a particular command that the operator can require, the system configures the interface in order to restrict the overall field of specification for this command.

4 Augmented Reality, the other way around

If we represent the preceding examples on our model, as shown in figure 2, we easily notice that the different information paths affected by the various augmented reality processes are mostly directed in the perception sense, and always towards the operator. This is what we call the "bias" of Augmented Reality. In this section, we propose a reasoning model which let us correct this imbalance [8]: each example described in the previous section was summarized with a formal description. By using the obvious central symmetry of our model, we can turn this formal description the other way around, hence getting a new formal description for dual augmented reality processes. This reasoning method leads us to systematically envision new processes and examples that are not usually seen as Augmented Reality.

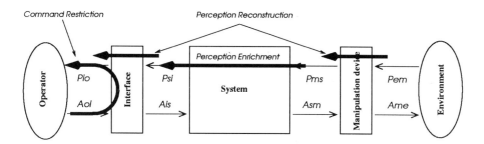

Fig. 2. Positionment of the examples

4.1 Mixing real and virtual... actions

The formal description of the first example ("Perception Enrichment") can be turned into the following one:

Action enrichment

> *Given a goal of an actional nature, the system is able to add supplementary information of the same actional nature, in order to help achieving this goal.*

Consider that an operator controls a robotic arm which is able to grasp and transport a full glass somewhere in the scene. In a standard approach where the robot arm is fully controlled, the operator is in charge of both moving the arm and preserving the verticality of the glass. In order to ease the operator's work, we can imagine to add some "intelligence" to the system, and let it detect automatically whether the glass is full, and if so, take care of the verticality. The operator will then have exactly the same command to use in both cases. The affected information path in this example is $A_{is} \rightarrow A_{sm}$, which is the counterpart of the original one: the system needs A_{is} to understand where the glass should go, and generates the supplementary actions A_{sm} in order to maintain the verticality. Whereas in the original example, "augmenting" reality meant enriching the perceptions with artificially generated ones, here augmenting reality means enriching the *actions* with artificially generated ones.

4.2 Reconstructing a missing... action

The formal description of the second example ("Perception Reconstruction") can be turned into the following one:

Action reconstruction

> *Given that a particular* action *is originally missing, a system uses substitute information in order to recreate this action in a synthetic way.*

Controlling human body avatars or robotic arms can be done in an isomorphic way, for instance by using an integral data suit to mimic the avatar's movement, or by using an exo-skeleton to capture the arm's motion. In those cases, the original action exists, and the work of the system is just to reproduce it on the manipulation device. However, there are cases in which this original action doesn't exist. For instance, when a robotic arm is controlled with a trackball, there isn't any original operator's arm motion to reproduce. The system must then use some substitute information (from the trackball) to produce the desired action. This example illustrates cases where the input device is too simple. On the other hand, there are cases where the desired action is too complex to exist in reality. David Sturman[5] illustrates the control of a virtual creature thanks to a whole-hand input device. The creature has too many degrees of freedom for an operator to mimic its whole movement. Consequently, the system tracks the operator's "walking fingers" ($A_{oi} \rightarrow A_{is}$) and reconstructs the walking of the creature ($A_{sm} \rightarrow A_{me}$).

While this idea of substituting an action information to reconstruct another one has obviously been used for a long time in robotics, the relation between those systems and Augmented Reality does not seem to have been pointed out before. We find it interesting to show that such a priori distant areas actually belong to the same conceptual domain.

4.3 Restricting the... execution field

The formal description of the third example ("Command Restriction") can be turned into the following one:

Execution Restriction

> *Given a particular command that the environment can* undergo, *the system configures the manipulation device in order to restrict the overall field of* execution *for this command.*

In other words, we do not restrict the way a command is specified this time, but the way it is *executed*. To illustrate this process, consider again our robotic arm, and the action of grasping an object. Different objects will need different hand pressure to be grasped (you would not grasp an egg as you would grasp a book). In a basic system, adjusting the pressure would be part of the operator's task, which can be rather difficult, especially if no haptic feedback is available. Imagine now that an intelligent assistance system detects the type of the object the operator is grasping, and configures the manipulation device to apply the proper pressure. This process is thus occuring on the $P_{em} \rightarrow A_{me}$ information path: the manipulation device needs P_{em} for getting the current pressure feedback, and modifies A_{me} to adjust it.

In this example, the pressure information, computed automatically, would be useless for the operator and shouldn't be returned to him. While it can appear surprising to talk of "augmented" reality whereas the operator's perceptions are actually "diminished", his actions are still augmented since he doesn't provide the pressure information.

5 Anticipated Reality

The figure 3 summarizes the examples we described in both section 2 and section 3, showing that the way we see Augmented Reality gives a more balanced concept.

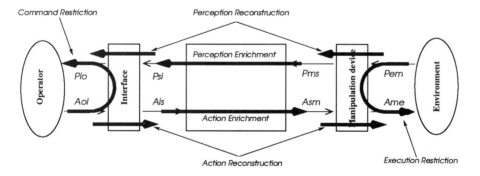

Fig. 3. Positioning the examples

In this section, we would like to propose yet another extension to the concept: Augmented Reality by *anticipation*. The idea is that the augmented reality processes are not based anymore on existing information, but on information that is *expected* to exist in a near future. To illustrate this idea, a prototype application called Toast[2] was implemented. This application simulates a robotic arm that is

---

[2] Toast is an acronym for "Tele-Operation Assistance SysTem"

154

able to grasp objects like a glass. The system features a knowledge representation model describing how actions like object grasping or transportation should be executed. Along with all other examples described in the previous sections, this application has *command correction* and *intention detection* capabilities.

5.1 Command Correction

Assume that during a transportation operation, the object falls (the command is then interrupted because an error occured). The system recovers by grabbing back the object *without any operator's intervention* (autonomously), and simultaneously generates a virtual scene to let the operator proceed as if nothing had happened. Figure 4 shows Toast in the process of command correction: the glass has fallen and the system is currently grabbing it again. The error recovery process is drawn in wireframe on the operator's screen while a simulation drawn in normal mode let the operator proceed the normal action as if no error had occured. In this example, Reality is "augmented" not only by producing the

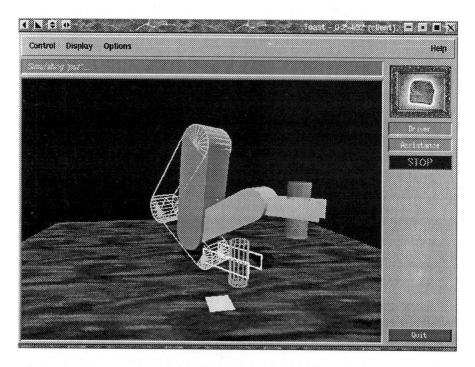

Fig. 4. Command Correction

synthetic "grasp" action, but by generating virtual perceptions that are *expected* to have happened if the actions had completed successfully.

5.2   Intention Detection

The knowledge representation model provided in Toast allows the system to watch the operator's commands, and *detect* his intentions (like grasping an object). Once an intention has proven to be highly probable, the system interrupts the operator's commands, optionally asks him to confirm the detected intention, and proceeds automatically to complete the action. Figure 5 shows Toast in the process of intentions detection. The operator was moving the arm towards the object, and the system detected that the intention of grasping was probable enough to ask for a confirmation. In this example again, Reality is "augmented"

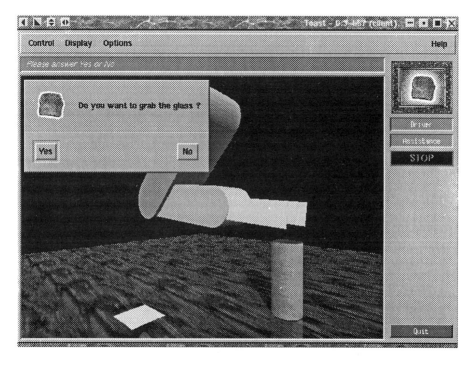

Fig. 5. Intentions Detection

by generating an action that is *expected* to become real in a near future.

6   Conclusion

In this paper, we tried to precise and widen the notion of Augmented Reality. We proposed a generic model describing virtual reality situations, and especially tele-operation ones. Provided with this model, we examined several examples of Augmented Reality, among those that we consider the most representative of the concept as it is currently envisioned. Those examples were examined following two axis: which information paths are affected by the augmented reality process, and how information is modified by this process. This study permitted to demonstrate that the notion of Augmented Reality is currently biased towards the operator and his perceptions. By systematically applying the central symmetry of our model to the previously described examples, we were able to show how this imbalance can be corrected, and how Augmented Reality can be seen the other way around, that is towards the environment and its undergone actions.

We believe that the proposed reasoning method has major benefits:

- On a semantic field, our approach enlarges the concept of Augmented Reality: if it usually means adding virtual components to a real scene, those "components" shouldn't be restricted to perceptual information, but should include actions as well.
- As far as existing tele-operation applications are concerned, our view of the concept shows that even very mature tele-robotics applications, such as trackball-driven operations do belong to Augmented Reality, even if this relation is not commonly stated or realized.
- As far as future tele-operation systems are concerned, and especially in the field of computer aided Tele-Operation [3], our reasoning method demonstrates how, from existing examples, we can systematically envision new applications that would otherwise be more difficult to design from scratch.

References

1. Côté, J., Lavallée, J.: Augmented Reality Graphic Interface for Upstream Dam Inspection. In SPIE, Photonics East, 1995.
2. Dubois, E., Nigay, L., Troccaz, J.: Interaction Chirurgien-Système: Gestes Médico-Chirurgicaux Assistés par ordinateur. In proceedings of IHM'97, pp. 207-208. Poitiers, France (1997).
3. Grumbach, A., Verna, D.: Assistance cognitive à la téléopération en monde virtuel. In proceedings of: Journées Nationales Réalité Virtuelle, GT-RV, GDR-PRC, pp. 38-46. Toulouse, France (1996)
4. Mellor, J.-P.: Enhanced Reality Visualization in a Surgical Environment. M.I.T. Technical Report No. 1544.
5. Sturman, D.: Whole Hand Input. M.I.T. Ph.D. (1992).
6. Verna, D.: Téléopération et Réalité Virtuelle: Assistance à l'opérateur par modélisation cognitive de ses intentions. In proceedings of: IHM'97. Poitiers, France (1997).
7. Verna, D.: Can we define Virtual Reality? The M_RIC model. In proceedings of: Virtual Worlds 98. LNAI 1434, pp. 29-41, 1998. Paris, France (1998).
8. Verna, D.: Sémantique et Localisation de l'Assistance en Réalité Virtuelle. In proceedings of: Journées Nationales Réalité Virtuelle, GT-RV, GDR-PRC. Issy-les-Moulineaux, France (1998).

Interaction Techniques on the Virtual Workbench

Rogier van de Pol[1,2], William Ribarsky[1], Larry Hodges[1],
and Frits Post[2]

[1]GVU Center, Georgia Tech, [2]Delft Technical University

Abstract

This paper evaluates interaction methods within the general framework of navigation, selection, and manipulation. It considers large display environments and, in particular, the virtual workbench, comparing this system to HMD and CAVE systems. The paper addresses three issues: (a) identifying the characteristics that set the workbench apart from other virtual environments; (b) determining types and examples of interaction techniques; (c) evaluating how these techniques perform on the workbench to determine which perform best. The evaluations are based on an extensive set of user observations. Also discussed are some problems that stereoscopic display coupled with interaction bring out.

1 Introduction

The availability of economical, bright, high resolution large displays, especially projected displays, has significantly increased their use. In particular this is true for tracked immersive or semi-immersive systems. CAVE-like immersive systems [3] with two, three, four or more displays are used in a variety of engineering, design, and scientific applications. In the last few years, the semi-immersive virtual workbench [5,7,11] with its horizontal or slanted display has come into use for engineering and scientific applications, often involving collaboration. In the future we can expect to see an even wider use of large displays, often with (frequently wireless) tracking.

In spite of the interest in immersive and semi-immersive large display environments, there has been relatively little work that provides an overall classification and evaluation of interaction techniques for these environments. This lack is compounded because these environments tend to use stereoscopic display more frequently than, say, head mounted display (HMD) systems. Stereoscopic display coupled with interaction provides its own special problems, some of which are heightened in semi-immersive environments. In addition there have been essentially no usability studies testing performance of interaction modes. For these reasons we address interaction in semi-immersive environments in this paper. We also discuss the design of user studies for interaction and present some preliminary results.

For the virtual workbench our goals are
- To find what the characteristics are for the workbench that set it apart from other environments, like HMD and CAVE systems
- To determine the types and organization of interaction techniques
- To see how these techniques perform in the workbench and to determine which might be best for that environment.

In this paper we present results for each of these goals. Several of our conclusions on interaction can be extended to other environments.

2 Related Work

Although the CAVE has been around longer than the virtual workbench and there have been several papers on the design of the environment [3] and on applications, there has been relatively little work looking in detail at the types and behavior of interaction. Recently there have been tools, such as CALVIN [8], developed for collaboration in systems such as the CAVE. These tools have been used on architectural design and other applications. But here again there is little evaluation of interaction methods. In the present paper several of the methods evaluated are applicable to the CAVE and other large display systems, not just to the workbench.

Recently, Cutler et. al. [4] focused on two-handed interaction in a workbench environment. Techniques were investigated to manipulate objects using both hands with Pinch Gloves as input devices. The described techniques adhered to Guiard's principles of two-handed tasks [6], where the non-dominant hand provides a reference for the dominant hand, which performs the actual task. However, there is no quantitative evaluation of the techniques, as we have begun in this paper. Also, we discuss both one- and two-handed interaction, gaze-directed interaction, and input devices in addition to the Pinch Gloves. In addition we compare and contrast the workbench to other immersive and semi-immersive devices. The workbench is also a natural environment for collaboration; a recent study [1] looked at ways to allow two (or more) people to work together effectively on the workbench. This involved two people being head-tracked simultaneously by multiplexing all four eye views. We discuss a few alternative ideas that would not involve simultaneous head-tracking.

A classification and description of interaction tasks in virtual environments is given by Mine [9], distinguishing navigation, selection, and manipulation as three general tasks. Bowman and Hodges discuss the need for constraints in virtual environments [2]. They consider both virtual constraints (software) and physical constraints (e.g., a tabletop), giving examples of how to constrain interaction tasks to improve efficiency and accuracy. We use here a classification scheme similar to that of Mine in discussing interactions in large display environments and also discuss the role of constraints. The importance of exploiting the proprioceptive sense is discussed in Mine et. al. [10]. Here it is argued that because the user is often unable to see his hands, proprioception can help improve interaction. By bringing an object close to his body and by using intuitive hand gestures, the user has a better understanding of the position and orientation of the object. We think that proprioception is important in large display environments, even though the user is able to see his body, and we discuss how it affects the interactive methods we describe.

3 Classifying Interaction

It is useful to provide a classification of techniques that can be used in a semi-immersive, large display environment. Three universal tasks that can be found in almost any virtual reality application are [2] *Navigation*, *Selection*, and *Manipulation.*

We have implemented some navigation techniques, but our main focus has been on selection and manipulation in the workbench environment. Furthermore, we have focused on direct interaction techniques, where the user directly interacts with objects using natural gestures (as opposed to using sliders or menus).

3.1 Navigation

In this paper we define navigation as the process of changing the position and orientation of the viewpoint in the environment. The most obvious navigation technique in a workbench environment is to let the user physically walk around the workbench to get different views of the scene. To accomplish this the user's head is tracked. Two other navigation techniques we implemented are *panning* and *scaling*. It can be argued that these are not really navigation techniques, since the user's viewpoint doesn't change. However, since these techniques affect the position of the entire scene relative to the viewpoint, we include them here.

Panning is important if the virtual scene is larger than the workbench screen, because invisible parts can be 'dragged' into view. In our environment, panning is activated through pinching together two fingers of the Pinch Glove (the thumb and middle finger). When the user moves his arm, the scene will move as if it were attached to the users left hand. Panning stops when the user releases the pinch. The user can only pan the scene parallel to the horizontal workbench plane. Scaling allows the user to scale the entire scene up or down by moving the pinched fingers closer or farther from the display surface. This technique is similar to moving the viewpoint nearer or farther. We chose scaling because this ensures that the objects remain above the workbench screen and therefore within reach of the user.

3.2 Selection

Selection is used to identify objects, usually to manipulate them in some way. It may also be used to identify a region of space and/or the objects inside. There are two general cases. First of all, the object can be within arm's reach of the user. In this case, the user can simply reach out and "touch" the object to select it. Secondly, the object can be out of reach (either because it is too far away or because it is below the workbench surface). Here the user must use a tool to select the object from a distance. We implemented ray casting, gaze directed selection, pointing, and virtual hands.

Direct picking. The most intuitive and easy way for the user to select an object is to simply reach out until his hand intersects it. After some trial, we decided that the most precise way to support this was to put a tracker on the forefinger of each Pinch Glove (see Fig. 1) and define a small, invisible box around it. An object is selected when this box intersects the object's bounding box. The size of the box can be adjusted to allow for a larger or smaller 'error margin'. This technique is always active, even when one of the other tools described next is active as well.

Ray casting. The user can activate a ray that shoots out from the tip of his index finger. To select an object the user has to intersect it with the ray. In our environment, a ray can be activated for both hands (Fig. 2). If several objects are intersected, the first object is chosen.

Gaze-directed selection. When this technique is active, the user can select an object by looking at it. The user's gaze direction is approximated with an invisible ray originating between the user's eyes. Instead of pointing straight ahead, the ray points down at an angle. Trials with different angles revealed that this is more comfortable for the user because he has to look down all the time to see the workbench screen. A small cube is placed at the intersection of the ray and the workbench surface to serve as a cursor providing the user with visual feedback on his gaze direction. Again, the first object is chosen if multiple objects are intersected.

Pointing. This technique allows the user to select an object by pointing at it with his forefinger so that its tip overlaps the object in the user's field of view. To determine where the user is pointing, an invisible ray shoots out from between the user's eyes to the fingertip. The object closest to the user's eyes is chosen.

Virtual hands. Virtual hands are virtual objects that mimic the movements of the user's real hands (Figs. 3,4). When the user extends his arms, the virtual hands will extend faster than his real hands. This stretching effect allows the user to reach distant objects. (This is related to the GO-GO method of Poupyrev [12]). An object can be selected by positioning one of the virtual hands inside it. The function that maps virtual hand to real hand position ensures that the user can reach any object visible on the workbench screen.

3.3 Manipulation

Manipulation is the act of changing certain parameters of an object (e.g. its position, orientation, shape, or color). Once an object has been selected, the user can manipulate it. Currently, only the basic manipulation tasks (translation, rotation, and uniform scaling) are supported in our application. If the object is within physical reach of the user, he can manipulate it directly with his hands. If the object is out of reach, there are three possibilities for manipulation:

- Close manipulation – bring object to user
- Distant manipulation
- Tele-manipulation – bring user to object

Close manipulation. Close manipulation brings the object to the user, after which he can manipulate it directly with his hands. In accordance with studies on the importance of proprioceptive feedback [10], we felt that close manipulation would be quite useful for detailed work on objects, especially work involving precise positioning and orientation. If the object is within reach, the user can pick it up by first selecting it with the direct picking technique and then pinching together his thumb and forefinger. This will attach the object to the user's hand, allowing him to move and orient the object by moving his hand. When the object is out of reach, the user can navigate towards it by panning and scaling the scene (or walking around the workbench). We implemented two other techniques to bring an object close to the user, *popping* and *copying*. When active, popping causes distant objects that have been selected to 'pop' into the user's hand when he makes a pinch gesture. Copying works the same way, except that a copy of the original object is placed in the user's hand. When the user manipulates the copy, the original object will mimic the rotations of the copy. When the user releases the pinch, the copy will disappear.

Distant Manipulation. The user can perform distant manipulation by selecting an object with one of the distant selection tools (ray casting, gaze directed, or pointing). After this the user can make a pinch gesture, attaching the object to the current tool.

Tele-manipulation. Tele-manipulation lets the user manipulate distant objects as if they were close to his body. The virtual hands can be used for tele-manipulation. As was described in the section on selection techniques, the user can pick up a distant object with the virtual hands (Fig. 3) and then manipulate it as if he were holding the object in his real hands.

3.4 One Versus Two-Handed Manipulation

In many cases the use of two hands to perform tasks could improve performance significantly. To investigate this, we extended several of the aforementioned techniques to allow two-handed manipulation. Of course the user is still able to select and manipulate different objects with either hand. Besides two-handed manipulation, we implemented two-handed panning as well, since using one hand can be annoying when traversing large distances. Therefore, we changed this technique so that the user can alternate hands (like pulling himself forward along an invisible rope).

An object picked up with one hand is attached to this hand. This allows the user to move and rotate the object. However, people usually use both hands to examine an object; they pass it back and forth between both hands and let it 'roll' through their hands to quickly examine it from all sides. In our system, the user can pass an object from one hand to the other by selecting the object with the free hand while letting it go (releasing the pinch) with the other hand. The user can also switch to two-handed manipulation by picking an object with both hands. The object can then be rotated, translated and uniformly scaled by moving the hands relative to each other. This can be visualized by imagining a sphere between the fingertips of the user's hands. Rotation of the object can be seen as moving the fingertips across the surface of this sphere. Translation can be seen as moving the center of the sphere by moving both hands in the same direction. Finally, scaling can be seen as moving the hands further apart or closer together. This works the same way when the user is employing the virtual hands (Fig. 4). We changed the distant manipulation techniques (ray casting, gaze directed, and pointing) as well, but these techniques didn't work very well. This is because these techniques are like manipulating an object with two sticks (Fig. 2).

3.5 Aids to Interaction

Constraints.   When manipulating real objects, there are usually all kinds of constraints that restrict the user's movements (e.g. gravity, or physical surfaces like rulers, tablets or tabletops). People often depend on these things to perform precise tasks. In most virtual environments such natural restrictions are not present. However, the workbench does provide a physical screen that can be used as a constraint. The manipulation techniques as described above are excellent for quick examination and rough placement of objects. However, these unconstrained techniques are often not suited for more precise manipulation. Therefore, we implemented in-the-plane interaction, where manipulation is constrained to the workbench screen. When in-the-plane interaction is active, objects can only move parallel to the horizontal workbench surface. When the user picks up an object, it will therefore continue to rest on the surface, even when the user moves his arm up and down. When the user is holding an object with just one hand, he is only able to translate it. If he wishes to rotate or scale it, he has to grab the object with both hands. Rotation is only possible about the axis perpendicular to the workbench surface.

3.6 Combining 2D and 3D

The workbench is better suited than other virtual environments to displaying 2D elements like windows, menus, and dialog boxes because of its nature (3D objects resting on a 2D physical surface). We have also implemented a simple *grid* to further constrain interaction and a *virtual sheet*. When the grid is activated, horizontal and vertical gridlines are displayed on the workbench surface. This causes objects to snap to grid intersections between the gridlines. One could also extend this to make rotation and scaling snap to the grid. The user could adjust the grid spacing by picking up two gridlines and changing the distance between them. The virtual sheet can be seen as a sheet of paper lying on the workbench surface. The user is able to move it around by placing his hand on top of it and sliding it across the workbench. This sheet could be used to make notes, or it could be made into a floating menu.

4 Hardware and Input Devices

We use the Immersive Workbench from Fakespace, Inc. It consists of an Electrohome Marquee 8500 Projection System, Polhemus 3Space Fastrak Tracking System, CrystalEyes emitter and glasses, and Fakespace Pinch Gloves. As an alternative to the Pinch Gloves, we used two button chord devices, one for each hand. The workbench is powered by a 4 processor SGI Onyx2 with IR graphics. We use three trackers: one for the user's head, and one for each hand.

Pinch Gloves. Fakespace Pinch Gloves do not recognize hand gestures, but instead they register 'pinches' (i.e. the user pressing together two or more fingers). The user can pinch two fingers of the same hand, but also one finger of each hand, or combinations of these. Obviously, this allows for a lot of different combinations. A later version of the gloves also has a big contact pad on the palms, allowing pinches that would otherwise be impossible (like forefinger and ring finger). Although intuitive, it remains to be seen if using the gloves is more intuitive than using, say, a normal button device. There are only a few pinch gestures that are really intuitive (e.g., pinching thumb and index finger to pick up an object). Furthermore, a user may not be able to remember and use as many combinations as the Pinch Gloves allow. However, it appears that people can more easily remember pinch gestures than button presses. Our qualitative observation is that this is so. Also the Pinch Gloves offer the advantage that the user can pick up and hold different tools while wearing the gloves. Disadvantages that we encountered were that using the keyboard becomes very difficult, and that the gloves are one-size-not-really-fits-all. Furthermore, inexperienced users often make pinch gestures unintentionally. Finally, pinches have to be precise (the contact pads really have to make contact). More experiments are needed testing the usability of Pinch Gloves for different tasks and comparing them with other devices.

Button chord devices. Besides the Pinch Gloves we used button chord devices, one for each hand, to provide user input. We made these from plastic tubes on which we attached a tracker and five buttons (Fig. 1). The latter are placed so that the user can access each button with a finger while comfortably holding the device. Giving commands with these devices seemed to work better (a user notices fairly easily that a button is not correctly pressed down). The button chord devices seemed to be more suitable for (distant) selection than Pinch Gloves. Because of their shape, the direction in which they are pointing is obvious to see. They also suffered less from the "arm lever problem". This is the problem of a small movement of the user's hand resulting in a large displacement of the tip of the selection ray. On the other hand the Pinch Gloves seemed to be much more suitable for close manipulation. Using the button chord devices for manipulation seemed like sticking two sticks in an object and then manipulating it, which is less natural.

5 Workbench Characteristics

One of our main goals was to find what characteristics of the workbench set it apart from other types of virtual environments. After extended evaluation, the workbench seems to have the following dominant characteristics, summarized in Table 1.

Semi-immersive. The workbench environment is not fully immersive. In the HMD and CAVE, the general goal is to completely immerse the user in the environment. Both result in the user being able to see only the virtual world, although in the CAVE he can also see his body and any tools he is using. By contrast the workbench brings virtual objects into the real world rather than bringing the user into the virtual world. Instead of being inside the scene, the user is looking down on it. This difference is reflected in the interaction modes. For example, instead of walking through the virtual environment, the user walks around the workbench to obtain different views.

Workbench Characteristic	Description
Semi-immersive	Brings virtual objects into the real world; causes occlusion and boundary effects; user looks down on scene; walk around rather than walk through
Flat, limited size display	horizontal display; heights of objects above display and extents constrained; object positioning important
Physical surface	Introduces barrier to grabbing objects; requires alternatives besides direct grabbing; can provide a useful constraint
Collaboration	Naturally collaborative; hardware solutions or new interaction methods needed to handle head-tracked viewing

Table 1. Workbench characteristics affecting interaction methods and applications

Flat display of limited size. In most environments, the display screen is vertical. However, the workbench surface is horizontal or nearly horizontal. Furthermore, although the screen is large, its size is still limited. The horizontal screen allows the user to look on top of the scene, but its limited size constrains the heights and extents of objects sticking out of the screen. If an object is not projected completely inside the screen, its perceived stereo effect will tend to collapse. Therefore, objects can't be higher than the user's eye position (at least for a horizontal screen). Usually objects should be lower than this, for example to allow the user to bend his knees to look at the side of an object without having the object project outside the screen. Because of this, the object(s) of interest should be positioned somewhere in front of the user, in the center of the screen. An improvement might be to have another (vertical) display behind and integrated with the workbench. This would allow the user to really look at an object from the side (and even from the bottom).

Physical surface. In the workbench environment there is a physical surface directly in front of the user. In HMD setups such a surface is not present. Although CAVE systems do have physical walls and floors, they are usually relatively far away from the user. The physical surface introduces a barrier that sometimes prevents the user from grabbing virtual objects that seem to be within reach. In fact, if the interaction technique is not appropriately designed, the user will continually bang his hand into the display surface! Because of this barrier, other techniques besides direct grabbing have to be implemented, as we discussed above. In the CAVE, the goal usually is to hide the fact that the physical walls are present. However, for the workbench it might be an advantage in many cases to have the physical barrier. An example of this is using the screen as a physical constraint, like we did with the constrained manipulation methods. As we've discussed, the screen could be used to display 2D items like menus, grids, or information windows [4,5]. The workbench surface makes these elements easier to use.

Collaboration. The workbench is a naturally collaborative environment. Unfortunately the use of head-tracking impedes two or more people working together because the untracked person will get a distorted view which can become extreme (e.g., when the tracked person moves to the opposite end of the workbench or leans well over to one side while the untracked person remains upright). Recently new methods have been developed that permit two people to be tracked simultaneously by multiplexing all four eye views [1]. However, this is expensive and does not appear scalable to more than a few people. As alternatives, we plan to implement and evaluate virtual trading of tracking between collaborators, turning tracking on and off through gesture or voice commands, and the "best" averaged viewpoint for a group of users when head tracking is turned off.

6 Results on Effectiveness

We built a simple scenario for the workbench that we used consistently in the evaluation of all interaction methods and input devices. The scenario consisted of a room with various pieces of furniture positioned so that they appeared to rest on the workbench surface. We added a textured ground plane to this scene that coincided with the workbench surface, making it look opaque and solid. To prevent objects from disappearing below this ground plane, we implemented a crude collision detection scheme. The user looks down on this scene and by using the selection and manipulation techniques he can pick up and manipulate the furniture. An object turns red to indicate selection. We observed people using this scenario on the workbench during countless lab demonstrations and several planned observation sessions. In this way we observed several hundred users. This feedback permitted us to make the several updates of techniques described in this paper and is the basis for the evaluations in this section. The results of our evaluations and observations are summarized in Table 2. Some initial formal user studies are described below.

Type of Interaction	Evaluations of Workbench Effectiveness	Comparison to Immersive
Navigation	God's eye view; mostly panning and scaling; pinch gestures are intuitive.	Navigation is often from within scene.
Selection	Objects can be inadvertently moved out of the display area & lost.	
Direct picking	Cursor necessary in case object too far above screen or too close to viewer.	Not a problem in monoscopic env.; less of a problem in CAVE.
Distant selection	Ray casting best for object selection; gaze-directed good for less precise selection; virtual hands effective but require learning.	Workbench evaluations also apply to immersive envs.
Manipulation Close Distant	Both one & two hands especially effective. Ray casting for rough positioning; virtual hands reasonably good.	Workbench evaluations also applicable to CAVE.
Constrained	For precise placement & orientation in scene.	
Unconstrained	For working on hand-held objects; two hands important here.	

Table 2. Results for interaction technique effectiveness

Navigation. We found that navigation does not play as big a role as in other types of virtual environments. The scene is often relatively small (model-sized), and therefore there is no need for the user to cover large distances. Head-tracking allows the user to physically walk around the workbench. Since no special tool is required, the user's hands are free for other tasks. The other navigation techniques we implemented (panning and scaling) are necessary because of the limited size of the screen. Invisible portions of the scene have to be dragged into view. Using pinch gestures and arm movements to achieve this proved to be very natural and easy to use. These gestures give proprioceptive feedback as well as visual feedback so that the user quickly learns the relationship between arm position and, for example, the size of the scene.

Selection. Although direct picking is very intuitive, we noticed that users were having difficulty selecting objects that were floating relatively high above the workbench. This appears to be partly caused by the fact that the user receives false occlusion cues. Because the user's physical hand is always in front of the workbench screen, virtual objects will be projected beyond it, even when the virtual object is actually between the users head and hand. This causes the user to think that the object is farther away when it could in fact be closer to his eyes. In addition stereo images of objects located relatively close to the face cannot be fused, which further erodes depth information. To solve this, we put a small virtual cursor near the tip of the user's forefinger or of the button chord device. This definitely made selection easier, because the depth cues of this cursor relative to an object are always correct.

Of all distant selection techniques, ray casting seemed to work best. We think that this is because the selection ray is always visible, whereas with gaze directed selection or pointing it is invisible. However, when we included the cursor near the user's fingertip, pointing (a very intuitive technique for selecting distant objects) worked just as well. A drawback of ray casting is that, due to the limited screen size, the illusion of the ray shooting out of the user's hand breaks down when the hand is relatively far from the workbench (part of the ray doesn't project on the screen). A problem of the pointing technique is that the user's hand can completely obscure small objects, making selection difficult. Gaze directed selection absolutely requires the cursor. We placed this cursor at the intersection of the users gaze direction and the workbench surface. However, this results in the user selecting an object not by simply looking at it, but by trying to place the cursor behind the object (the user doesn't focus on the object anymore, but on the cursor). Gaze directed selection is probably more suitable for selecting general regions of space (e.g., a traveling direction), instead of objects.

Often in VEs, arm extension techniques like the virtual hands make selection more difficult. This is because the virtual hand has to be inside an object, whereas a ray only has to intersect the object. However, we found that our virtual hands worked pretty well, due to the limited size of the workbench.

Manipulation. Close manipulation is without a doubt the best way to manipulate objects on the workbench. The user holds objects in his hands, close to his body, which allows him to take full advantage of proprioception. The user can rest his elbows on the edge of the workbench, roll the object through his hands, and pass it from one hand to the other. Distant manipulation is useful for very rough object placement. However, if a certain level of precision is required, the user should strive to bring the object right in front of him before manipulating it. If the user wishes to inspect an object, or he has to have quick access to all sides of an object, unconstrained manipulation is the most suitable. However, if the goal is to precisely position and orient an object in the scene, the more constrained techniques should be used. When an object's movement is restricted to the workbench plane, relatively precise placement and orienting of an object is possible simply by sliding the hands across the workbench surface. Even more precise placement is possible when grids are used. Close manipulation has the drawback that small objects may get obscured by the user's hands, and the user may get false occlusion cues. Tele-manipulation (using the virtual hands) removes this problem. However, the user now seems to have four hands (because his real hands are still visible) which can be confusing. We noticed that many people had trouble using virtual hands. Because real hand movements are exaggerated by the virtual hands, they tend to quickly move around on the screen. They often even disappear from the projection screen. Also, because of this exaggeration of movement, it is difficult to keep an object at its old position while manipulating it. An improvement to the virtual hands might be to let them mimic the movements of the real hands exactly once an object has been selected for manipulation (i.e., without scaling). However, once a user gets experience using them, virtual hands can be a valuable tool for manipulation, because the user can reach any object on the screen.

One vs. Two Hands. It appears that the proprioceptive feedback of relating one hand to the other makes fine manipulations faster and more accurate. For example if the user were attaching one object to another or placing a part in a slot in another object, it would be easier to do having an object in each hand rather than, for example, laying one object down and then using just one hand to insert the other object. Preliminary experiments support this speculation. In addition it should be faster to, say, make multiple attachments to different sides of an object with two hands than one.

7 User Studies

We set up an experiment to test the above ideas about one vs. two hands. A virtual box with an opening in one side and a rod were placed on the workbench surface (Fig. 5). Subjects were required to orient the box so that the rod could be placed inside without touching the sides (Fig. 5). Each subject was given several trials with different positions and orientations of the box and rod. For each collection of trials they used one-handed glove and button chord device, and the same devices with two hands (4 sets altogether). The order in which the devices were used was randomly set for each subject. After trials with over 40 subjects, preliminary results are that two-handed manipulation is better than one-handed in performance time and accuracy. However, the button chord device is better than the gloves in both performance time and accuracy, even though the subjects believe they do better with the gloves. We will soon present complete results for this experiment including statistical analyses.

8 Conclusions

In this paper we have studied and described the dominant characteristics of the workbench. These characteristics have to do with its semi-immersive nature, its flat, limited size display that presents a physical barrier, and its natural capability for collaboration. Interaction method effectiveness is affected by these characteristics. We discuss effectiveness in the three main interaction categories of navigation, selection, and manipulation, concentrating mainly on the latter two. Based on observations and demos involving several hundred users, we have evaluated and adjusted many interaction techniques. We find that although there are problems caused by limited screen space size and stereoscopic display, these can be minimized with proper cues and adjustments. The results given here on interaction methods provide design parameters that can increase the effectiveness of a wide variety of applications.

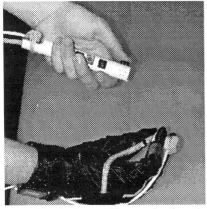

Fig. 1 Pinch glove and button chord devices showing placement of trackers

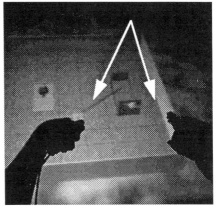

Fig. 2 Manipulation of object using ray casting (indicated by arrows).

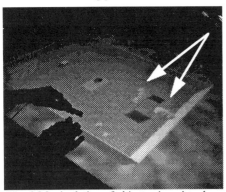

Fig. 3 Manipulation of object using virtual hands (indicated by arrows).

Fig. 5 Close-up of error condition where rod intersects box edge in user study of Sec. 7.

Fig. 4 Close-up of virtual hand manipulating lamp in the evaluation scenario.

Building on the results in Sec. 7, we plan to follow up with controlled user studies for a number of interaction techniques where we will be able to quantitatively evaluate performance. We will also look at the possibility of finding new interaction and display methods to minimize head-tracked viewing problems among multiple collaborators on the workbench.

Acknowledgments

This work was performed in part under contracts from the Naval Research Lab and the Office of Naval Research. We thank Frank Jiang for help in setting up the workbench and David Krum and Fleming Seay for designing initial user studies.

References

1. M. Agrawal, A.C. Beers, B. Frohlich, P. Hanrahan, I. McDowall, and M. Bolas (1997). The Two-User Responsive Workbench: Support for Collaboration Through the Individual Views of a Shared Space. Proceedings, ACM SIGGRAPH 1997, pp. 327-332.
2. D. Bowman, D. and L. Hodges (1997). An Evaluation of Techniques for Grabbing and Manipulating Remote Objects in Immersive Virtual Environments. Proceedings of IEEE VRAIS '97, pp. 35-38.
3. C. Cruz-Neira, D.J. Sandin, and T.A. Defanti (1993). Surround-Screen Projection-based Virtual Reality: the Design and Implementation of the CAVE. Computer Graphics Proceedings, ACM SIGGRAPH 1993, pp. 135-142.
4. L.D. Cutler, B. Frohlich, P. Hanrahan (1997) Two-Handed Direct Manipulation on the Responsive Workbench. 1997 Symposium on Interactive 3D Graphics.
5. J. Durbin, J.E. Swan, B. Colbert, J. Crowe, R. King, T. King, C. Scannell, Z. Wartell, and T. Welsh (1998). Battlefield Visualization on the Responsive Workbench. To be published, Proceedings of IEEE Visualization '98.
6. Yves Guiard (1987). Symmetric Division of Labor in Human Skilled Bimanual Action: the Kinematic Chain as a Model. Journal of Motor Behavior 19(4), pp 486-517).
7. W. Krueger, C. Bohn, B. Frohlich, H. Schuth, W. Strauss, and G. Wesche (1995). The Responsive Workbench: A Virtual Work Environment. IEEE Computer, pp. 42-48.
8. J. Leigh, A.E. Johnson, C.A. Vasilakis, and T.A. DeFanti (1996). Multi-Perspective Collaborative Design in Persistent Networked Virtual Environments. Proceedings of IEEE VRAIS '96, pp. 253-260.
9. M.R. Mine (1995). Virtual Environment Interaction Techniques. University of North Carolina, Tech Report TR95-018.
10. M.R. Mine, F.P. Brooks Jr., C.H. Sequin (1997). Moving Objects In Space: Exploiting Proprioception In Virtual-Environment Interaction. Computer Graphics Proceedings, ACM SIGGRAPH 1997, pp. 19-26.
11. U. Obeysekare, C. Williams, J. Durbin, L. Rosenblum, R. Rosenberg, F. Grinstein, R. Ramamurthi, A. Landsberg, and W. Sandberg (1996). Virtual Workbench - A Non-Immersive Virtual Environment for Visualizing and Interacting with 3D Objects for Scientific Visualization. Proceedings of IEEE Visualization '96., pp. 345-349.
12. I. Poupyrev, M. Billinghurst, S. Weghorst, and T. Ichikawa (1996). The Go-Go Interaction Technique: Non-Linear Mapping for Direct Manipulation in VR. UIST '96, Seattle, WA, pp. 79-80.

A General Framework for Cooperative Manipulation in Virtual Environments

David Margery, Bruno Arnaldi and Noël Plouzeau

IRISA/INRIA, Rennes, France
[David.Margery|Bruno.Arnaldi|Noël.Plouzeau]@irisa.fr

Abstract. Whereas cooperation and collaboration have become two popular words in virtual reality, the problem of cooperative manipulation has been mainly left aside due to the great number of other challenges facing anyone trying to setup multi-user worlds. We define cooperative manipulation as a situation where two or more users interact on the same object in a concurrent but cooperative way. The focus of this paper is to describe an experiment whose goal was to experiment problems specific of cooperative manipulation setups. Those problems include synchronizing user's input over the network, mapping user's input into a meaningful 3-D movement thanks to what we call a model of activity and giving him relevant visual information. In this paper, we present a general framework able to take into account these problems.It is compatible with physically simulated objects and has been implemented using Java, VRML and a distributed approach.

1 Introduction

Multi-user worlds are becoming an increasingly popular research subject, especially since the definition of VRML (the Virtual Reality Modeling Language), a multi-platform 3-D exchange format for Internet. Research in that field essentially focuses on the network architecture underlying such worlds [1–3] and on ways of reducing the network traffic required by using the spatial distribution of users in the world [4, 5]. The main expected uses of shared virtual reality are :

- social interaction such as in *Habitat* [6] or more recently *Virtual society* [7] or commercial web-oriented projects.
- teleconferencing such as in *Massive* [8].

Other potential uses include cooperative information retrieval and education, such as described in the *Nice* project [9]. All these applications enable some form of cooperation between participants, but little work has been devoted to classifying the cooperation modes multi-user worlds may support. Nevertheless, in order to compare any proposed network architectures or projects, one needs to be able to compare the cooperation level they enable.

In that context, we will focus our attention on the application level of shared multi-user virtual reality, sometimes called *cooperative virtual environments* (CVEs).

At first, we will define a classification for the different cooperation levels already present in various environments, before we explore the notion of cooperative manipulation, a subject largely uncovered by the existing literature. We define cooperative manipulation as a situation where two or more users interact on the same object in a concurrent but cooperative way. To enable such a manipulation, two problems have to be solved:

1. How can we combine the input from different users to act on a specific 3-D object?
2. What metaphors are needed to enable the users to understand the movement of an object, especially when they are acting on it?

Section 2 of this paper introduces a cooperation level classification. In Section 3 we discuss the specific problems tied to cooperative manipulation. We will then in Section 4 introduce a general framework to solve these problems before we present in Section 5 our current implementation of that framework. We will then conclude with a first assessment of our work and future research directions.

2 Classifying Cooperation

For the time being, the main research direction in collaborative virtual environments deals with the underlying network architecture. For that reason, the different kinds of tools provided to the user for collaboration (we focus on collaboration in 3D spaces) tend to be quite different from one system to the other. Nevertheless, the way a system supports user interaction has a direct influence on the design complexity, especially in respect to network requirements. One can identify two network load factors: richness of communication media (text, gesture, audio or video) and impact of collaboration on scene management. Because audio and video streaming are research domains of their own and that adequate software already exists for that kind of communication, we chose to look at the existing systems from the point of view of scene management. This led us to the following classification of existing work.

2.1 Cooperation level 1

We define collaboration (cooperation level 1) as the basic cooperation level. This is done by enabling users to perceive each other in the virtual world thanks to avatars (the 3D representation of an user) and providing ways of communicating between these users. This cooperation is common to all multi-user systems. Nevertheless, the strain on the system is not the same between text-based communication, gesture (as in Community Place [7]) and audio (as in Massive [8]). Yet, all these systems share a simple scene consistency model.

2.2   Cooperation Level 2

As far as scene management is concerned, the next step is to enable the user to act on the scene. When each user can change the scene individually, the system is said to support level 2 cooperation. This level can be divided into two sub-levels:

1. **Level 2.1** All possible scene modifications are constrained by scene design. For instance, users can trigger animations or switch different items on and off.
2. **Level 2.2** Modifications made by a single user are not constrained. The most obvious example is the ability to move an object anywhere in the scene.

Level 2 cooperation can be found for example in *Community Place* [5] where users can trigger shared behaviors through scripting. This scripting mechanism is event driven, which means it is essentially aimed at supporting level 2.1 cooperation, even though it can be used for level 2.2. An example of a system designed for level 2.2 is Calvin [10]; its purpose is to provide tools for cooperative architectural design. Every user of Calvin can act on the scene in very diverse ways, in order to provide full latitude to change the location and properties of objects and walls.

2.3   Cooperation Level 3

The main limit to cooperation level 2 is that users cannot cooperate on the objects present in the scene. For example, if two users want to move the same object, a lock mechanism would ensure that only one user can perform this action. Cooperation level 3 enables such cooperation on an object. As with level 2, this level is divided into two sub-levels, depending on the kind of cooperation possible on the object .

1. **Level 3.1** enables two or more users to act on the object in independent ways: for example someone would be moving a piece of furniture while someone else would be opening it. Thus two users can concurrently modify independent properties of a same object (e.g. location and color).
2. **Level 3.2** enables two users to act in a codependent way: the resulting reaction of the object is then a combination of the different inputs. Thus two users can concurrently modify the same or linked properties. This level is requested to perform cooperative manipulation.

For example, *Smallview* [11] has implemented level 3.1 cooperation, users being able to move a briefcase and open it to see its contents at same time.
Document [12] discusses concurrent interactions, a notion similar to our level 3.2 definition. Broll's paper focuses on means of interaction detection and therefore on the strain such interactions put on the distribution layers. Hereafter we focus our attention on a general framework implementing a system capable of cooperative manipulation.

3   Cooperative Manipulation: Problems and Solutions

A simple example of a cooperative manipulation is the following: two people cooperate to move a heavy or voluminous object. Should such an operation take place in a virtual environment, two main problems would arise:

1. Distribution issues: how will the input of users using different machines be combined? We will address this in 3.2.
2. The need for appropriate metaphoric information. This will be the focus of the next section.

Besides these two main problems, another issue arose: how to map user input (from a mouse or 3D pointer) into a meaningful action for the considered world? To address this, we chose to define an activity model that filters any input from the scene and transforms in a meaningful action in the virtual world.

3.1   Metaphoric Information

In a computer system, technical constraints add to the constraints of the represented reality. On top of that, means of perceiving that reality are quite poor in a computer system compared to those existing in the real world. Therefore, different types of information need to be added to the representation of the scene to keep it understandable to the user. For instance:

1. **Activity Metaphor** In our example, if two users are going to cooperate, they need to share such notions as left, right, in front of, etc. Therefore, users need to be represented in the system by information-rich avatars, that show at least the position and the view direction. More generally, avatars need to represent the state of the activity model they are in (walk, grab, carry), thus the notion of activity metaphor. This activity metaphor is aimed at all participants in the virtual environment, whereas the informative metaphor presented thereafter is local to each user.
2. **Informative Metaphor** Unlike real world situations, interactions in a virtual world happen through a computer system. Hence, users put the blame for unexpected behaviors on the computer. For instance, if an user cannot grab an object, he will not be able to distinguish between a network failure and the fact that the object was to far away in the virtual world for his avatar to grab it. In order to address such needs, informative metaphors which are local to one display are needed.
3. **Action Metaphor** In real life, when two people act on the same object, each one of them can feel through different sensorial channels the actions performed by the other. When interacting through a computer system, very few sensorial channels can be used to transmit such information. Therefore, the missing information needs to be redirected to the existing sensorial channels through special objects called action metaphors. These objects (eg. 3D arrows) make the missing information (eg. direction and intensity of the other's moves) available, provided that the object representation changes so that for

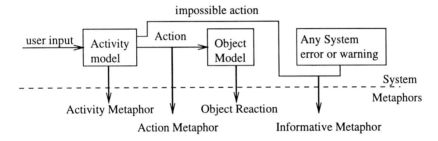

Fig. 1. Data Flow and Metaphors

example, two users located on either side of a voluminous object can see the other's arrow. For example, an active object could be made transparent.

Figure 1 sums-up all the different metaphors presented here and their role during data transmission between the user and the manipulated object.

3.2 Combining the Input

During a cooperative manipulation, the input from at least two users needs to be combined to produce a resulting movement. In order to have a general solution not limited to two users, the computation of the movement has to be based on a double model: an input model and an object model. The ideal object model would be a complete physical model and the input (from the point of view of the object) the corresponding physical forces. But for performance reasons, any complete enough model for the represented world is satisfactory.

Having this double model is necessary but not sufficient to make cooperative manipulation possible. Indeed, in order to combine actions, the system needs to be able to decide when they are simultaneous and when they are not [12]. If there is no notion of simultaneity in the system, all we have is a succession of elementary moves made by each user (cooperation level 3.1) and not a combination of those elementary moves (level 3.2).

Even if those two points are solved, the problem of consistency still remains: how will the system maintain consistence between all the computers? The system can either replicate the calculation or elect a master copy of the object whose changes will be propagated through the network layer. This last solution has two main drawbacks: first it introduces asymmetry in the treatment of all the interactors and secondly the bandwidth consumed can be much greater (eg. in the case of a deformable objects, a lot of changes can occur). Indeed, with a master simulator the changes to geometry have to be transmitted through the network whereas with replicated simulators the changes are known locally.

In the next section, we present the general framework we used to enable cooperative manipulation, with a special focus on the methods used to combine the inputs.

4   A general Framework for Cooperative Manipulation

One of the objectives of the framework we present here is to be able to combine the input of users according to the laws of physics. To do so, the reaction of an object manipulated by one or more users will be computed by a simulator. To be general, this simulator has to be able to accept any number of inputs, those inputs being expressed as physical entities (application point on the object, direction of movement, intensity, etc) called actions in this framework. As shown in fig 1, user input is mapped into actions by an activity model, and these actions are the input of the simulators.

What we have here is an abstract view of the combination process. We have yet to address the issues of distribution of the system and the methods used to keep the virtual world consistent. Our approach in that context is to replicate the database where necessary (partial replication) and the computation on every machine participating in the same region of the virtual environment. Indeed, provided all the simulators get the same data in the same order, the same simulation code should produce the same result. Of course, the notion of same data needs some explanation, and it will be presented now.

4.1   Feeding the Replicated Simulators with the Same Data

Having the simulator replicated on each machine, symmetry of treatment between the local user and remote users is fundamental. If that wasn't the case, the data received by each copy of the simulator would be different leading to divergent results. Therefore, any action produced by the activity model is sent to the network. The network is then in charge of transmitting that information to all the replicated simulators. Providing that the network is able to deliver all messages in the same order at all sites, all copies of the simulators will get the same data. Fig 2 sums up the complete process.

One remaining problem has to be solved: the delay between the arrival of two actions to be combined is not guaranteed by the network. Therefore, two replicates of the same simulator may not take the same decision regarding which actions are simultaneous and which actions are not if no further action is taken. The way we guarantee that the same decision is taken is the topic of the following section.

4.2   Architecture of a Simulator

The simulation process must be designed in a way that ensures that two actions that are considered simultaneous on one machine will be considered simultaneous on all machines. To ensure such a property each user acting on an object must first subscribe to the simulator of that object. This is done in a transparent way for the user by the activity model (a selection will subscribe the user and send the first actions). All users subscribed to a simulator are considered as acting on the object. Therefore, a simulator knows exactly how many actions it has to combine and each copy of the simulator will wait until it receives that number

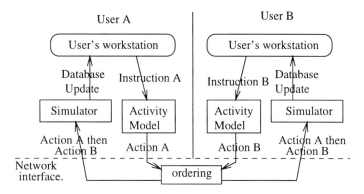

Fig. 2. How Two Simulators Get the Same Data

of actions before computing the result of the combinations of these actions.
For this system to work, there are three requirements:

1. First, subscription and unsubscription must be completely synchronized with
   the action flow. Indeed, each copy of the simulator must subscribe one user at
   the same time. To ensure that, subscribing and unsubscribing are considered
   as special action and as such are ordered by the network interface.
2. Secondly, the activity model must send actions in a data flow mode. Indeed,
   if that property was not true, we could have the following situation. Of two
   users acting on an object, one is trying to maintain the object in the current
   position. To do so, he stays active on the object but does not move his input
   device. The activity model analyses the situation correctly, and does not
   send any action. The simulator is then waiting for an action from that user.
   In that situation, the system is blocked, thus the need for an action data
   flow. This data flow can be simply implemented using a timer that sends
   a specific action (depending on the activity model) if no input has been
   provided by the user during a certain amount of time.
3. And at last, the network interface has to ensure secure message passing,
   complete message ordering and that a maximum delay for the delivery of
   messages can be guaranteed in order to ensure reactivity to the system.

In order to test the complete framework presented here, an experimental platform was developed. It provides a full implementation of the concepts and mechanisms described in this document and it is presented in the section thereafter.

5 Experimental Platform

To validate the framework presented in the preceding paragraph, we chose to
implement and test a simple case of cooperative manipulation. The test case
of our work is to enable any number of users to move an object in a simple

environment. The whole scene is described using VRML, and evolution of the scene is managed by a Java applet using the External Authoring Interface (EAI). The network interface we used was developed by a local team called Rusken, presented thereafter.

5.1 Rusken: our Network Architecture

Our experimental platform uses a simple implementation of the Rusken communication interface. The work carried out within the Rusken project is transversal to research projects within Irisa and is linked to different fields such as distributed application architectures, 3D graphics management, distributed data consistent management protocols, service quality control in distributed algorithms [13], tool boxes for distributed application building.

Our current implementation relies on a centralized message broadcasting system. This system ensures that messages exchanged between platform nodes are transmitted with a user-defined delay. Nodes that cannot meet these requirements are excluded from the node's group and may return later if they meet the requirements again. When such exclusions take place, users are informed through an appropriate metaphor. We plan to add the distributed services developed in 1999 ([13]: quality of service, [14]: coherent group management). The services provided include those needed for our platform (Sec. 3).

5.2 Implementation of the Activity Model

The activity model is implemented using both VRML interactors and software control. VRML interactors such as `PlaneSensor, CylinderSensor` already provide most of the mapping of 2D movement into 3D and enable the software developer to know if the user is active on an object or not. The activity model we implemented has two possible activities: `walk` when the user is moving in the scene, and `carry` when the user is moving an object. Switching is done by selecting an object. The activity model is then advised that the user is trying to grab an object. If the object is too far away, an informative metaphor is displayed. If not, the user is subscribed to the selected object's simulator and actions are provided to it. When the object is released, the simulator's built-in gravity makes the object fall.

5.3 Results

The screenshot of Fig 3 shows two users manipulating the same object. Therefore, their actions on it are materialized by the arrows (action metaphor), and the object is rendered semi-transparent to enable the two users to see each other. With such metaphors, it is easy to anticipate the direction the object will take. Cooperative manipulation has been tested successfully with up to five users for the same object on a local network. Experience showed that the interactivity of the whole system is more dependent on network latency than on the number of

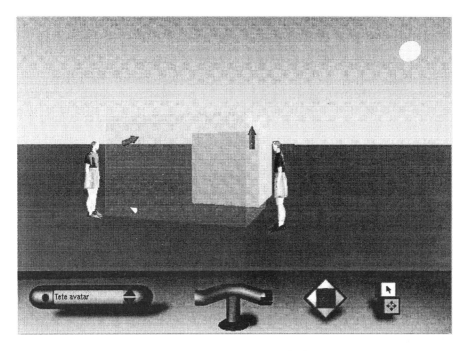

Fig. 3. A Cooperative Manipulation from a third user's point of view

users interacting. In fact, no difference was felt when an user joined the group interacting.

Computational limits were experienced when more objects were added to the scene. This is due to two factors: the use of Java and VRML inside a web browser, and the cost of collision detection 25 times a second with Java.

6 Conclusion and Future Work

In this paper, we have presented a general framework to enable cooperative manipulation on a distributed system. This framework was successfully tested with an experimental platform developed using VRML, Java and the EAI. Due to the computational limitations described above, it would be difficult to enhance the system with a complex physics model and with complex avatar animation. Despite these drawbacks, we think the framework has proved its viability and we plan to use the gained experience in integrating multi-user technologies in the Siames team's General Animation and Simulation Platform (GASP) [15].

References

1. M. R. Macedonia, M. J. Zyda, D. R. Pratt, P. T. Barham, and S. Zeswitz, "Npsnet:

A network software architecture for larger scale virtual environments," *Presence*, vol. 3, no. 4, 1994.

2. Y. Honda, K. Matsuda, J. Rekimoto, and R. Lea, "Virtual society: extending the WWW to support a multi-user interactive shared 3D environment," in *1995 Symposium on the Virtual Reality Modeling Language (VRML '95)* (ACM, ed.), (New York, NY, USA), pp. 109–116, ACM Press, 1996.

3. W. Broll, "DWTP — an Internet protocol for shared virtual environments," in *Proceedings VRML 98: third Symposium on the Virtual Reality Modeling Language, Monterey, California, February 16–19, 1998* (S. N. Spencer, ed.), (New York, NY, USA), pp. 49–56, ACM Press, 1998.

4. S. Benford and L. E. Fahlen, "Awareness, focus, and aura: A spatial model of interaction in virtual worlds," in *Proceedings of the Fifth International Conference on Human-Computer Interaction*, vol. 2 of *III. Media*, pp. 693–698, 1993.

5. R. Lea, Y. Honda, K. Matsuda, and S. Matsuda, "Place: Architecture and performance," in *VRML 97: Second Symposium on the Virtual Reality Modeling Language* (R. Carey and P. Strauss, eds.), (New York City, NY), ACM SIGGRAPH / ACM SIGCOMM, ACM Press, Feb. 1997. ISBN 0-89791-886-x.

6. C. Morningstar and F. R. Farmer, "The lessons of lucasfilm's habitat," in *Cyberspace:First Steps* (M. Benedikt, ed.), MIT press, Cambridge, Mass., 1990.

7. R. Lea, Y. Honda, and K. Matsuda, "Virtual society: Collaboration in 3D spaces on the internet," *Computer Supported Cooperative Work*, vol. 6, no. 2/3, pp. 227–250, 1997.

8. C. Greenhalgh and S. Benford, "MASSIVE: A collaborative virtual environment for teleconferencing," *ACM Transactions on Computer-Human Interaction*, vol. 2, no. 3, pp. 239–261, 1995.

9. A. Johnson, M. Roussos, J. Leigh, C. Barnes, C. Vasilakis, and T. Moher, "The nice project: Learning together in a virtual world," in *In the proceedings of VRAIS '98*, pp. 176–183, Mar 1998.

10. J. Leigh, A. Johnson, and T. DeFanti, "Calvin: an immersimedia design environment utilizing heterogeneous perspectives.," in *In Proceedings of IEEE International Conference on Multimedia Computing and Systems '96*, pp. 20–23, June 1996.

11. W. Broll, "Extending vrml to support collaborative virtual environments," in *Proceedings of CVE'96, Workshop on Collaborative Virtual Environments*, pp. 47–54, Sept 1996.

12. W. Broll, "Interacting in distributed collaborative virtual environments," in *Proceedings of the IEEE Virtual Reality Annual International Symposium - VRAIS'95*, pp. 148–155, IEEE Computer Society Press, March 1995.

13. S. Lorcy, N. Plouzeau, and J. Jezequel, "A framework managing quality of service contracts in distributed applications," in *Proc. of the 26th Int. Conf. on Technology of Object-oriented Languages and Systems (TOOLS USA '98)*, pp. 125–137, Aug. 1998.

14. S. Lorcy and N. Plouzeau, "A distributed algorithm for managing group membership with multiple groups," in *Proc. of the Int. Conference on Parallel and Distributed Processing Techniques and Applications (PDPTA '98)*, pp. 1643–1649, July 1998.

15. S. Donikian and R. Cozot, "General animation and simulation platform," in *Computer Animation and Simulation '95* (D. Terzopoulos and D. Thalmann, eds.), pp. 197–209, Eurographics, Springer-Verlag, Sept. 1995. ISBN 3-211-82738-2.

Occlusion in Collaborative Augmented Environments

Anton Fuhrmann, Gerd Hesina, François Faure
and
Michael Gervautz

Department of Computer Graphics,
Vienna University of Technology

Abstract. Augmented environments superimpose computer graphics on the real world. Such augmented environments are well suited for collaboration of multiple users. To improve the quality and consistency of the augmentation, the occlusion of real objects by computer-generated objects and vice versa has to be implemented. We present methods how this can be done for a tracked user's body and other real objects and how irritating artifacts due to misalignments can be reduced. Our method is based on simulating the occlusion of virtual objects by a representation of the user modeled as kinematic chains of articulated solids. Registration and modeling errors of this model are being reduced by smoothing the border between virtual world and occluding real object. An implementation in our augmented environment and the resulting improvements are presented.

1 Introduction

One of the main advantages of using an augmented environment [1, 8] for collaboration as opposed to an immersive setup is the direct interaction of participants in reality. While the collaborators in an immersive setup always have to rely on more or less satisfying representations of each other, ranging from disembodied hands or heads to complete bodies visualized in plausible poses, users of an augmented environment always are able to see each other and the interface devices they are using. This combination of reality and virtuality leads to the problem of correct occlusion between real and virtual objects, which does not exist in an immersive environment.

Wrong occlusion can hide gestures or facial expressions of participants. When applied in a video-based augmentation setup virtual objects can completely hide real objects if not occluded properly. Even discounting the importance of the social interaction, wrongly occluding virtual objects subject the users brain to conflicting depth clues: stereo-cues give a farther distance than the occlusion suggests. This not only leads to misconceptions of spatial relations by the user, resulting in errors when trying to grab objects, but also increases eyestrain and the probability of motion sickness.

1.1 Influences of the display system

As already mentioned, the properties of the display system influence the severity of the occlusion problem, as outlined in the following table:

Table 1. occlusion order vs. display system

occlusion order display system*(example)*	virtual object occluding real object	real object occluding virtual object
back-projection/ screen based *(CAVE [6],responsive workbench [11])*	impossible	inherent
semi-transparent HMD *(Studierstube [20])*	inherent	semi-visible / software solvable
video + immersive HMD *(UNC [18])*	inherent	software solvable

In screen-based augmented environments or projection based setups occlusion of virtual objects by real ones is simple: real objects are always between the display surface and the eye and therefore always occlude virtual objects. This yields excellent results as long as no real object is placed behind (nearer the projection screen) a virtual one. In this case the real object incorrectly occludes the virtual object in front of it. The only exception for this would be the projection-based virtual office [15], where front projection is used. Since the virtual objects are projected on top of the real ones, pictures or windows can be excluded from this projection by displaying black in the relevant portion of the display area. Nevertheless the occlusion of the display surface by real objects still shows: users hands and arms for example may drop shadows on the surface, thereby occluding parts of objects virtually in front of the shadow.

When using HMDs, the display is always between the eye and real objects. Without further processing virtual objects always occlude real ones. The only difference exists between HMDs using semi-transparent mirrors and immersive HMDs being fed video images by headmounted cameras: the first only overlays semi-transparent images over reality while the second one may display completely opaque objects.

We concentrate on setups where the displayed virtual objects overlay images of reality, since this is the only case where the occlusion problem is solvable.

1.2 Influences of the tracking system

Tracking of users (heads), input devices and real objects is a major task which influences strongly the quality of the augmentation. Immersive environments can tolerate discrepancies between reality and computer generated images which would be impossible to ignore in an augmented setup. Since in an immersive situation the user only relies on computer generated images for hand-eye coordination, errors between hand position in reality and projected hand/cursor position in the environment almost never lead to problems when interacting with the virtual environment.

In an augmented environment however, misalignment between tracked real objects and their representations in virtuality can cause severe problems for interaction in the environment. Additionally, lag between reality and the computer-generated environment is much more noticeable than in an immersive situation, since the position of virtual objects in respect to the real surroundings can be immediately compared. This results in "swimming" motions of the virtual environment, which may also lead to motion sickness.

When addressing the problem of occlusion, another quality of the tracking system matters: the ability to supply the simulation with additional information about the occluding objects. Ideally, we would like the tracking system to deliver complete geometric information which enables us to determine which parts of virtual objects to occlude.

This yields the following classification by tracking system:

Table 2. occlusion order vs. display system

Supplies only positional data	supplies additionally geometric information
Magnetic tracking	video tracking delivering depth map from stereo [25]
Mechanical tracking	
Optical tracking using beacons [18]	video tracking delivering contour data [4]
	video range tracking [15] using invisible structured light
	laser range tracking

Tracking systems providing occlusion data

A very efficient and self-contained approach would be video-based augmentation using stereo headmounted cameras and a HMD. Stereo video data could be used for inside-out tracking of the users position and orientation and also to generate a dense depth map of the visible scene usable for occlusion. While this approach seems to be the most promising in respect to versatility the computational complexity of the depth map reconstruction allows only coarse approximations of the scene depth to be computed in real-time. Wloka and Anderson [25] only produce coarse approximations of occlusion in acceptable time. This will probably be solved with increasing computing speed of future systems. Another drawback is the line-of-sight problem: objects not visible in the video images cannot be tracked. While tracking of these objects is not needed for solving occlusion, tracking of the users hand outside the viewing frustum may is necessary when using two-handed interaction as we do when using the Personal Interaction Panel (PIP) [19]: The user must be able to use his proprioceptic sense alone to use virtual input devices without relying on his hand-to-eye coordination.

Berger [4] presented a contour-based approach to occlusion which delivers outstanding results while using essentially only 2D image processing methods. This reduces the computational costs drastically, but also suffers from line-of-sight problems.

Approaches using special hardware, e.g. laser range scanning devices, while providing excellent data are in most cases prohibitively expensive and suffer in many cases from line-of-sight problems, especially in a collaborative situation where users standing close together examine and object between them, as for example in [9].

Tracking systems providing only positional data

At the moment most virtual environments use tracking systems providing only position and orientation. This includes commercial magnetic and mechanical tracking devices and advanced beacon-based optical tracking systems like the one developed at UNC [22] or the structured-light approach of [15].

Sophisticated optical tracking systems like this, or hybrid optical/magnetic solutions like the one used in [18] deliver high precision tracking data but unfortunately no additional data usable for occlusion.

1.3 Registration problems

The problem of registering the users head position with the position of the virtual camera and the virtual objects with the real environment has already been covered extensively [2, 17, 21, 24]. Here - like in the previously cited approach to occlusion by [4] - a 2D image-based approach presented by Kutulakos [12] seems to be an adequate solution for video-based systems.

The registration errors present us with especially annoying artifacts when occluding virtual objects. Slight errors produce a visible gap between virtual and real object (Figure 1) or overlapping effects which occlude a slice of the real object that is supposed to appear in front of the virtual.

Since registration of the commonly used magnetic trackers is notoriously instable, these errors tend to appear in most augmented environments. We try to present a solution for reducing the visual impact of these artifacts.

2 Requirements for occlusion in "Studierstube"

The collaborative augmented environment we have developed allows multiple collaborating users to simultaneously study three-dimensional scientific visualizations in a "study room" - German: "STUDIERSTUBE". Each participant wears an individually head-tracked see-through HMD providing a stereoscopic real-time display. This provides stereoscopic, undistorted images for every user. The see-through HMDs allow users to see each other and avoids the fear of bumping into obstacles.

Objects in Studierstube may appear - unlike in projection based display systems - both between and beside users. Interaction and collaboration within arm reach of the users is possible and supported by scientific visualization applications we have presented in [9] and [10]. Since the resulting scenarios lead often to situations where users heads, hands or bodies or the PIP had to occlude virtual objects, we had to find a method for efficient handling of these occlusions.

The properties of Studierstube and our chosen hardware and software setup presented us with the following requirements for solving the occlusion problem:

View independence supporting multiple users: Studierstube supports multiple users. Occlusion methods therefore have to support a view independence of methods, ideally holding the computational cost proportional to the number of users.

Minimize number of trackers: Representation of users bodies has to be supported with a minimal number of additional trackers. Otherwise the tracking requirement of multiple users could exceed hardware capabilities.

Minimize rendering overhead: The tolerable overhead for correctly simulating occlusion is relatively low. We have to keep rendering passes, additional geometry or image-processing to a minimum.

Since our environment Studierstube uses - like most virtual environments at the moment - commercial magnetic trackers we need another approach to the occlusion problem which does not rely on tracking of geometry or depth.

3 Occluding with phantoms

Since we are using a tracking system which does not supply geometric information of real objects, we have to acquire this information offline. This can be done by modeling or digitizing coarse representations of the objects offline and placing them inside the virtual scene.

We call these mockups of real objects "phantoms". By rendering them in an appropriate way occlusion of the virtual objects by real objects can be simulated (Figure 5). Rendering of phantoms depends on the display system used:

Semi-transparent HMDs only need black areas where reality should be visible. To correctly occlude objects in this setup phantoms have therefore only to be rendered in black, without any special rendering order. This is fast and easy to implement.

When combining images for a video-based approach externally using a luminance- or chroma-keyed system the same method can be applied. For presentation purposes or when generating movies of our environment we usually apply digital compositing using one machine - an SGI Octane - for simultaneously digitizing video data and rendering virtual objects overlaying the video information.

The previous rendering approach would only produce a black avatar in front of the video image. Therefore we render the phantoms before any other geometry into the z-buffer without overwriting the video image.

This can be done in a pre-processing step and does not influence rendering times. The following OpenGL sequence is executed for each frame:

Table 3. OpenGL rendering sequence for occlusion

reset z-buffer
⇓
render video background
⇓
enable z-buffer testing & writing,
disable RGB writing
⇓
render phantoms
⇓
enable RGB writing
⇓
render visible part of scene

This results in "invisible" phantoms, which only are registered in the z-buffer of the rendering hardware. Normal geometry is only rendered where it lies nearer to the viewpoint as a phantom.

184

3.1 Occlusion of static objects

The simplest case of occlusion of real by virtual objects is when the real objects are previously known and static over the duration of the simulation. Examples for this would be furniture and fixtures of the room used as workspace.

We have applied this method to simulate occlusion of virtual objects by laboratory furniture in Studierstube, like already shown in [5].

3.2 Occlusion of tracked rigids

The occlusion of virtual scenery by non-stationary rigid real objects can be handled in much the same way as for static objects. The position and orientation of the have to be coupled to the real object, in our setup by an additional magnetic tracker sensor on each occluding object. We have used this approach to model occlusion of virtual objects by tracked real objects like the PIP and pen in Studierstube (Figure 5).

3.3 Occlusion for tracked articulated objects

A more general case than tracking simple rigid objects for occlusion purposes is the use of tracked articulated objects for occlusion. The primary application of this in our environment was the occlusion generated by participant's bodies moving in front of virtual objects.

To achieve this under the requirements stated above we modeled a coarse articulated representation of a user. This approximation is used as a "phantom avatar", which mimics all poses and gestures of the tracked user to implement correct occlusion. It consists of rigid segments corresponding to body parts, which have to be animated in real-time according to incoming tracker data. To achieve this we have to mount additional trackers on the user as shown in Figure 6. Since the head position is already tracked via the HMD, only three additional tracker sensors were used: two on the lower arms and one on the back of the user, a scheme comparable to the one used by Badler [3]. Similar results have been obtained by Waldrop [23] with the use of three sensors per arm for implementing avatars in a distributed virtual environment.

Based on the reduced number of sensors our simulation has to implement a number of additional constraints regarding joint stiffness and degrees of freedom to correctly simulate the posture of the user. Since our system is based on rigids we also are not able to simulate deformations of the body.

Compensate registration errors by "blurring" the phantom

As already stated before, slight registration errors between phantom and real object result in annoying artifacts when occlusion occurs. This can be caused by errors between tracker data and real position of the sensor, due to time lag or misregistration of real and virtual environment or by differences between the shape of the user and phantom geometry. The first two causes can be addressed in one of the ways cited above, whereas the last case defines a new problem.

While theoretically possible, a pixel-perfect representation of the user is in most cases unnecessary. Even discounting remaining errors from the tracker misregistration, deformation of the body and even changed clothes can reduce the similarity between body part and phantom. Furthermore a precise and therefore finely tessellated model of the avatar would consume too much of our polygon budget.

We are therefore proposing to represent this margin of error in our phantom avatar. We do not render a hard edge between occluded object and occluding phantom but a smooth transition covering the error margin (Figure 3). This transition enables the user to perceive details of both virtual and occluding real object, while not significantly reducing the visual occlusion clue.

A further application of this transitional "blurring" effect are body parts where much additional tracking effort would have to be spent just to implement precise occlusion: the users hands. Without using the almost always cumbersome and inaccurate gloves to track exact hand and finger positions, not enough data is available to correctly occlude the users hands. When using some kind of "probability blurring" in this area, which renders the avatar the more occluding, the higher the probability of a part of the hand appearing in it is, we are able to provide satisfactory occlusion (Figure 2). Since finger and hand gestures are desirable social interactions we want each user to be able to see them.

4 Implementation

4.1 The Studierstube-setup

As mentioned before, each participant in our collaborative augmented environment STUDIERSTUBE wears an individually head-tracked see-through HMD providing a stereoscopic real-time display.

The HMDs we use - Virtual I-O i-glasses - are very lightweight and unobtrusive, but only of limited resolution and small (30°) field of view. As input devices we use a 6DOF pen with multiple buttons and the Personal Interaction Panel (PIP) [19]. The PIP allows both intuitive three-dimensional manipulations such as placement of objects and the input of numerical data or commands via traditional 2D sliders and buttons (Figure 5) - historically one of the weak points of VEs. The pen, the PIP and the HMDs are tracked by an ASCENSION flock of birds magnetic tracker.

Integration of the necessary extensions for occlusion into Studierstube proved to be relatively straightforward. The whole system is based on the OpenInventor [16] Rendering/Simulation library, which reduces the addition of new functionality to the Studierstube environment to the simple process of adding a new dynamically loadable module. The necessary tracker data is delivered by the Studierstube tracker interface, which delivers positions and orientations in OpenInventor fields, a high-level interface element, which allows easy connections to the dynamics simulation library [7].

4.2 Kinematic simulation of avatar posture

The phantom avatar used for occlusion is modeled as articulated solids representing a human body (Figure 7). Some of the solids are directly connected to the trackers attached to the user, as illustrated in figures 4 and 6.

Dynamics is used to animate the avatar. This allows us to intuitively rigidify the degrees of freedom of the joints using damped springs. An upward force applied to the body maintains a standing position. The resting positions of the springs define the natural, comfortable posture of the avatar.

Our simulator, detailed in [7], solves the inverse kinematics problem while taking into account masses and forces. Forces are applied at the beginning of each time step. The motion is then integrated over time, leading to new positions. In addition, the position of the solids bound to the trackers are set accordingly to the input data, regardless of forces or velocities. Possible violations of geometric constraints induced by forces, time integration and tracker input are then cancelled by computing appropriate displacements of the other solids.

The displacements are computed by solving the dynamics equation

Equation 1: $\quad (JM^{-1}J^T)\lambda = b$

where matrix M is a block-diagonal matrix which represents the mass of the system and J a sparse matrix which codes for the geometric constraints. Vector b represents the geometric errors to cancel. Vector λ gathers Lagrange multipliers of the constraints. They act much like integrated forces. The corresponding motion corrections are are thus $M^{-1}J^t\lambda$. Velocity updates are deduced from position corrections by applying Stoermer's rule [14]. This integration scheme considers displacements instead of velocities. This avoids us to differentiate the possibly noisy tracker data.

An iterative solution of equation (1) is performed. A minimization of the norm of the error is performed over the search space defined by the components of vector λ. This approach has two useful features for our application. First, in presence of over-constrained solids, such as the upper arms, a compromise between the constraints is found. Second, the iterative minimization allows the user to trade-off accuracy for computation time, making it suitable for real-time simulation.

4.3 Implementing "blurred" phantoms

There are essentially two approaches to implement the "blurring" of the avatars:

Image-based blurring

The first method that comes to mind when an operation like "blurring" is requested is of course an image-based approach. Rendering an avatar blurred by some kind of convolution operation seems to be the simplest way to implement the desired effect.

But a convolution of a video-resolution image may not be completed in real-time without the use of special hardware. Convolution techniques utilizing OpenGL hardware as presented in [13] are not fast enough on all OpenGL implementations. Using the OpenGL accumulation buffer provides an elegant solution for this problem, but unfortunately requires N^2 rendering passes of the scene for an N×N convolution.

Furthermore certain properties of the image-space approach may not result in the desired appearance of the occlusion: we want the margin of error to be specified in absolute, real-world measurements, to allow for a fixed error produced by e.g. different clothing or hairstyles. An image-based approach would deliver the same amount of blurring for near and far parts of the avatar. The above mentioned "probabilistic blurring" would also not be implementable using a single convolution over the avatar.

Object-based blurring

Another approach to the implementation of smooth transitions for occlusion is to implement a "blurred geometry" of the avatar. This consists not of a single surface representation of the geometry representing a body part, but a layered approach of successively bigger and more transparent shells around the geometry (Figure 2). These shells can be modeled as the same geometry rescaled around the centroid of the object, since most of the avatars geometry is convex.

Of course this approach does not yield a smooth transition, but a discrete number of steps. We found it to be sufficient to use a reasonable small number of steps - say three to ten - to obtain satisfying results in most cases. Since this geometry undergoes the same perspective transformations as everything else, the error margin can be specified in real-world measurements as opposed to the image-based approach above.

A further advantage of this method is the ability to implement "Levels of Detail": for phantoms: with increasing distance we can "switch off" more and more of the intermediate shells, to reduce geometric complexity and therefore polygon count for objects farther away. This allows us to vary the number shells and of transition steps according to distance. In distant phantoms only one or two transitions, covering maybe an equivalent amount of pixels of distance between two shells in image space are rendered. Phantoms nearer the observer are represented by more shells, resulting in approximately the same number of pixel per transition step. This behavior is implemented using the standard OpenInventor LoD-node.

5 Evaluation and Results

Registration of the avatar geometry to the user is relatively time consuming. Since misregistrations of the sensors' position relative to the geometry results not only in visual artifacts (Figure 1) but also in artifacts of the simulation, registration has to be done very carefully. A further problem is an additional time-lag introduced by the kinematic simulation, which could only partially be corrected in this version. The visual results in a typical scientific visualization situation as in (Figure 3) were satisfying and gave users a much better overall impression of the situation and the spatial relationship between real and virtual scene.

In cases where hand-gestures made rigid modeling difficult, object-based blurred phantoms gave a satisfactory compromise between correct occlusion and tracking effort (figures 2 and 3). The artifacts along the intersections between shells of different rigids can be corrected by using stencil masks, a correction which will be implemented in the next version of our occlusion system.

The main difficulty for the animation of the avatar is to have it coincide with the image of the user (figures 8). The positions of the trackers and of the joints with respect to the geometry have to be interactively registered. Joint positions are difficult to adjust because they are inside the body of the user, thus invisible. We adjust them

188

iteratively using different postures.

There are several sources of error in the final result (figure 9) The geometric models do not fit perfectly to the body of the user. The human body is a much more complex structure than our avatar. Limbs are not rigid, especially when covered with cloth, and the joints of the human body differ from our simple joints. If the calibration of the virtual camera does not fit perfectly to the real camera used for video input, the avatar may overlap the user in some postures but not in others. Future work include a more realistic body structure, especially for shoulders, back and neck, and semi-automatic calibration of the virtual camera.

6 Future Work

We are planning to introduce a calibration scheme for rescaling the phantom avatar to fit different users. The basic idea for this is to let the user strike a small number of predefined poses, which should enable the system to infer body measurements.

We plan eventually to eliminate the sensor on the users back by additional constraints in the head/back joint and to introduce certain assumption of the body posture (vertical) for our preferred work situations, standing and seated.

For further information contact fuhrmann|hesina|faure|gervautz@cg.tuwien.ac.at or access the latest results on http://www.cg.tuwien.ac.at/research/vr/occlusion/

7 References

1   Ronald Azuma. A Survey of Augmented Reality. Presence, 6(4): pp.355-385, 1997
2   Ronald Azuma and Gary Bishop. Improving Static and Dynamic Registration in an Optical See-Through HMD. Proc. of SIGGRAPH'94, pp. 197-204, 1994.
3   Norman I. Badler, Michael J. Hollick and John Granieri. Real-time control of a virtual human using minimal sensors. Presence 2(1), 1993, pp. 82-86.
4   M.O. Berger. Resolving Occlusion In Augmented Reality: A Contour Based Approach Without 3D Reconstruction. Proceedings of Conference on Computer Vision and Pattern Recognition, IEEE, 1997, Poster Session 1.
5   David E. Breen, Ross T. Whitaker, Eric Rose and Mihran Tuceryan. Interactive Occlusion and Automatic Object Placement for Augmented Reality. Computer Graphics Forum (Proceedings of EUROGRAPHICS'96), 15(3):C11-C22, 1996.
6   C. Cruz-Neira et al. The CAVE: Audio Visual Expirience Automatic Virtual Environment. Comm. of ACM, 35(6):65,1992.
7   Francois Faure. Interactive solid animation using linearized displacement constraints. Proc. Eurographics Workshop on Animation and Simulation, 1998.
8   S. Feiner, B. MacIntyre, and D. Seligmann. Knowledge-Based Augmented Reality. Communications of the ACM, 36(7):53-62, 1993.
9   Fuhrmann, H. Löffelmann, and D. Schmalstieg. Collaborative Augmented Reality: Exploring Dynamical Systems. In IEEE Visualization '97 Proceedings, pages 459-462. IEEE Computer Society, October 1997.
10   Anton Fuhrmann, Helwig Löffelmann, Dieter Schmalstieg, and Michael Gervautz. Collaborative Visualization in Augmented Reality. IEEE Computer Graphics and Applications, 18(4):54-59, July/August 1998.

11 W. Krueger and B. Froehlich Visualization Blackboard: The Responsive Workbench (virtual work environment) IEEE Computer Graphics and Applications, 14(3), pp. 12-15, May 1994.

12 Kiriakos N. Kutulakos and James R. Vallino. Calibration-Free Augmented Reality. IEEE Transactions on Visualization and CG, 4(1), pp. 1-20, January 1998.

13 T. McReynolds, D. Blythe, B. Grantham, and S. Nelson. Advanced Graphics Programming Techniques Using OpenGL. SIGGRAPH `98 Course notes

14 Press, Teukolski, Vetterling, and Flannery. "Numerical Recipes in C", Cambridge University Press, 1992.

15 R. Raskar, G. Welch, M. Cutts, A. Lake, L. Stesin and H. Fuchs. The Office of the Future: A Unified Approach to Image-Based Modeling and Spatially Immersive Displays. Proc. SIGGRAPH 98 Annual Conference Series, pp. 179-188, Addison Wesley, July 1998.

16 P. Strauss and R. Carey. An Object Oriented 3D Graphics Toolkit. Proc.SIGGRAPH'92, (2):341-347, 1992.

17 A. State, G. Hirota, D. T. Chen, W. F. Garrett, and M. A. Livingston. Superior Augmented-Reality Registration by Integrating Landmark Tracking and Magnetic Tracking. Proc.SIGGRAPH 96, ACM SIGGRAPH, pp. 429-438.

18 A. State, M. A. Livingston, G. Hirota, W. F. Garrett, M. C. Whitton, H. Fuchs, and E. D. Pisano (MD). Technologies for Augmented-Reality Systems: realizing Ultrasound-Guided Needle Biopsies. Proc. SIGGRAPH 96, ACM SIGGRAPH, pp. 439-446.

19 Zs. Szalavári, M. Gervautz: The Personal Interaction Panel - A Two-handed Interface for Augmented Reality. Proc. EG 97, Budapest, Hungary, 335-346, 1997.

20 Zs. Szalavári, D. Schmalstieg, A. Fuhrmann, and M. Gervautz. Studierstube - An Environment for Collaboration in Augmented Reality. Virtual Reality: Research, Development & Applications, (3):37-48, 1998.

21 T. Oishi and S. Tachi. Methods to Calibrate Projection Transformation Parameters for See-Through Head-Mounted Displays. Presence, 5(1):122-135, 1995.

22 Mark Ward, Ronald Azuma, Robert Bennett, Stefan Gottschalk, Henry Fuchs. A Demonstrated Optical Tracker with Scalable Work Area for Head-Mounted Display Systems. Proceedings of 1992 Symposium on Interactive 3D Graphics (Cambridge, Mass., March 29 - April 1 1992), 43-52

23 M. Waldrop, Marianne S., Pratt, Shirley M., Pratt, David R., McGhee, Robert B., Falby, John S. and Zyda, Michael J. Real-time Upper Body Articulation of Humans in a Networked Interactive Virtual Environment. Proceedings of the First ACM Workshop on Simulation and Interaction in Virtual Environments, University of Iowa, 13 - 15 July 1995, pp. 210-214.

24 R. Whitaker, C. Crampton, D. Breen, M. Tuceryan, and E. Rose. Object Calibration for Augmented Reality. Proc. EUROGRAPHICS'95, pp. 15-27, 1995.

25 M. Wloka and B. Anderson. Resolving Occlusion in Augmented   Reality. Proc. Symposium on Interactive 3D Graphics, ACM SIGGRAPH, 1995, pp. 5-12.

190

Figure 1: Occlusion with head phantom, misregistration (in circle) due to time lag

 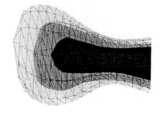

Figure 2: "Probabilistic" function of hand and corresponding phantom

Figure 3: "probabilistic" occlusion

Figure 4: trackers (circles) and joints (squares)

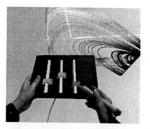 

Figure 5: PIP occluding geometry

Figure 6: User with 4 sensors and HMD

Figure 7: geometry of user "phantom"

Figure 8: Occlusion of background

Author Index

SpringerEurographics

Bruno Arnaldi,

Gérard Hégron (eds.)

Computer Animation
and Simulation '98

Proceedings of the Eurographics
Workshop in Lisbon, Portugal,
August 31–September 1, 1998

1999. VII, 126 pages. 82 figures.
Softcover DM 85,–, öS 595,–, sFr 77,50
ISBN 3-211-83257-2. Eurographics

Contents:
- J.-D. Gascuel et al.: Simulating Landslides
  for Natural Disaster Prevention
- G. Besuievsky, X. Pueyo: A Dynamic
  Light Sources Algorithm for Radiosity
  Environments
- G. Moreau, S. Donikian: From
  Psychological and Real-Time Interaction
  Requirements to Behavioural Simulation
- N. Pazat, J.-L. Nougaret: Identification
  of Motion Models for Living Beings
- F. Faure: Interactive Solid Animation
  Using Linearized Displacement
  Constraints
- M. Kallmann, D. Thalmann: Modeling
  Objects for Interaction Tasks
- M. Teichmann, S. Teller: Assisted
  Articulation of Closed Polygonal Models
- S. Brandel, D. Bechmann, Y. Bertrand:
  STIGMA: a 4-dimensional Modeller
  for Animation

Eduard Gröller,

Helwig Löffelmann,

William Ribarsky (eds.)

Data Visualization '99

Proceedings of the Joint EUROGRAPHICS
– IEEE TCCG Symposium on Visualization
in Vienna, Austria, May 26–28, 1999

1999. XII, 340 pages. 230 figures.
Softcover DM 118,–, öS 826,–, sFr 107,50
ISBN 3-211-83344-7. Eurographics

In the past decade visualization established
its importance both in scientific research and
in real-world applications.
In this book 21 research papers and 9 case
studies report on the latest results in volume
and flow visualization and information visualization. Thus it is a valuable source of information not only for researchers but also for
practitioners developing or using visualization applications.

All prices are recommended retail prices

 SpringerWienNewYork

Sachsenplatz 4–6, P.O.Box 89, A-1201 Wien, Fax +43-1-330 24 26, e-mail: books@springer.at, **Internet: http://www.springer.at**
New York, NY 10010, 175 Fifth Avenue • D-14197 Berlin, Heidelberger Platz 3 • Tokyo 113, 3-13, Hongo 3-chome, Bunkyo-ku

SpringerEurographics

Martin Göbel,

Jürgen Landauer, Ulrich Lang,

Matthias Wapler (eds.)

Virtual Environments '98

Proceedings of the Eurographics Workshop
in Stuttgart, Germany, June 16–18, 1998

1998. VIII, 335 pages. 206 partly coloured figures.
Softcover DM 128,–, öS 896,–, sFr 116,50
ISBN 3-211-83233-5. Eurographics

Ten years after Virtual Environment research
started with NASA's VIEW project, these
techniques are now exploited in industry to
speed up product development cycles, to
ensure higher product quality, and to encour-
age early training on and for new products.
Especially the automotive industry, but also
the oil and gas industry are driving the use of
these techniques in their works.
The papers in this volume reflect all the different tracks of the workshop: reviewed technical papers as research contributions, sum-
maries on panels of VE applications in the
automotive, the medical, the telecommunica-
tion and the geoscience field, a panel discussing VEs as the future workspace, invited
papers from experts reporting from VEs for
entertainment industry, for media arts, for
supercomputing and productivity enhance-
ment. Short industrial case studies, reporting
very briefly from ongoing industrial activities
complete this state of the art snapshot.

Panos Markopoulos,

Peter Johnson (eds.)

Design, Specification and Verification of Interactive Systems '98

Proceedings of the Eurographics Workshop
in Abingdon, U.K., June 3–5, 1998

1998. IX, 325 pages. 119 figures.
Softcover DM 118,–, öS 826,–, sFr 107,50
ISBN 3-211-83212-2. Eurographics

Does modelling, formal or otherwise, have a
role to play in designing interactive systems?
A proliferation of interactive devices and
technologies are used in an ever increasing
diversity of contexts and combinations
in professional and every-day life. This
development poses a significant challenge
to modelling approaches used for the design
of interactive systems. The papers in this
volume discuss a range of modelling approaches, the representations they use, the
strengths and weaknesses of their associated specification and analysis techniques
and their role in supporting the design of
interactive systems.

SpringerWienNewYork

Sachsenplatz 4–6, P.O.Box 89, A-1201 Wien, Fax +43-1-330 24 26, e-mail: books@springer.at, **Internet: http://www.springer.at**
New York, NY 10010, 175 Fifth Avenue • D-14197 Berlin, Heidelberger Platz 3 • Tokyo 113, 3-13, Hongo 3-chome, Bunkyo-ku

Springer-Verlag
and the Environment